Germanna Road

Three Hundred Year History of Lower Orange County, Virginia, with particular attention to the Alexandria Tract and Lake of the Woods

by Dr. Peter G. Rainey

authorHOUSE®

AuthorHouse™
1663 Liberty Drive
Bloomington, IN 47403
www.authorhouse.com
Phone: 1-800-839-8640

First published by AuthorHouse 6/24/2010

ISBN: 978-1-4520-3639-7 (e)
ISBN: 978-1-4520-3638-0 (sc)

Library of Congress Control Number: 2010909001

Printed in the United States of America
Bloomington, Indiana

This book is printed on acid-free paper.

Dedication

To Roger Trask

I started this work a three years ago with my friend and neighbor, Roger R. Trask. Roger had a long career as a historian, both as a university professor and as the historian for several government agencies. He was a past president of the Society for History in the Federal Government. Roger was a long-time resident of Lake of the Woods. He died April 18, 2008, in Bradenton, Florida.

Roger was a recognized expert in recording oral histories. He taught me to understand that memoirs may not always reflect historical documents and to try always to find at least two sources for any important event. He also taught me there is a fine line between prose and history. His most valuable lesson was that the repetition of a statement from author to author, or generation to generation, does not necessarily make it the truth.

Acknowledgements

Without the support and assistance of my brother and other friends, this work would never have been realized. James M. Rainey financed a major portion of the publishing. Josef W. Rokus spent countless hours editing several revisions of the manuscript. Dan McFarland provided use of his vast collection of photographs and took many more at my request. Both Josef and Dan have authored histories of this area that are referenced herein. John Howard provided the resources of the Memorial Foundation of the Germanna Colonies in Virginia, Inc. Thank you.

Interviewing the principals involved was the key that unlocked the door to the actual events in 1965 and beyond. They are an amazing group of people who did extraordinary things. These pioneers and several other community leaders who followed have all provided their recollections of what actually happened to create, nurture and preserve the Lake of the Woods.

- Atwell Somerville, descendant of three of the original justices of Orange County, Commonwealth Attorney for Orange County, attorney for Boise Cascade, and long-time attorney for Lake of the Woods.
- William T. Goodwin, surviving member of the Goodwin Timber Company, a man who hauled lumber to Washington, D. C., who saw the conversion from axe to hand-held power saw, who owned vital portions of the future Lake of the Woods and to this day owns large acreage across from Route 601 and Route 3.
- C. Daniel Clemente, of Taylor and Clemente Law Office, Falls Church, Virginia, lawyers for Virginia Wildlife Club, Inc., (VWCI) and one of the three initial directors of Lake of the Woods Association, CEO of Clemente Development Co. Inc., a man who has built a real estate and banking empire in Northern Virginia.
- James C. Foote of Eastern Land & Timber, Inc., Annapolis, M.D., a man of 29 years in 1965 who "had fun" giving landowners their first helicopter ride as he negotiated acquisition of their property. He had the vision to create wealth for Orange County, himself and others by spending five million dollars to improve and sell land worth less than one hundred thousand dollars just one year earlier.
- William Ray Apperson, resident farmer and landowner, one of those that sold the family farm to form Lake of the Woods. His father built the White House.
- John R. Henry, surviving member of the first all-member Board of Directors.
- Carolyn Nowakoski, surviving founder of LOW Church and spouse of Don Nowakoski, deceased, a Director of LOWA for six years. Lyn has continuously served on numerous committees and clubs since 1971.
- Sonny Weedon is one of the surviving "rock pickers" who played golf with President

Gerald R. Ford at LOW and one of the local Virginians who moved his family into LOW. His daughter was the first LOW student to ride the school bus to Orange.

- Bill Howard was at his LOW lakeside house with his wife and 3 year old daughter when hurricane Camille passed by. He was a marshal at the 1975 Lee Elder tournament and escorted the President Gerald R. Ford's foursome. He is an avid collector of LOW memorabilia.

- Ruthan O'Toole has been a resident and member since her childhood. Her parents were the principal leaders in LOW clubhouse activities in the 1970s. She has a photo and document collection from the Wilderness Bottle Club, Inc.

- Alan Polk has been President of LOWA twice, separated by a decade. He was principally responsible for several of the financial reforms during the 1990s.

- Many others are credited with supplying vital bits of information, photographs and a few darn good stories, each and everyone is cited for their contribution in the endnotes.

Table of Contents

Preface

"Dedications and Prefaces, which are prefixed to most Books, being regarded by few Readers, I think it best for my present Purpose briefly to mention in an Introduction, what I would have known concerning the Occasion, Nature, and Use of this Treatise, before I enter upon the main Work itself." - Hugh Jones, *The present state of Virginia*, London 1724

This is a history of the land and the landowners along Germanna Road and connecting roads, from the Rapidan River to Wilderness Run. The chapters that follow provide the history of the lower end of Orange County, especially the Alexandria Tract, with particular attention to the land in and around Lake of the Woods.

My brother asked me, "Why should I care about the Alexandria Tract?" My simple answer was, "Because we are descendants of Alexander Spotswood." He got me to thinking about what motivates anyone to write and especially to research and record one's findings for posterity. When the English settler came to Virginia, he brought his law and his library. The concept of land boundaries and personal ownership were foreign until then, as was the concept of written records. The land records, journals and family records of the five generations of Spotswoods, their relatives and neighbors that lived on and near the Lake of the Woods area have been preserved, but their story has not previously been written. Similarly, the modern pioneers that came in the late 1960s and later to form the community of Lake of the Woods should have their story preserved.

W. W. Scott's classic "A History of Orange County, Virginia" provides the history of the county up to 1870. Almost a hundred years later, the Orange County Historical Society published "Remembering: A History of Orange County, Virginia" by Frank S. Walker, Jr. These two histories provide the background for activities in the county for the last 300 years.

Alexander Spotswood is recognized as a remarkable man who had the foresight to see past just looking to London and instead looked for the future in western exploration. Little else is written about the pioneers and landowners along Germanna Road. The apparent lack of historic interest in the eastern portion of Orange County is related to the result of Ann L. Miller's research. In 1988, the Orange County Historical Society published her book *Antebellum Orange, the Pre-Civil War Homes, Public Buildings, and Historic Sites of Orange County, Virginia*. Of the 150 sites that she reported and photographed, only eight are east of Mine Run. A similar very small percentage of properties of historic interest are listed in the Works Progress Administration of Virginia Historical Inventory of Orange County.

In addition to the resources described above and the files of the Orange County Historical Society, we are very fortunate to have pristine and complete volumes of deeds, wills and other court records dating from the formation of the county. Closer than even the county courthouse are the files of the Memorial Foundation of the Germanna Colonies in Virginia, Inc. and the historical files of the National Park Service Fredericksburg and Spotsylvania National Military Park. The vast resources of the Library of Virginia and the Virginia Historical Society are a couple of hours away, and both have indexes that are Internet accessible. A large, diverse and at times surprising amount of applicable material is available by searching the Internet. With all this information, I have constructed snapshots of the families that pioneered, cultivated and survived along Germanna Road over the span from 1714 to 1964.

Of all the places within a few hours of Washington, D.C., why pick the Wilderness to develop a large lake recreational community? The answer to this question cannot be found in any published history of Orange County. Why would families sell their home of generations including the family cemetery? The simple answer of "for the right price" is not the only explanation. *The fascinating History of the Lake of the Woods Area* written in 1976 by Arnold E. Chase provides the early history of the Lake of the Woods Association (LOWA) from 1969, Mr. Chase having been one of the first year-round residents in 1970. It does not explain how and why Lake of the Woods was built in Orange County, nor describe the individuals responsible for building a new community in The Wilderness. The Story of Lake of the Woods and its impact within Orange County is the story of the people who built it and made it grow. The official records of the Lake of the Woods Association and the archives of local newspapers provided useful background. The true story was obtained by interviewing the people that made it happen. *Que est veritas?*

Lt. Gov. Alexander Spotswood - A fine portrait of Alexander Spottswood, (i.e. Spotswood) artist unknown, hangs in the Governor's office of the Capitol at Richmond. The picture is part of the collection of photographs prepared for the Virginia Room Exhibit at the 1939 World's Fair in New York City. On computer file at the Library of Virginia.[1]

1710 – 1964

B E Y O N D Col. Spotswood's Furnace above the Falls of Rappahannock River, within View of the vast Mountains, he has founded a Town called Germanna, from some Germans sent over thither by Queen Anne, who are now removed up farther: Here he has Servants and Workmen of most handycraft Trades; and he is building a Church, CourtHouse and Dwelling-House for himself; and with, his Servants and Negroes he has cleared Plantations about it, proposing great Encouragement for People to come and settle in that uninhabited Part of the World, lately divided into a County.
- Hugh Jones, London 1724

"Miniature painting, Alexander Spotswood First half 18th C.," Museum & Photograph Collection accession No. 1963.23. Printed with permission from the Virginia Historical Society. © Virginia Historical Society all rights reserved.

Chapter 1   The Alexandria Tract

The Alexandria Tract is bounded by the Rapidan River, Wilderness Run and Russell Run.[2,3] It is bisected by Flat Run. A quarter of the acreage is the Flat Run watershed. The edges of the watersheds, the natural high ground, became a network of roads in a future Orange County. This land was initially in Essex County. It became part of Spotsylvania County in 1721 and finally the eastern part of Orange County in 1734. This section of Orange is frequently called lower Orange as the elevation of the land, and especially the Rapidan River, are lower than other parts of Orange County.

Taking Up the Land

The Germanna tract containing 3,229 acres was granted to Wm. Robertson by patent the last day of October 1716 and was conveyed to Colo. Spotswood in the following November. A tract containing 3,065 acres was granted to Richard Hickman by patent on 2nd day of November 1719 and was conveyed to Colo. Spotswood the following December. The tract in the fork of Rappahannock River containing 1,920 acres was granted to Harry Beverley by patent the 2nd day of November 1705 and conveyed by him to Colo. Spotswood the 22nd day of April 1720.[4]

Alexander Spotswood was appointed Lieutenant Governor of the Virginia colony by Queen Anne on February 18, 1710. He arrived in Virginia the following June. Within three years, he established Ranger companies to patrol and explore west of the colony, built Fort Germanna and Fort Christianna, and signed the Tobacco Act into law. He obviously took a strong interest in the northwest frontier, which at that time was the Rapidan – Rappahannock Rivers. By 1717, his relations with the Virginia Council, House of Burgesses and the Anglican Church were strained, and he started to accumulate vast tracts in that area in his own name.

Answer of Lt. Governor Spotswood to the anonymous queries etc., written Feb'ry 7th, 1715 [1716] To ye L'ds Comm'rs of Trade and Plantations.[5]

"As to the other settlement, Germanna, there are about 40 Germans … who having quitted their native country upon the invitation of the Herr Graffenreidt, and being grievously disappointed by his failing to perform his engagements to them, and they also arriving just at a time when the Tuscaruro Indians departed from the treaty they had made to settle upon the northern frontiers, he, in compassion to those poor strangers,

1

and regard to the security of the country, placed them upon a piece of land several miles without the inhabitants, where he built them habitations and subsisted them until they were able by their own labour to provide for themselves. ...

I know of no restraint upon any of H.M. subjects from taking up land in any part, but it is true that some time after my arrival here, observing many undue practices in relation to the unpatented lands ... I therefore judg'd it best, and had the Council's concurrence, that the Surveyors should no longer have liberty to admit, solely of themselves, these excessive large entrys; but that for all tracts exceeding 400 acres, leave should be first obtained from the Governor in Council to enter for the same etc. No man has been denied the liberty of taking up as much land as he could reasonably be suppos'd of ability to cultivate etc. Instead of 12,000 acres which the Querist says were taken up, to my own use, in the name of William Robertson, and leased to the Germans, the whole quantity surveyed at the time of composing his queries, amounted to no more than 1287 acres. And tho by the Patent for that tract, whereon the Germans are seated it will appear to contain 3429 acres, yet what is added to the first survey is part of a tract taken up by one Mr. Beverley, and voluntarily yielded by him for the conveniency of that settlement. And as I don't know that H.M. has in any of his Instructions restrained a Governor from taking up land to his own use, as well as any other of his subjects, so I hope it will not be accounted any breach of my duty if for the security of that part of the frontiers, and for the settlement of a number of indigent people, I have been at the expence of surveying and purchasing rights and patenting a tract of land to which no other person had any pretensions. But because the entring for this 1287 acres in a borrowed name, may carry with it some colour of fraud, I beg leave to inform your Lords that patents for land being sign'd by the Governor, it would be improper for him to grant a patent for himself; and therefore it is necessary to make use of another person's name in the original grant, and such has been the constant practice of former Governors, whenever they had a mind to take up land for themselves ... I hope your Lordships will be of opinion, that my taking up land, and building houses for people who were not able to take it up or build for themselves; my advancing money for their transportation and subsistance, when they must have been sold (according to the custom of this country) into servitude or have famish'd; and my allowing them to live at such easy rents, is far from what the Querist would here charge me with. I shall very readily yield him up the profit I have made by those people, provided he reimburses me what I have expended on their account etc....I bid defiance to all mankind to produce a single instance of my accepting any sort of gratification for any place or office in my disposal, though privately pressed to do so etc., or of taking any fee, but what has been look'd upon as the undoubted right of my predecessors ..." - (signed) A. SPOTSWOOD.

In 1720, Spotsylvania County was established, and the courthouse was at Germanna. In that year, the laws governing the patenting and development of land were eased, with relief granted from quit rents. In April of 1722, King George relieved Spotswood of his office.[6] He soon thereafter moved to take ownership of the entire Alexandria Tract.

"Which three tracts lye together." July 1722, a patent was made out in the name of

> *Richard Hickman in trust for Colo. Spotswood for 28,000 acres, which includes these three tracts; the new land contained in that patent is 19,786 acres.*[7]

A Court held on October 5, 1725, also accounted for 15,000 acres called the Iron-tract (in Spotsylvania County), 3,650 acres at Massaponax and 40,000 acres in a tract called the Spotsylvania Company (partially in Orange and Culpeper Counties). On the Spotsylvania Tract, there were 30 plantations at this time. The Spotsylvania Tract was valued at 1,515 pounds, which implies that the average tenement was worth 50 pounds.[8] The Alexandria Tract with 21 tenements was worth 11,000 pounds, implying that Spotswood's seat, Germanna, was worth 10,000 pounds.

Alexander Spotswood's rights were challenged, and he had to travel to England to defend those rights. He was successful but at a price. His main source of wealth, the iron works at Tuball, suffered under the wretched management of John Graeme, Spotswood's cousin.[9]

> *... the state of Colo. Spotswood's Seating, Cultivation & Improvements saved his Lands from lapsing, according to the laws of Virginia. On the Alexander tract containing 28,000 acres and 21 Plantations or Tenements: houses, mills and their dams valued over 11,000 Lbs; cleared land at 30 acres per plantation, one with another making 630 acres; 263 head of cattle and 56 horses.*[10]

Alexander Spotswood intended to keep his tract and wished his descendants to hold the land. He also realized that his patent would be at risk if the 28,000 acres were not settled. His workforce at the furnaces and the staffing of the Germanna fort was but a few dozen families. As of October 1725, the Germanna parcel in the Alexandria Tract contained only 21 tenement houses of 30 acres each for a total of 630 acres. He populated the area by leasing to tenant farmers small parcels, usually less than 300 acres. In this way, he and his descendants received income for decades. There were 14 leases duly recorded in Spotsylvania County in 1734 for lands that soon thereafter became Orange County.[11] There were 38 leases duly recorded in Orange County between July 15, 1735, and August 27, 1741.[12]

The terms of these contracts required the farmers to establish a home, an orchard and raise a crop, usually including tobacco, or livestock. In return for an annual payment in pounds of tobacco, they received the rights to the land for themselves and their descendants until Christmas 1775. The lease to Thomas Sims, duly recorded in Spotsylvania Co. Deed Book C-(1734-1742), is an example. The terms of the lease also required them to provide one laboring hand for making the water dam or race of any gristmill which Spotswood, his heirs or assignees desired. It provided that if Rebecca or Thomas Jr. should die before Thomas Sims, Sr., or December 25, 1775, the latter or his assigns could choose the person to take their place. These conditions were common to all of Spotswood's leases.

> *Tho Sims and his assignees for & during the natural lives of Rebecca, the wife, and Thomas ye son ... yielding and paying therefore yearly ...on the 25th of December...624 pounds weight of ... marketable top tobacco...delivering it at a convenient landing in the County of Spotsylvania.*

In his will, Alexander Spotswood empowered his executors to continue leasing parcels. Between August 27, 1741, and August 27, 1746, his executors leased an additional 58 parcels. His son John took control of the estate in 1745. John established his seat at New Post, Spotsylvania, his father's mansion near Massaponax.[13] His brother died in a battle with Indians in 1756. John died only two years later, and once again, the estate was in the hands of trustees.[14] John left two minor sons at the time of his death in 1758. Col. Moore of King William County, John's brother-in-law, was appointed guardian to the boys and trustee of the estate.[15] Alexander Spotswood's will provided generously for his wife and sons and daughters. All the income from the tenements was insufficient to cover those debts. In 1761, the executors of John Spotswood were authorized to sell certain lands for payment of debts. When the income from those land sales was also determined insufficient to cover the debts and maintain the minor children, the executors were then permitted to use "the profits of the whole estate."[16]

> *… although it appears to have been Major-General Spotswood's intention that the said lands should be all settled with tenants, yet his executors being all dead, and the issue in taille an infant, it is doubted whether the same can be leased …*[17]

> *Bernard Moore Exor of Will of John Spotswood Esq. … to be raised by such sale … not more than six thousand pounds …*[18]

Given the combination of lease expiration of December 25, 1775, and the dissolution of the crown government, the record of land ownership became clouded after the Revolutionary War. As late as 1791, there were still Spotswood tenants in Orange County. Sometimes the tenants ultimately obtained deeds to the land, but in most cases, the tenants suffered to remain on the land, and they ultimately claimed title without benefit of deed.[19] Many parcels of Orange County land trace their titles to Spotswood leases.[20]

The Alexandria Tract was never much good for crops. The soil, for the most part, is of poor drainage, rock and clay. Unlike the early patents in other parts of Orange County, which were established for agriculture, the Spotswood patent was established for mining. The native forest that Alexander Spotswood found in the early 1700s was cleared to shore the mines and fire the furnaces. Red Oak was especially favored for the furnaces. Ancient trees were naturally replaced by young growth and bush. Relatively little agriculture was successful between the Rapidan River and Russell Run. The clearing of large land parcels for planting seldom occurred. The average farm was less than a few hundred acres, two-thirds of which remained unused. There were exceptions, especially Ellwood where the black walnut trees grew.[21]

Alexandria Tract Land Patent

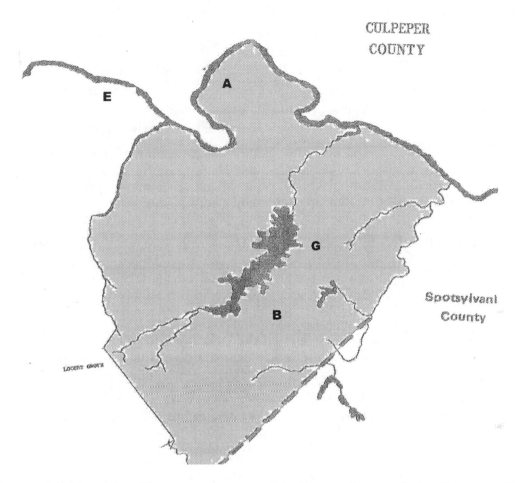

The plot of the Alexandria Tract was drawn by Mr. Joyner, former clerk of Orange County. The large lake shown is the main lake at Lake of the Woods, formed by a dam constructed on Flat Run. **A:** Germanna (Site of Alexander Spotswood's "Castle"), **B:** The Wilderness (Site of Civil War battle), **E:** Indiantown (Site of early Indian village), **G:** Orange Grove (Home of John Spotswood).[22]

Crossing Germanna Ford

Lt. Gov. Alexander Spotswood arrived in Virginia a hundred years after John Smith explored the Rappahannock River. During those hundred years, settlement remained close to the month of the river. At the start of the 18th century, the charts of the Rappahanock River area downstream of the fork were based on descriptions by the natives and not the survey of the settlers. Prior to the founding of Fort Germanna, the only transportation routes in this area were the waterways and a few forest paths created by Native Americans. Whatever motivated Alexander Spotswood in 1714 to establish Fort Germanna several miles west of the limits of the Ranger patrols and west of the fork in the river, it was a pivotal decision.

> *Besides general colonization, one of Spotswood and the German's most important contributions to north-central Virginia was transportation routes. Most of the roads were built to or from a site developed by Spotswood, including the town of Germanna, Germanna Ferry, Tubal Iron Works, and Massaponax Wharf, which indicated his great wealth, power, and control over the landscape. A study of area road orders from 1721 to 1740 showed that over one-quarter of all road orders contained roads leading to or from a Spotswood-influenced property.[23]*

The key feature of the Alexandria Tract was the natural crossing of the Rapidan at Germanna Ford. Alexander Spotswood named this branch of the Rappahannock River the Rapid Anne. Rapid for its rate of flow and because it quickly rises in a storm, and Anne for his benefactor Queen Anne of England. In April 1723, a petition for a ferry at Germanna was approved. The first mention of the ferry in Spotsylvania Road Orders 1722-1734 appears in March 1724. The Germanna ferry was the subject of one of the first businesses conducted at the court of the new County of Orange.[24]

> *In Complyance to an Order of Court dated 21st day of January 1734 We the Subscribers went to Colo. Spotswood to know upon what terms he would let his Land for a Ferry at Germana and his Honor was pleased to say that he would let the plantation at the Ferry together with land Sufficient for two hands to work for the Term of Seven Years for Six hundred and thirty pounds of tobacco pr: Year but debars the keeping of a tipling house or hoggs runing at large at the Ferry Plantation...*

Alexander Spotswood received an annual stipend of tobacco for his ferry crossing at Germanna. At the time of the death of Alexander Spotswood in 1740, Germanna Ford was an important commercial link to his tenants to the west in today's Culpeper and Madison counties, to the commercial town of Fairfax, now the town of Culpeper, and to the east to Fredericksburg. After his death in 1740, his trustees, and later his descendants and their trustees, continued to receive this income. In 1758, his son, Col. John Spotswood, died and left his estate and guardianship of his children to his brother-in-law, Col. Bernard Moore. Col. Moore, bankrupt, claimed in a letter to George Washington to have not taken from the Spotswood trust, "as I owe Spotswood's Estate not one farthing."[25] However, in December 1763 the court expressed concern for his lack of care of the Germanna Ford ferry.[26]

Ordered That Nathaniel Pendleton Gent do Acquaint Bernard Moore Esqr. of John Spotswood Esqr. decd. that unless there be better Attendance given and better Cannoes kept for the Transportation of Tobacco &c at Germanna ferry for the future that this Court will withdraw the salary that they Annually have Allowed: and pursue such Steps as by Law pointed out in Such Cases.

John Newport in behalf of himself and others presented a petition into Court as a Proposition and Grievance to have a bridge built at Germanna Over Rappahannock River the ferry being very ill kept wch: is ordered to be certifyed to ye Genl Assembly

There was interest in building a bridge at Germanna Ford across the Rapidan as far back as April 27, 1742.[27] A committee was appointed to take subscriptions for a bridge at Germanna and agreements for workmen to build it. If subscription was insufficient, the balance was to be levied by the County not to exceed 3,000 pounds of tobacco. In 1752, the Court of Culpeper County ordered a bridge over the Rapidan at Germanna. Again in 1754 the court again so ordered a bridge.[28]

In 1844, Captain Ambrose Powell Hill of Culpeper was appointed one of the commissioners of the Culpeper County Court to consider the construction of a bridge spanning the Rapidan River between Culpeper and Orange counties. He maintained records as superintendent of the building of Germanna Bridge, including orders of the County Court, specifications, a bond of the contractor, William T. J. Richards (in the hand of William Green), and accounts.[29]

The bridge existed at the start of the Civil War.[30]

William G. Reynolds, her father, and Jim Roach, her uncle, ran a store at Germanna before the War Between the States. John Willis ran a woolen mill at the same place. It stood near the bridge – Mrs. Dolly Roach.

Two accounts of the events at Germanna Ford and associated bridge building during April and May 1863 are presented below.

On Thursday (May 7th 1863) ... Lieut. Sumner went to Germanna Bridge ... Information obtained from residents near Germanna Bridge satisfied Lieut. S. that it would not be prudent to go further ... To sum up Gen. Stoneman moved about within the enemy's lines at will for nine days ... disabled every line of communication between the army of the Rappahannock and the rebel capital... by destroying all bridges over large streams ... [31]

Federals poured across the Rapidan fords through the night of April 29 and into the morning of April 30, 1863 ... A Southern bridge-building party had just begun work at Germanna Ford, obviously not intending their labors as a benefit for an enemy column they did not expect. During the afternoon of April 29, Slocum's Federal 12th Corps had descended on the Germanna crossing. They surprised Confederates inadequately *protected by skirmishers, drove them back into a road cut, and eventually captured most of them. Some troops splashed right into the Rapidan through a fast and deep current. Others awaited the cobbling together of a rude bridge and then crossed by the light of bonfires. Howard's 11th Corps troops followed close on Slocum's heels.*[32]

A skirmish occurred during the first week of October 1863.

A day or two ago the rebels made a vigorous attempt to cross the river at Germanna Mills, with a force of six hundred infantry as a storming party. One hundred of Gen. BUFORD'S dismounted cavalry, who were on picket duty at that point, kept the enemy at bay, and finally repulsed them with severe loss.[33]

During the Mine Run Campaign, the Army of the Potomac crossed at Germanna Ford on November 26, 1863. An A. R. Waud sketch published in "Harper's" January 1864 showed Brook's brigade of Warren's Corps crossing Germanna Mills Ford. In the sketch, the bridge was destroyed, they crossed on boats, and a pontoon bridge was under construction.[34] The army again crossed Germanna Ford returning to Stevensburg a few days later.[35] When the Army of the Potomac crossed the Rapidan at Germanna Ford in May 1864, they used a system of pontoon bridges. This event was captured in both photographs and sketches.[36] During the Civil War, Spotswood's Germanna disappeared. While the ford was recognized as an excellent river crossing, it was in a location that did not lend itself to being strongly defended. From the Confederate viewpoint, it was only the best of several isolated fords in that part of the Wilderness, all too far from either Fredericksburg or Orange to be incorporated into the Rappahannock or Rapidan defensive lines. Union forces also appeared to see no wisdom in trying to control the ford.[37]

Virginia's Department of Transportation could not provide any information on the bridging of Germanna Ford prior to 1934. In August of that year, construction was completed on a two-lane bridge.[38]

Building the First Road

The Governor therefore proposed to settle them above the falls of Rappahannock River to serve as a Barrier to the Indians and desiring the opinion of the Council whether in Consideration of their usefulness for that purpose the Charge of building them a Fort, clearing a road to their settlement … may not properly be defrayed by the publick.[39]

The Germanna path was developed by the Fort Germanna settlers, and led from Tappahannock to the falls near the Leaseland and on to the fort. This soon became known as the Germanna Road. This roadway, the first European-based in the area, was ordered by the Virginia council in April 1714. It was no more than a bridle path. A bridle path was very narrow and primarily used by travelers on horseback. Though they were the shortest route between two points, they were often the most treacherous.

A few years later, a rolling road was built through this area. Rolling roads were the widest and best-maintained roads of early Virginia. They were used to roll hogsheads of tobacco to a market or wharf, and they had to be away from all stream crossings to keep the tobacco dry. The new road connected Germanna to both Tubal Iron Works and Massaponnax wharf.[40]

Germanna Road was not along any watershed boundary, it was far from being on the high ground as it crossed Wilderness Run and Flat Run before crossing the Rapidan River. Spotsylvania Road Orders 1722-1734 document the problems faced by the colonial settlers who maintained this route.

> *6 August 1728, On complaint & Information made to this court Benjamin Cave Overseer of the Road from the markt Stones to Germanna that John Graeme Gentn: Attorney to Collo: Alexander Spotswood will not suffer any of his male labouring tithables to come & help cleare the road with him pretending they are excused a late act of assembly as belonging to ye Mines & c which if thay are taken away from him, he hath none other left to clear the said road that is now much out of repair…*

> *3 November 1730, On Petition of John Gordon Overseer of the road from the Markt Stones to Germanna, for to have the Wilderness Run bridge built at ye County Charge reason his gang Chiefly Consisting of Collo. Alexander Spotswoods Mine People Which now are Exempted Law is granted, and Ordered that Goodrich Lightfoot, William Bledsoe, and Robert Green, Gentlemen or any two of them, do agree with Some Person to build the same on the Cheapest Terms they Can and Make return of their Proceedings to the Next Court.*

The tobacco census of 1726 listed 18% of the tobacco crop of (then) Spotsylvania County as produced from west of Wilderness Run, mainly on the lands of Augustine Smith and Goodrich Lightfoot.[41,42] In 1730, the Crown ordered that all tobacco must be shipped through 70 designated inspection stations. Fredericksburg was appointed such a station. In 1732, the warehouses were built by Henry Willis, the inspection station opened, and all tobacco henceforth was carried there. This terminated the old arrangement with Col. Alexander Spotswood and required modifying the roads leading to the Massaponax wharves. By this tobacco inspection decree, the town of Fredericksburg was born and began the waning of both pillars of Spotswood's fortune, Germanna and Massaponax. One of Henry Willis' earliest tasks was to open an ordinary and recruit John Gordon to move to the still-empty town of Fredericksburg as his ordinary keeper.[43] John Gordon had immigrated to Virginia from Scotland in 1721. He had been a tavern keeper at Germanna when it was the county seat. Spotsylvania Road Orders 1722-1734 document that he also had been the overseer of the road.

> *3 September 1732, On Petition of John Gordon Overseer of the road from the Markt Stones to Germanna to be Discharged from the Same, (he being removing from that Precint) is granted …*

The place for holding courts in the County of Spotsylvania was relocated from Germanna to Fredericksburg in August 1732. Upon formation of Orange County from Spotsylvania, the March 1734 session of the Orange County Court was charged with selecting the location of the Orange County courthouse. Col. Alexander Spotswood wrote to the court. The offer was acknowledged, but never considered.

> *"Whereas I have been desired to declare upon what terms I will admit the Courthouse of Orange County to be built upon my land in case the Commissioners for placing the*

same should judge the most convenient situation thereof to be within the bounds of my Patent. And forasmuch as I am not only willing to satisfy such commissioners that no obstruction in that point will arise on my part, but am also disposed to make those terms as easie to the County, as can well be expected; I do therefore hereby declare that consent to the building of a courthouse, prison, pillory and stocks on any part of my lands not already leased or appropriated; and that I will convey in the form and manner which the justices of the County can in reason require such a quantity of land as may be sufficient for setting the said buildings on, with a convenient courtyard thereto, for the yearly acknowledgment of one pound of tobacco. And moreover, that I will allow to be taken gratis off my land all the timber or stone which shall be wanted for erecting and repairing the said buildings. Given under my hand at Germanna the 6th day of January 1734-5." - (signed) A. SPOTSWOOD

After the death of Alexander Spotswood, the road was in such disrepair as to require action by the court on May 24, 1744.[44] A bridge over Flat Run was built in 1753.[45]

Flat Run in this County below Germanna is very difficult & bad to pass over with Tobacco, for want of a Bridge over the same …

Seventeen years later, on June 25, 1761, James Roach was appointed overseer of the road from Germanna Ford to the Wilderness Run Bridge.[46, 47] Years later, on April 28, 1785, James Gordon (no relation to the previously mentioned John Gordon) was appointed overseer of the road.[48] Descendants of James and John Roach and James Gordon were prominent in the history of lower Orange County for almost the next two centuries. Part of their descendants' lands eventually became Lake of the Woods.

Little changed in the way roads were maintained during the 19th century. John Samuel Apperson described in his diary the condition of current Route 20 between Orange Court House and Locust Grove in November of 1862.

The Plank road is in a bad fix showing that plank roads are a humbug.[49]

Twenty-five years after the Civil War, Virginia's roads were far worse than when the war began. This was true despite the fact that in the reconstruction period, the General Assembly enacted much road legislation.[50] After the Civil War, magisterial districts were responsible for maintaining the roads. There was a time when the Gordon District floated its own road bonds and had the best roads anywhere around. The tithe system, a museum piece from the colonial era, was struck down by the courts in 1894. Roads were then maintained by the "road gangs" of local prisoners. In 1918, Virginia organized a state road system and took over maintenance of Germanna Highway, then called Route 37. On a 1925 highway map, that single-lane Route 37 was shown as "non-hard surfaced" and "improved" which meant it was a modern width of eighteen feet.[51]

By authority of the Virginia Route Commission, order issued March 26, 1969, Route 3 from Culpeper to Fredericksburg was designated Germanna Highway.

Germanna Ford May 1864

UPPER: "Germanna Ford, Rapidan River, Virginia. Ruins of bridge at Germannia (sic) Ford, where the troops under General Grant crossed, May 4, 1864." Grant's troops seen crossing downriver of the bridge location. Wet plate glass negative made on May 4, 1864 by Timothy H. O'Sullivan. Library of Congress, Civil War Photographs.[52]

LOWER: "The crossing of the Rapidan at Germanna Ford, May 5, 1864--Wilderness campaign." Edwin Forbes pencil drawing created May 5, 1864. Library of Congress, Morgan collection of Civil War drawings.[53]

Chapter 2   Mines: Silver, Iron and Gold

Colonel Spotswood and His Mines

It was first believed by friends and business associates of Alexander Spotswood that silver would be found in the branches of the Rappahannock. For several years in the early 1700s, they had petitioned the Queen for rights to this area. Through a series of false starts, it culminated in the first wave of German miners to Virginia. The German miners' story is documented by the Memorial Foundation of the Germanna Colonies in Virginia, Inc., and the writings of John Blankenbaker.[54,55] Although the projected silver mine was only a few miles from his Fort, Spotswood would not let the Germans work on the mine until questions about the ownership of the ore were resolved. He explained this in a letter to the Lord Commissioners of Trade in London in a letter of July 21, 1714:[56]

> "They (the Germans) are generally such as have been employed in their own country as Miners, and say they are satisfied there are divers kinds of minerals in those upper parts of the Country where they are settled, and even a good appearance of Silver Oar, but that 'tis impossible for any man to know whether these Mines will turn to account without digging some depth into the Earth, a liberty I shall not give them until I receive an Answer to what I represented to your Lordships concerning your Ascertaining her Majesty's Share ..."

Lt. Gov. Spotswood was able to mitigate the expenses to himself and the Germans by an act of the Council.

> The Governor acquainting the Council that Sundry Germans to the number of forty-two men women & children who were invited hither by the Baron de Graffenried are now arrived but that the said Baron not being here to take care of the Settlement, The Governor therefore proposed to settle them above the falls of Rappahannock River to serve as a Barrier to the Indians and desiring the opinion of the Council whether in Consideration of their usefulness for that purpose the Charge of building them a Fort, clearing a road to their settlement & carrying thither two pieces of Canon & some ammunition may not properly be defrayed by the publick.
>
> It is the unanimous opinion of this Board that the Said Settlement, tending so much to the Security of that part of the Frontiers, It is reasonable that the expense proposed

by the Governor in making thereof should be defrayed at the publick charge of the Government, and that a quantity of powder & ball be delivered for their use out of her Majesty's Magazine. And because the said Germans arriving so late cannot possibly this year cultivate any ground for the[ir] Subsistence, much less be able to pay the public Levies of the Government, It is the opinion of this Board that they be put under the denomination of Rangers to exempt them from that charge. And for better enabling the Said Germans to supply by hunting the want of other provisions, It is also ordered that all other persons be restrained from hunting on any unpatented Lands near the Settlement.[57]

While visiting Germanna, John Fontaine recorded his view of the silver mines.

German-town, 25th August 1716 - "After dinner we went to see the mines, but"could not observe that there was any good mine. The Germans pretend that it is a silver mine; we took some of the ore and endeavoured to run it, but could get nothing out of it, and I am of opinion it will not come to anything, no, not as much as lead. Many of the gentlemen of the county are concerned in this work. We returned to our hard beds." [58]

Two years later, nothing had been accomplished at this silver mine except the investors had become discouraged about the prospects. The Germans had hardly been allowed to scratch the surface. By 1716, the prospects for silver had been totally discounted.

" ... In Feb. 1717 [by the new style calendar, this would be 1718] ... to set up iron works in Virginia, and desires people might be employed to find out the oar, and some thousands of acres taken up for that purpose. Accordingly I set my Germans to work to look for such oar which search cost me upwards of three score pounds ... I chose to join in with several Gentlemen here who were willing to carry on the project, and bear their proportion of the charges I had already been at; and so, the mine tract, consisting of 15,000 acres of land, was in 1719 [1719 by the patent book; this was in 1720 on the modern calendar] taken up by nine or ten Adventures." – Alexander Spotswood[59]

The mine tract containing 3,065 acres was granted to Richard Hickman by patent on November 2, 1719, and was conveyed to Col. Spotswood the following December. Robert Beverly conveyed his ten shares of the Ironmine Land to the Hon. Alexander Spotswood in 1722. Their co-partnership was for the carrying on the design of smelting and casting of Iron.[60]

Robert Beverly and Thomas Jones hold in trust by patent, 20 February 1719, 15,000 acres commonly know by the name Ironmine Land.

John Blankenbaker, the unofficial historian of Germanna, has corrected the often repeated "erroneous facts."[61] There is no evidence that the Germans participated in the building of the iron furnace, which was not operational until about 1723.[62] At the time of the settlement of the second group, the First Germanna Colony had just commenced the search for iron ore. The second group of Germans, known eventually as the Second Germanna Colony, had no part of the search for iron ore or the building and operation of the iron-smelting furnace. They were placed on the north side of the Rapidan, each having a small farm upstream from Germanna. Headrights to this second group secured the Spotsylvania Tract. After the Germans' servitude period was over in 1725, they migrated to farmland on the Robinson River Valley in today's Madison County or to an area southeast of Mt. Pony in today's Culpeper County.[63] Spotswood replaced them with a mix of black slaves and white indentured servants. At this time, the Germanna community was at its zenith. Spotswood received income from his iron business, mills on various tributaries of the Rapidanne, the ferry at Germanna Ford, a small number of tenants in the Alexandria Tract and a large number of tenant farms in his other lands in current Madison, Culpeper and Spotsylvania counties.

In his visit to Colonel Spotswood and his mines in 1732, Col. William Byrd described the furnaces and iron foundries.

> "I came to be instructed by so great a master in the mystery of making of iron, wherein he had led the way, and was the Tubal Cain of Virginia ... Then I inquired after his own mines, ... He told me he had iron in several parts of his great tract of land, ... the mine he was at work upon was 13 miles below Germanna. That his ore (which was very rich) he raised a mile from his furnace, and was obliged to cart the iron, when it was made, fifteen miles to Massaponax, a plantation he had upon Rappahannock River; but that the road was exceeding good, gently declining all the way, ... He said it was true his works were of the oldest standing: but that The Colonel has a great deal of land in his mine tract exceedingly barren, and the growth of trees upon it is hardly big enough for coaling. However, the treasure under ground makes amends ... They raise abundance of ore there, great part of which is very rich."[64]

Alexander's rights were challenged, and he had to travel to England to defend those rights. He was successful but at a price. The iron works at Tuball suffered under the wretched management of John Graeme, Spotswood's cousin.[65]

> *Deed of Lease ... Alexander Spotswood ...on trust for Jno Grame Gent and Katheriune Grame, their heirs ... two plantations Bear Quarter and Wildcat Quarter near Germanna ...on Wildcat, sometimes called Flatt Run, ... not to include Germanna 3,229 or Wilderness 3,065 ... Jno Mackmath, their trustee.*[66]

Col. William Byrd wrote in 1732 that Alexander told him:

> *... his long absence in England, and the wretched management of Mr. Graeme, whom he had entrusted with his affairs, had put him back very much. That, what with neglect and severity, above eighty of his slaves were lost while he was in England, and most of his cattle starved. That his furnace stood still a great part of the time, and all his plantations ran to ruin...*[67,68]

It seems highly probable that Graeme's shortcomings were partially counterbalanced by Spotswood's financial agent, the industrious Reverend Robert Rose, and his furnace manager, Mr. Chiswell, who was experienced in mine operations.[69]

By 1736 … 175 tithables, most of them undoubtedly Negroes, both men and women, were employed at Spotswood's iron works.[70]

Lt. Governor Gooch wrote to the Council of Trade and Plantations in July 1735 his annual accounts of laws made, manufactures set up and trade carried on in the Colony. He seems to consider the ironworks of little importance, and the search for minerals, other than iron, as a waste of money. His list of minerals did not include any precious metals.[71]

" … There are four ironworks in this Colony employed in running pig iron only, which they send to Great Britain to be forged, and these works are thought rather beneficial to the trade than inconsistent with it; forges for barr iron have been long talked of, but since the first settlement there is but one in this Government, nor can I learn any more are intended ; a sure sign the attempting to manufacture iron for the use of the Plantations, more than is necessary for agriculture and planting, for mending as well as making tools, is a tiling impracticable and unprofitable ; at the furnaces, as the people call for them, they make pots, backs and and irons for fire places. There is one air furnace at work, which does the same. They have yet had no manner of success in either tinn, lead or copper mines, though the searches have been very expensive to many gentlemen."

The will of Alexander Spotswood, Esq., of Orange Co., Virginia, contains in part the following description of the ironworks in circa 1739.[72,73]

The Mine Tract is set apart for an ironwork, and at least 80 working slaves and 20 children belonging to them must be employed on the Tract; any deficiency shall be made good by slaves from other plantations; all tradesmen, servants, stock, implements, etc. on the tract shall remain there till his son John is twenty-one and shall them be given to him; or if he dies, the Tract etc. go to his son Robert, at twenty-one; the executors are empowered to maintain and lease the Mine Tract.

Alexander Spotswood's will provided generously for his wife, sons and daughters but prohibited using income and assets from the mine-tract to pay for those expenses. All the income from the other tracts in Spotsylvania, Orange and Culpeper counties where insufficient to cover those debts. The law enacted by the General Assembly in March 1761 authorized disposal of certain lands in Spotsylvania, Orange and Culpeper for payment of debts to enable the executors of the will of John Spotswood, Esquire, deceased, to pay the debts and legacies due. When the income from those land sales was also determined insufficient to cover the debts and maintain the minor children, the executors were then permitted to use "the profits of the whole estate." The profits from the iron works are stated as "very considerable."[74] No longer were the profits and assets of the mine-tract used exclusively for improving the ironworks.

There is evidence that the executors failed to maintain production of Wilderness iron.[75] With the passing of the Spotswood properties, iron manufacture in eastern Virginia came to a virtual standstill.[76] There was a brief resurgence at the start of the Civil War, which Federal forces destroyed when they crossed the Rapidan.[77]

Gold Mines at Lake of the Woods

The same belt of minerals that runs along and either side of Wilderness Run that contains iron was also found to contain gold. The Virginia Division of Mineral Resources has documented 301 gold and silver mines, prospects and occurrences in Virginia, with the majority of them in the gold-pyrite belt shown below. About 100,000 troy ounces of gold were produced in Virginia from 1804 through 1947, when gold was last produced in the State.

About 1826, on a 266-acre tract of Mr. William Jones, some children returning from a Sunday school found a considerable piece of gold. The discovery created great excitement, and such an amount was found that the earth containing the surface gold was removed and washed in a common rocker. In ten months, Mr. Jones and his son-in-law, Judge Coulter, received $10,000 from the labor of eight hands. John Spotswood, Jr., of Orange Grove, also received income from the mining.[78] The 1850 census lists Robert Hartshorn of New Jersey and family as a goldminer under the enumeration of John R. Spotswood. Following that listing is a Mr. Alexander E. Riddle from Ohio, occupation: engineer. The Spotswood estate at that time was valued at $2,250.[79] The remains of the Orange Grove Mine are shown in a map drawn in the 1950s.[80]

> *According to Robert A. Hodge, a Fredericksburg historian, there were 84 gold mines in the vicinity between 1837 and 1966, and mercury was used at all of them to get gold from ore ... state officials have confirmed the presence of mercury in the sediments near the site of a former gold mine. Gary Moore of the State Water Control Board's Northern Virginia office, said ...tributaries of the Rapidan River near Lake of the Woods, contain mercury.*[81]

Peyton Grymes, son of Benjamin and Sally Grymes, established the Vaucluse gold mine, the most renowned and longest lasting of the several mines to be established within the Alexandria Tract. In the record of his sale of 200 acres within the Vaucluse tract in 1852 to the Liberty Mining company is listed a steam engine, mill and pumps, clearly indicating an ongoing mining operation at that location. Hannah Grymes, his unmarried sister, conveyed the property to him. On the following page of the deed book is recorded his sale to Liberty Mining for $11,000.[82] Hannah remained on another 100 acres of the original Vaucluse tract and lived with her unmarried sister Lucy in the family mansion. Seventy-seven years later, Henry Ford purchased the Vaucluse tract in Orange County for a reputed price of $10,000.[83] He removed the circa 1832 mining equipment and displayed it in his museum in Dearborn, Michigan.

> *That pump is an enormous affair and must have cost a great many pounds sterling. It is a Cornish pump, the only one of its kind in America. It was brought to Virginia a century ago and was installed in the Vaucluse gold mine in Orange County, then owned by British interests. At that time this was one of the most prominent of the American mines, and like the others was worked to the water level and then abandoned.*[84]

It is said that more money was made by trading in land than in the actual mining of that land. There is no better example of this than the Supreme Court case of GRYMES v. SANDERS, 93 U.S. 55 (1876).[85]

The land survey of Germanna Road area in the Wilderness by E. J. Woodville made in 1937 shows six mining companies with rights to a total of 1,815 acres. Several mines were located within the Lake of the Woods area.[86] In 1957 there were pit and trench cuts with quartz dumps just east of the intersection of Liberty Blvd. and Wakefield Drive, and just southwest of Harpers Ferry Drive, about 0.1 mile by road southeast of its intersection with Lakeview Parkway. The Orange Grove Mine was located near the present location of a boat ramp on the main lake of Lake of the Woods. The Partridge Mine was located on both sides of the Rapidan-Stratford Park Road approximately 0.5 mile by road north-northeast of its intersection with Route 3. In 1975, a caved shaft and three caved pits were observable. Other mine open pits and dumps were evident on both sides of Route 3 between Lake of the Woods and Route 20.

The deed for C. H. Kuper and wife Mary purchase of 196 acres in 1901, for $3,000, from Wilderness Mining and Milling Company includes a plat by E. Woodville that shows the location of a "Gold Mine Shaft" on the 189-acre Wilderness Mining parcel. Flat Run bisects the parcel, and the mineshaft was located about a half mile west of Flat Run.[87]

As recently as 1947, Harry W. Jones, 77, of Five Mile Fork, panned gold from several of the small streams that wind gracefully through the (LOW) lake's surrounding woodland.[88] In 1988, the Orange Planning Commission heard a proposal by spokesmen for Sterling Exploration, Inc., who want to prospect for gold and other minerals on a site north of Lake of the Woods. Warren Lodge (GM), general manager at that time of Lake of the Woods, now the largest community in Orange County, asked the commission to take no action on the proposal. The Commission denied the permit.[89]

Mineral Rights

Alexander Spotswood retained all rights to minerals in the leases he wrote. Since that time, the transfer of land and mineral rights within the Alexandria Tract have frequently been separate transactions. It is ironic that Alexander Spotswood never knew that his land was rich in gold. It is equally ironic that his grandson and namesake, Brig. Gen Alexander Spotswood, failed to retain the mineral rights when he sold parcels in the Alexandria Tract to Benjamin Grymes and the Jones brothers at the time of the Revolution.

John A. Partridge of Washington, D.C., bought 100 to 200 acre parcels in the Flat Run, Germanna Road area over a period from 1875 to 1890.[90] On March 15, 1890, he sold 636 acres to Edward Woodman of Portland, Maine.[91] The land is described as southside of Germanna Road, the same tract conveyed in March 1841 by John H. Gordon and wife.[92] Edward Woodman of Maine may have been buying for timberland or mineral rights or both. In 1918, he sold some of his land along Flat Run and Germanna Plank Road to J. W. Masters, "subject to the reservation of the mineral rights." It eventually became part of Lake of the Woods.

As recently as 1955, the sale of land in the area of the future Lake of the Woods did not include the mineral rights.[93] The property deeds for some lots in Lake of the Woods contain reservation of mineral rights.[94]

> *All the certain property ... described as Lot ... Section ... Lake of the Woods ... this conveyance does not include the oil, gas and mineral rights in, to and in respect of the above described property inasmuch as the Developer, Virginia Wildlife Clubs, Inc., reserved the same at the time of development.[95]*

Mining Companies along Germanna Road

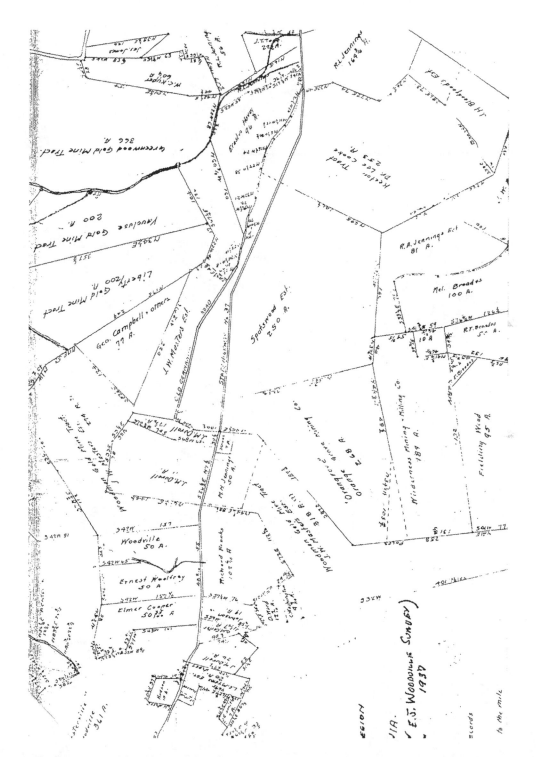

E. J. Woodville survey of 1937, rights of mining companies along Germanna Road. Reproduced from Orange County Clerk's Office files.

Chapter 3   American Revolution

Retreating rapidly before Cornwallis, the latter boasting "the boy cannot escape me,"
LaFayette crossed the Rapidan, probably at Germanna Ford ...

While no other significant event occurred in lower Orange County during the Revolutionary War, many of her sons served with honor and distinction. The grandsons of Lt. Gov. Alexander Spotswood, Alexander and John, returned from Eton circa 1764 when their guardian, Col. Moore, failed to provide their support. Alexander, the older brother, arrived of age circa 1772 and took control of the estate.[96,97] Both grandsons served in the Continental line. Alexander's service spanned the entire war from April 1775 as one of the Gentlemen of the Independent Company of Fredericksburg, soon after as major of militia at Great Bridge and later as Brigadier General of Spotswood's Legions 1781 – 1783.[98] Alexander sold or leased land in the Wilderness to his distant cousins Benjamin Grymes and Churchill Jones. He later relinquished his rights to the remaining inherited land in the Wilderness to his younger brother John Spotswood.[99]

Four Gentlemen - Patriots

The principal landholders along Germanna Road were Benjamin Grymes of Orange County, Churchill Jones of Woodville, James Gordon of Germanna and John Spotswood of Orange Grove.[100] Marriage and social ties closely related these four. James Gordon's aunts were the wives of the Jones brothers.

> *The two brothers (Churchill and William Jones)...fell in love with the two daughters of their guardian, Judith Churchill and Betty Churchill. When my father was twenty-one years of age the brothers determined to seek their fortunes in what was then literally "The Wilderness" in Spotsylvania County. They were accompanied by two other young men, Benjamin Grymes and Dudley Diggs. They leased a large tract of land from the estate of Governor Spottswood[101]... In 1773, they brought their brides to the new homes they had prepared for them in the Wilderness – Elizabeth Churchill Jones Lacy.[102]*

In September 1775 and January 1776, Benjamin Grymes leased and later was deeded land from Alexander Spotswood.[103] He established his seat and named it Vaucluse. Years later, this was the location of the Vaucluse Gold Mine. In 1777, he was a Gentleman Justice of the Orange County Court.[104]

Virginia had declared her independence of the Crown on the 29th of June, 1776, five days before the general Declaration in July. The public officers appear to have simply held over by taking the Convention oath. But in May, 1777, commissions from Patrick Henry, the first governor of the new "Commonwealth", directed to James Madison … Benjamin Grymes … were received: and they constituted the first bench of justices under the new regime.[105]

In 1780, he was listed as providing provisions and in 1782, the Orange County Court allowed his claim of public service to be just and reasonable.[106]

Churchill Jones was commissioned a captain, 3rd Continental Dragoons, January 1, 1777.[107] He transferred to Baylor's Consolidated Regiment of Dragoons, November 9, 1782, and served until the close of the war.[108] In January 1776, Churchill Jones along with his brother William and sister-in-law leased 305 acres adjoining Grymes' land from the Spotswood estate.[109] Churchill named his seat Woodville.

John Spotswood is memorialized by the DAR in Lake of the Woods' Spotswood Park. He was wounded and captured while a captain of the 10th Virginia Regiment.[110] He was paroled by the intervention of Gen. George Washington and sent back to Fredericksburg.[111] He established his seat circa 1773 that became known later as Orange Grove.[112] Years later, this was the location of Lake of the Woods. In 1787, John Spotswood was a Gentleman Justice of the Orange County Court.[113]

James Gordon of Germanna was known as "James of Orange," to distinguish him from his first cousin, the second James of Lancaster. He was the eldest son of John Gordon and Lucy Churchill Gordon, daughter of Col. Armistead Churchill and his wife, Hannah Harrison. James Gordon served in the Revolution as a civilian; he represented Richmond County in the House of Delegates in 1781. The people of Orange elected him at the age of 29, along with James Madison, as their representative in the convention called to pass upon the question of the adoption or rejection of the new Federal Constitution. On February 17, 1788, we find him writing from Germanna to James Madison, then in New York, as follows:[114]

"Dear Sir: Being favored by Colonel Monroe with a sight of your letter of the 27th of January, and finding no mention therein of your being in our country in a short time, I take the liberty as your friend to solicit your attendance at March Orange court. I am induced to make such a request, as I believe it will give the country in general great satisfaction to hear your sentiments on the new Constitution. Your friends are very solicitous for your appointment in the convention to meet in June next. I trust, were it not practicable for you to attend, your election will be secured; but your being present would not admit a doubt … The sentiments of the people of Orange are much divided. The best men, in my judgment, are for the constitution; but several of those who have much weight with the people are opposed … Upon the whole, sir, I think it is incumbent on you without delay to repair to this State: as the loss of the constitution in this State may invoke consequences the most alarming to every citizen of America."

I am, Dear Sir, Your most obedient servant,

(signed) JAMES GORDON

Of the 57 families listed by Benjamin Grymes in 1782, the four gentlemen aforementioned owned 67% of the black slaves in lower Orange County.[115] The majority of all the other families were farmers who held very few or no slaves. William and Reuben Hawkins, were neighbors of Capt. John Spotswood. William had purchased 246-acres "on the Flat run" from John's older brother Alexander Spotswood, Esq., and his wife Elizabeth Washington for the sum of 116 pounds Virginian.[116] In the census of 1782, William is listed after James Gordon with seven white and three black and Reuben is listed as five white and no black. William was acknowledged as a patriot for furnishing supplies to the Orange militia.[117] Several of the neighbors served in the militia. Reuben Hawkins was a captain. John Almond had served in the Orange County militia and at age 86 is listed in the 1840 Census of Pensioners Revolutionary or Military Services.[118] Absalom Roach of Orange, at age 72 in 1832, proved two years service in the Revolution.[119] There is a record of his declaration of being present at the surrender of Yorktown.[120]

Although there were no battles fought on this land, the people sacrificed materially to support the militia and Continental troops and spiritually as families divided between Crown and Commonwealth. John Randolph Grymes, cousin of Benjamin Grymes of Vaucluse, "served the royal cause," joined the Queen's Rangers until he left for England in 1778. He later returned to Orange County. Although they fought on opposite sides, Benjamin named his third born son John Randolph. While Churchill Jones fought in the Continental Line, his brother William opposed the movement to establish American independence.[121] Whether willingly or not, William Jones did furnish supplies to the militia and Continental line, as did his neighbors including the Brooke, Bledsoe, Coleman, Cooke, Gibson, Gordon, Grymes, Jennings, Johnson, Jones, Payne, Spotswood, and Willis families.[122] In addition, William Jones entertained Lafayette twice in his life.

> *Jean La Fayette camped for the night on the hill opposite Ellwood, and was entertained with his officers at the house ... He for the second time enjoyed the hospitality of Ellwood, when on his return to this country ...* [123]

> *Lafayette never forgot the kindness, and breakfasted with him (Wm. Jones) at Ellwood during his 1824-25 grand tour of the United States.*[124]

> *In the campaign of 1781, the Marquis de Lafayette marched through the Wilderness to rendezvous with Brig. Gen. "Mad Anthony" Wayne. On 3 June 1781, Lafayette's army camped south of the Wilderness Bridge across Wilderness Run from Ellwood. The next day, Lafayette reconnoitered Ely's Ford while the army crossed Germanna Ford to reach Culpeper Church. Afterward Lafayette marching south, recrossed the Rapidan River. During his Grand American Tour, Lafayette retraced his campaign and visited the Wilderness twice. In November 1824, Lafayette attended a reception at the Wilderness Tavern, and in August 1825 he breakfasted at Ellwood.*[125]

The Four Gentlemen - Patriots Pass On

James Gordon built a large, two-story frame home at the site of Lt. Gov. Alexander Spotswood's mansion in the 1790's. The Gordon family cemetery is located on these grounds.[126] James died intestate at age 40 at his home at Germanna December 14, 1799, and was buried there in the

Gordon family burying ground.[127] He possessed considerable land in both Orange and Culpeper counties, but left his estate more or less embarrassed.[128]

> *In "The Journal of a Young Lady of Virginia, 1792," written by Miss Lucy Lee, which preserves a very sprightly and vivid picture of the social life of the period in the new Commonwealth, frequent mention is made of the Gordons of Germanna, in whose hospitable home the writer appears to have been a welcome guest ... This vivacious journal ... contains in its many passages concerning Germanna and its residents a number of interesting references to "old Mrs. Gordon," widow of John of Richmond, who had come to Orange to reside with her son James, after his father's death.* – Armistead C. Gordon[129]

John Spotswood of "Orange Grove" was afflicted by his wounds and died in 1801. His will is dated October 23, 1800, and recorded May 9, 1801, in Fredericksburg District Court.[130] It reads, in part, "All to wife for life: then all Orange land to Jno: and all Culpeper land to other four sons and to children of Mary Voss, my deceased daughter. My children except Jno to be residuary legatees."[131] His wife, Sallie Rowzie Spotswood, died four years later.[132]

Benjamin Grymes of Orange County died in 1805 at the age of 55. His will was recorded in Fredericksburg October 1, 1805.[133] He left everything to his wife, Sarah, and children, each child to have its part on arriving at age. The will of his wife, daughter of Peter Robinson of King William County, was recorded in 1827.[134]

> *Benjamin Grymes, who had accompanied the Jones brothers, married Miss Steptoe, a cousin of Speaker Robinson of the House of Burgesses. He built "Vaucluse", about two miles from Ellwood, and raised a large family. One of his sons, John R. Grymes, ranked among the most distinguished lawyers of his day in New Orleans, and married the widow of Gov. Claiborne of Louisiana. Two unmarried daughters, Hannah and Sallie, kept up the old house after the rest of the family had scattered, and were true Virginia gentlewomen of the olden type. Of their mother, when she was a stately and well preserved old lady, John Randolph said that she reminded him of the last piece left of a rare and costly service of old china.* – Elizabeth Churchill Jones Lacy

> *Benjamin Grymes, Esq., age 55, late of the Wilderness, in Orange County, on Tuesday last at Auburn, the seat of William Bayly, Esq., in Stafford County.*[135]

Churchill Jones bought Chatham and 1,288 acres near the town of Fredericksburg in 1806 for the sum of $20,000.[136] Woodville became Jones's spring and summer home. In 1820, he commissioned Joshua Long to build him a toll bridge across the Rappahannock River at Chatham.[137] He died in 1822 at Woodville and lies buried in the Ellwood cemetery.

Churchill Jones portrait located at Chatham. Courtesy of Donald Pfanz, staff historian, Fredericksburg & Spotsylvania National Military Park.

Capt. John Spotswood "Images, Spotswood, John Grandson of the Governor," Museum & Photograph Collection accession No. IMG08939. Printed with permission from the Virginia Historical Society. ©Virginia Historical Society all rights reserved.

Chapter 4   Neither a Salubria nor a Chatham

The following is meant to convey the changes that occurred within the Alexandria Tract between the Revolutionary War and the Civil War. The antebellum period has been romanticized in literature. Along Germanna Road in lower Orange County, there were no large columned mansions. The Willis home was a small three stories, with attached one story, frame house. The largest two story houses were the Jones' and the Spotswood's farmhouses. The descendants of the original tenants that remained tended to enlarge the original small two-room houses to create larger farmhouses. One such house still exists and is located in Lake of the Woods. The only palatial home, Alexander Spotswood's "Enchanted Castle," had burned down a century earlier. All the families, except for Jones, had several children. Birth, marriage and death were the major social events and all occurred at home. Most of the homes had a family cemetery, many of which are still known to exist, a few on the Lake of the Woods Association property.

The families in the Alexandria Tract over the generations became intertwined by marriage.[138] The land records of Orange County are pristine and complete; however, since birth, marriage and death were family affairs, these records are not, and sorting the genealogy can be difficult.[139] By the start of the 19th century, the center of commerce and population of Orange County had moved over twenty miles southwest of Germanna Road. No longer were the plantations along Germanna Road mainly quarters of gentlemen that resided elsewhere. With the exception of the farms of Larkin Willis, Payne, Spotswood and William Jones, most of the properties were smaller than a couple of hundred acres and held no more than a few black slaves.

The Wilderness

"Offer our best respects to Mrs. Spotswood and the old lady, your mother ... also to all my old friends of the Wilderness" – letter to John Spotswood Esquire, Wilderness Virginia from John Randolph Grymes. 140

By 1757, the lands of Col. John Spotswood in Orange County had been divided into several quarters. One of these quarters was called Wilderness, another Germanna. "Quarter" in this case does not mean a fourth; it is a term for a substantial parcel of land with usually a mansion but not the permanent residence of the landowner. The quarter may serve as a summer home, may be home of a relative, or may only be inhabited by an overseer.

Wilderness Post Office, Orange County, first appears in 1812 and it existed until 1942. That post office was located two miles south of Vaucluse and half mile south of the Wilderness Mine. A deed in 1890 placed it near the John R. Spotswood estate and the Greenwood Gold Mining

Company.[141] A Wilderness Post Office, Spotsylvania County, also first appears in 1812; it closed in 1890. That post office was probably located at the Wilderness tavern. Germanna Post Office had been established earlier in 1804, but it disappeared after the Civil War. The Locust Grove Post Office was opened in 1839, and it continues to serve all of lower Orange County.[142] This Post Office was probably located at Robinson's Tavern. Locust Grove is located near the southwest border of the original Alexandria Tract. In the 18th Century, its earlier name was Old Trap, and many Road Orders of Orange County refer to it as such.[143]

Wilderness Run was the eastern boundary of the Alexandria Tract. When Orange County was formed out of Spotsylvania, it became part of the eastern boundary. The earliest record of the name Wilderness in the Spotsylvania Road Orders pertains to the Wilderness Bridge in 1722. This bridge was necessary to cross from Germanna to the furnaces east of Wilderness Run. This bridge must have failed in a storm, since in August of 1736 a road order was written:

> *On the motion of Elliot Benger Gent in behalf of Alexr Spotswood, Esqr: it is ordered that the sd Alexr Spotswood undertake to build the Wilderness bridge and finish the same by October next in order to be paid therefore at the next laying of the County Levy.* [144]

Germanna, the James Gordon Family

James Gordon and his wife Elizabeth along with 11 other white souls are listed by Benjamin Grymes in 1790. They had one dwelling and two other buildings. James Gordon acquired the Germanna Tract circa 1795 after several years of deeded transfers recorded in the Orange County Deed Books.[145] The house may have been, in part, constructed by 1790 and certainly by 1797.

On February 24, 1797, James Gordon sold to John Spotswood 600 acres of Germanna Tract being part of a tract sold Peter Conway by Alexander Spotswood. The price was 1,000 pounds paid over three years.[146] After his father's death, Rev. John C. Gordon received 550 acres including the house. His mother and unmarried daughters remained in the house. After the death of John C., his son, John Addison Gordon, bought out the other siblings, moved into the house and remained there until his death in 1883. He raised a family of 14 children. Lucy Harrison Gordon, his third child by his first wife, was born in 1837. After the Civil War, she married her Germanna Road neighbor, Alexander Dandridge Spottswood

> *The unmarried children of James Gordon, Armistead, Lucy and Elizabeth, continued to reside after the death of their parents at the family homestead at Germanna. Lucy died first…In 1852 it became know among the negro slaves on the Germanna plantation that Elizabeth Gordon had made a will, manumitting her slaves, … their freedom to ensue after the expiration of the life-estate of her brother…further provided that these negros … should be sent to Liberia … a short time thereafter both the sister and the brother died suddenly … from poison in the coffee … The emancipated slaves were sent to Liberia* – Armistead C. Gordon.

By the early 19th century, the thriving community on both sides of the Rapidan River at Germanna included Urquhart's gristmill, a sawmill operated by Lovell, dependencies for the

28

milling complex, a tavern, the ferry, several private schools, a general store and a number of homes.[147]

Charles Urquhart listed his buildings in 1816 for insurance by the Mutual Assurance Society as:[148]

1 story dwelling, walls and roof wood, 50 ft. by 18 ft. with attached porch

1 story kitchen, walls and roof wood, 20 ft. by 16 ft.

1 story store house, walls and roof wood, 25 ft. by 16 ft.

smoke house, walls and roof wood, 14 ft. square

3 story mill house, walls and roof wood, 60 ft. by 40 ft.

In 1820, Charles Urquhart advertised in the *Virginia Herald* that due to advanced period of life and precarious health and an earnest wish to settle all his affairs, he planned to move from Germanna and wished to sell his 288-acre farm, which was highly productive and with extensive orchards of selected fruit.

> *The Germanna Mills were in complete order, running two pairs of 5 foot burrs and one pair of country stones. The burr stones were quite new and of first quality; the machinery and gears were complete and new. The Mill was located 20 miles from the port town of Fredericksburg and convenient to the fertile counties of Culpeper, Madison, and the Shenandoah Valley.*[149]

William Reynolds and Jim Roach ran a store at Germanna before the Civil War. It stood near the bridge. John Willis ran a woolen mill at the same place.[150]

Somerset (Flat Run), James Somerville of Culpeper

The Somerset house was built circa 1834 for James Somerville's son.[151,152] As originally built, it was brick laid in Flemish bond, stood one story high, raised on an English Basement, and probably had a hipped roof.[153] Seventy-five years later, John Rowzie Spotswood's grandson, Alexander Gordon Spottswood, purchased this house, renovated it and added a second story. James Somerville of Culpeper never resided in Orange County but held a large estate therein.[154] James Somerville came to Virginia in 1795 and took possession of his uncle's large estate, which included the forestlands that were the scene of the Battle of the Wilderness in the Civil War. These lands had been purchased by his uncle from Brig. Gen. Alexander Spotswood and his wife Elizabeth Washington.[155] He married Mary Atwill of Fauquier County.[156]

Over a period of almost 40 years James Somerville of Culpeper sold his land on the east side of Russell Run in parcels of less than one hundred to five hundred acres to Daniel Dempsey, Charles Payne, John C. Gordon, William Jones, William Roach, Edwin Gibson, Joseph Webb, Mary Jones, Robert Roach, John R. Spotswood, Larkin Willis and Alfred Apperson.[157] The value of the land sold ranged from $4 per acre to $20 per acre. The family names listed appear on one or more Civil War maps in or nearby the current Lake of the Woods area.

Larkin Willis Family

Mary Gordon, granddaughter of James Gordon, married Larkin Willis on July 15 1823.[158] John Churchill Gordon deeded land to his son-in-law Larkin Willis in 1834. The house was completed in 1835 and still stands, unoccupied, at Meadows Farms Golf Course on Route 601. Their son, Larkin (Jr.), was born February 24, 1835. Larkin and Mary Willis sold Fox Neck, 1,400 acres in Culpeper County, to Charles Urquhart Lovell on May 1, 1837.[159] In 1848 and 1849, they bought several hundred acres in Orange County.[160,161] In addition to his farms, the Willis mills supplied much of the timber for the Orange Plank Road. His estate was valued in June 1856 at $39,982.[162] It included an 11-room house, seven other buildings, a steam saw mill, and over 2,200 acres. Over half of the value of his estate was slaves.

Ellwood, the William Jones family

William Jones purchased from Brig. Gen. Alexander and Elizabeth Washington Spotswood 642 acres for 600 pounds "beginning at the Wilderness Bridge…" duly recorded April 1, 1788.[163] William Jones became a major landowner along the eastern boundary of the Alexandria Tract, developing Ellwood into a very large estate spanning from Wilderness Tavern to the Trap property. He completed the Ellwood house by 1805. In 1822, he was willed his brother's land. The vast majority of his land was in Spotsylvania County, but he also held indenture trusts on property in Orange County.[164] He rose to be the wealthiest man along Germanna Road, while his neighbors' fortunes disappeared. A principal measure of wealth was the number of slaves held. William Jones reached a maximum of 107 slaves in 1820, and at his death in 1845, he owned 60 slaves.

The distance between the courthouses of Culpeper, Orange and Fredericksburg was such that overnight guests were frequent at the Wilderness houses. The most notable was Gen. Marquis LaFayette's visit to Ellwood. The National Park Service files contain a record of John Spotswood meeting with LaFayette at Ellwood in 1824.[165]

> "In the early days of my visit to the Lacy home, Ellwood in the Wilderness, I knew the father, the venerable John Spotswood, and frequently heard his memories and family traditions. He told me that when LaFayette passed through the wilderness, 1824, he a boy of sixteen joined the cavalcade, he was present at the ball … He said the Marquis at once took up one of his heels and said, "Mr. Spotswood, your grandfather the General, was wounded in the heel in the battle of Princeton."[166] – J. P. Smith, 1922.

Betty Churchill Jones died in 1823 and was buried at Ellwood. Five years later William married Lucinda Gordon, granddaughter of John Gordon and Lucy Churchill, the parents of James Gordon of Germanna. Betty Churchill Jones, the daughter of William and Lucinda, was born June 21, 1829. In 1845, William Jones died, leaving Ellwood to his wife, all other land to his two daughters. After her mother's marriage and her marriage to Horace Lacy in 1848, Betty Jones Lacy owned Ellwood.[167]

Payne's Farm

The old Payne plantation totaled nearly 1,000 acres. The Civil War Battle of Payne's Farm was fought on an adjoining tract. It remained in the Payne family until 1952.[168] All of the land parcels along Indiantown Road from Indiantown to Zoar Road, and further along Zoar Road, contain the description "Payne" in the Orange County land records. Several Payne family members built their homes in that area from as early as 1774 to the mid-1850s.[169]

Charles Payne married Lucy Jones in Orange County on November 8, 1814. They eventually had nine children: Eliza A., Jane, William H., Elizabeth, Susan, Charles, Mary A., John T. and Francis.[170] He established his home at the head of Russell Run adjoining Ikey Richards and John Robinson, 21 miles east by north of Orange County Court House. About 1830 his wife inherited from her father Francis Jones 125 acres on Middle Flat Run, which they sold in 1846.[171] He died in 1853 in Orange County. His will, dated February 5, 1852, named his neighbor, Larkin Willis, as executor.

Roach, Robinson and Almond Families

The Roach family maintained farms in the Russell Run and Flat Run watersheds for a period of over 200 years. The early records include:

> *Ordered that the Following Persons Vizt. all the Male Labouring Tithables of James Roach, John Roach,... work on the Road from the Wilderness Bridge to Germanna ford & that the sd Thorpe be Overseer of the same.*[172]

John Roach's property was located between Russell Run and Route 601. He received on July 14, 1769, a patent for 335 acres adjoining William Russell, deceased, Thomas Morris, and Spotswood's line.[173] He died in 1777.[174] In his will, Absalom Roach left the family's land to his son-in-law, Willy Morris. William (Willy) Morris had married Molly Roach on February 19, 1813, in Orange County, Virginia.[175] Elizabeth Morris sold to James Roach 97 acres for $291, duly recorded on April 26, 1813.[176,177] Henry D. Roach married Elizabeth Ann Payne on November 24, 1845.[178]

Along Zoar Road near Locust Grove, the land parcels contain the description "Almond" in the Orange County land records. John Robinson's wife, Nancy, was the daughter of James Roach and Elizabeth Lindsay.[179] Their daughter Mary Ann married John F. Almond in Orange County on January 20, 1834.

Robinson's Tavern

Brig. Gen. Alexander Spotswood and his wife Elizabeth Washington sold 168 acres to John Robinson, recorded on June 24, 1791, "On the east side of upper Flat Run, thence up the main Route unto the beginning."[180] Robinson's Tavern was begun in 1812 and finished in 1815. It was used as a tavern in stagecoach days and stood on the site of the Old Fredericksburg Swift Run Gap Turnpike, now Route 20.[181] The tavern was a two-story frame building with two chimneys and eight rooms. It was built by John Robinson, the great-grandfather of Mr. Walter Almond of Locust Grove.[182] By the time of the Civil War, it was occupied by John and Mary Ann Almond. Mary Ann was a daughter of John Robinson, who died in 1848.

At the time of the 1860 U.S. census, John Almond was 51 years old. He was listed as a farmer with real estate and personal property worth $5,110. The household included Mary Almond, age 45; Anne E. Almond, age 23; Thomas Almond, age 18; Mary L. Almond, age 15; and Juliett E. Almond, age 9.[183]

Gov. Almond Road

The road follows the high ground on the eastern boundary of the Russell Run watershed. Previously, it was the E. Fork Indiantown Road. The parcels along this road carry the names of, Payne, Roach and Willis. Only the Willis land is held in the same name as the original family. This parcel is 673 acres and carries the historic name Woodville. Mt. Zion Baptist Church is shown in many Civil War maps along this road.[184]

> ... road which leads from Locust Grove to Indiantown. Used as a farm road by owner, W. R. Almond, to this point. A sunken place indicates where it passed through the woods until it reached open field of J. L. Almond where it can be traced no further.[185]

Dempsey, Mason, and Sander Families

Daniel Dempsey leased a tenement containing 110 acres from James Somerville on the east side of the Germanna Road.[186] In 1846, his will was recorded in Orange County, witnessed by his neighbor John R. Spotswood.[187] P. Dempsey, age 45, is listed in the 1850 census as a neighbor of John R. Spotswood with the occupation of overseer. For generations, members of the Dempsey family were buried at the Alexander Wilderness Cemetery on the east side of Route 20.[188]

John Mason signed an indenture to George Faulconer in 1801 that clearly describes the location of his land as the lower end of Orange County.[189] Charles Mason, possibly his grandfather, was a resident of Orange County prior to 1788.[190] Charles, as most of his neighbors, had a very large family. Upon his death, Rebecca Mason was appointed guardian to the six orphan children of Charles Mason.[191] In 1834, John Mason in order to reduce his debt of $61.67 to James and John P Coleman sold a Negro girl named Jane.[192] A Charles Mason born in 1798 appears in the Orange County census of 1850 with his wife Lucy R. and 11 children.[193]

Nathaniel Sanders is listed in the Benjamin Grymes census of October 1782 with thirteen white and two black. Nathaniel possessed a considerable estate, both real and personal. From 1763 to 1780, he procured land along Mine Run.[194] His will of 1808 left his wife a life estate and after that, it was to be equally divided among his children. The deeds provide evidence that as some of the children left Orange County; they would sell to their siblings. In 1820, John and Joanna Sanders Gaine of Rockingham County assigned their rights of Nathaniel Sanders to one of his sons, John.[195] Benjamin Sanders' will appointed his son, Francis, executor; it was witnessed by his neighbors Charles Mason and Thomas Robinson.[196] Francis Sanders purchased 29 acres for $82.66 from Richard Webb in May of 1845.[197]

In 1781 Elijah Craig and Nathaniel Sanders, dissenting Baptist ministers recommended by the elders of their society, were licensed to perform the marriage ceremony. William Bell was appointed to administer the prescribed oath, "to oblige all the inhabitants to give assurance of allegiance to the State," and certain dissenting ministers, John Price, Elijah Craig, Nathaniel Sanders, Bartlett Bennett, and Richard Cave, took the oaths of allegiance and fidelity.[198]

Robert Gaines and Francis Jones Families along Flat Run

Alexander Spotswood leased 125 acres on Mountain Road and Flat Run in December 1772 to Robert Gaines.[199] Eighteen years later, Robert purchased 501 acres from Alexander Spotswood in the middle and upper Flat Run, on the south side of Mountain Road and adjacent to the Richards Plantation.[200] In 1799, Robert Gaines and his wife Elizabeth sold 180 acres to Francis Jones spanning from the east side of the Middle Flat Run to the west side of Middle Flat Run and corner of John Robinson.[201]

John Spotswood and wife Mary of Orange County conveyed to Francis Jones a parcel of land being of the tract of land the said John Spotswood "now lives on", 113 ¾ acres both sides of the Flat Run.[202] This parcel eventually became part of Lake of the Woods. Francis Jones continued to accumulate land around Flat Run for the next 15 years.[203] By May of 1828, he held 575 acres. He died at home only a couple of years later. Mary Jones, Milly Jones and neighbors Reuben Gaines, C. Payne and Roddy Hawkins were at his side.[204] His will was administered by Benjamin Sanders and witnessed by other neighbors, John Gibson and Richard Richards. He was a prosperous farmer with an estate worth over $2,000.[205] In January 1833, Reuben Gaines and his wife Sally, both living in Rockingham County, sold Sally's right.[206]

> *… at the division of the land belonging to Francis Jones dec'd of Orange … plat and division of estate of the said F. Jones dec'd filed in the clerk's office Orange.*

No record of division of this land has been found other than the 125 acres passed to Lucy Jones that eventually became the property of H. D. Roach, and later part of Lake of the Woods.

Orange Grove, the Spotswood Family

A portion of the Alexandria tract, near to Flat Run, remained in the Spotswood family for seven generations. Five generations, spanning almost 150 years, resided on the land that they named Orange Grove. During that time, the family sold off most of their thousands of acres.[207] Land was a better source of income than livestock or anything they could grow.

Capt. John Spotswood established his seat at Orange Grove, within the Wilderness quarter of his father, sometime after his marriage to Sallie Rowzie on September 19, 1771, and probably circa 1773.[208, 209][210] His second son was born in November 1781. On December 2, 1795, John purchased part of Germanna from James Gordon, expanding his holdings in the original Alexandria Tract.

> *The View of the Road Petitioned for by Adam Goodlet & others being returned it is Ordered that John Spotswood, James Somerville & Wm. Hawkins & Reubin Hawkins*

> *Owners of the Land Which the said Intended Road Will go throug Be Summoned to Next Court to Shew cause if any Why the said Road Should not be Established.*[211]

> *John Spotswood lived in the Wilderness a few miles from Germanna, and after the Revolution was known as "Col. Spotswood." He was noted for his hospitality, and his home was a favorite stopping place for Orange County gentlemen, going to Fredericksburg on business or for pleasure. He was once a candidate for the House of Delegates, but was defeated.*[212]

After the death of Capt. John Spotswood, his son John Spotswood, Jr., received his father's land in Orange County. The other sons were given the lands in Culpeper County. The Culpeper County lands were a principal source of income. The accounts of John Spotswood for 1792 show an income from 19 tenants. Apparently, without the income from the Culpeper tenants, John Jr. became indebted by 1811. He placed in indenture two parcels, the Orange Grove and Chesterville (a.k.a. Chesterfield) containing 2,500 acres and a saw and gristmill valued at 2,870 pounds money of Virginia, including the 21 Negro slaves of age 3 to 38.[213] John Spotswood, Jr., sold 517 acres in 1813. He placed his father's 1,200 acres sawmill tract, which may have been on Flat Run, for sale in 1816.

> *My saw-mill tract of land, situated on the lower end of Orange county, containing about 1200 acres. 5 or 600 acres of this land is of good quality for tillage, and lies well; the remainder contains a quantity of good pine fit for the use of the saw mill. There runs through the lower end of the tract, a stream that will afford water for a saw and gristmill at least 9 months in the year, and an excellent site for their erection. This property is distant 17 miles from Fredericksburg, and from the Wilderness tavern about 2 miles. From thence to Fredericksburg is a good turnpike, where there is always a ready sale for plank. The land also contains a considerable quantity of good oak timber, fit for barrels, which meets with a ready sale immediately in the neighborhood ...* - John Spotswood, Jr.[214]

George Thornton paid $2,844.87 to John Spotswood, Jr., and his wife Mary for 517 acres bounded by Germanna Road and on the west side of Flat Run adjoining James Gordon, John Spotswood, Somerville and Richards, duly recorded March 15, 1813.[215] George Thornton had previously purchased 402 acres from Benjamin Grymes and Sally Grymes, his wife, for indenture of $1,500, the land lately purchased from Alexander Spotswood, Esquire, survey of December 14, 1778. George Thornton bought additional land in Orange County.[216]

Chesterfield, sold to George W. Thornton in 1813, was later sold by Thornton's executors to Samuel Skinner in 1818, and Skinner later bought the adjoining Somerset (Flat Run) tract as well. He maintained ownership until 1870.

John Spotswood, Jr., does not have a will on file at the Orange County courthouse. He did transfer his estate to his son John R. Spotswood, with an indenture dated May 11, 1833.[217] It provided a life estate at Orange Grove for John, Jr., and his wife Mary. The death of John, Jr., at his residence in Orange County was reported in the *Virginia Herald* on April 18, 1835. Mary lived at Orange Grove another twelve years.[218] John R. Spotswood was the head of household in 1850. The enumeration included not only his wife and five children but also the Robert Hartshorn family of New York engaged in gold mining.[219]

In an indenture recorded December 24, 1827, between John's son, John R. Spotswood, and William Jones, Orange Grove is listed as containing 500 acres.[220] Twenty years later, in an indenture recorded January 2, 1845, Orange Grove contains 400 acres and 9 slaves, 10 cattle, 30 sheep and 15 hogs.[221] The release was recorded on April 16, 1850.[222] Although the estate was but a sliver of its original acreage, John R. Spotswood was honored with being a Gentleman Justice of the Orange County Court as his father had been 50 years earlier.[223]

Five generations resided at Orange Grove, 23 children were born there between 1772 and 1872, and some died as infants or young children. At least one marriage took place at Orange Grove.[224] The large house at Orange Grove burned down a second time after the Civil War, about 1873, and the family moved into what was the servants' quarters, a smaller house listed in the WPA of Virginia Historic Inventory Survey of Orange County in 1936. [225,226]

> *Mrs. Willis never saw the house, which burned, but feels that the Spotswood corner in the Richmond museum may have a description or possibly a picture ... Mr. Willis states that he remembers seeing a foundation somewhere in the vicinity of the (small) house.*[227]

All that remains of this historic estate, besides the pile of bricks, are two pages of the family registry written by Captain John's grandson, John R. Spotswood, and the written history of the last resident, Mrs. Lelia Spotswood Willis.[228] Mrs. Willis said that her parents, her grandparents, her great-grandparents and great-great-grandparents Spotswood are all buried at "Orange Grove."[229] The Spotswood family cemetery is located in Lake of the Woods section 14 between lots 3 and 4. The grave markers for Lelia's brother and parents are located there. Several fieldstones are also arranged in the cemetery. While impossible to date, they do appear to be lined up and could mark many gravesites.

> *It is the group's intention to try to identify a number of graves, marked only by small stones. In addition to restoring the Spotswood graveyard and its surroundings ... lake officials also are considering the building of a ... memorial to the Spotswood family -* James Foote, Vice President of Virginia Wildlife Club, Inc. [230]

Both the park and cemetery were inspected in November 2004 by Stephanie Jacobe, Secretary of the Virginia Archeological Society. She is certain the bricks are of 18th century origin, that both locations are valuable historic sites that should be preserved, and that probably several generations of the Spotswood family are buried in the cemetery. The number and age of the gravesites could only be determined by a preliminary survey of the cemetery, conducted by a state-licensed professional.

The Alfred Apperson Family

In 1846, Alfred Apperson purchased 200 acres from Thomas Robinson and Elizabeth, his wife, on old Mountain Road near the Lower Flat Run, adjoining Polly Jones, Robert Roach and James

Somerville.[231,232] Alfred Apperson conveyed his land to his son Eli, born June 2, 1849.[233] Part of this property would, 100 years later, become part of Lake of the Woods.[234] Some of the Apperson property became the Wilderness Battlefield, and another part was conveyed to the Lake of the Woods Church.

Alfred and Malinda Jones Apperson were a freeholding family that was farming in the Wilderness on the border between Orange and Spotsylvania counties.[235,236] Alfred Apperson was overseer for William Jones' estate.[237]

> *The Orange County farms Elmwood (Ellwood) and Hoodville (Woodville), both managed by Alfred Apperson, were in good land, but even this sparsely peopled piedmont of the Old Dominion was too confining for (his son) John Samuel, who was determined to make his own way. There were three brothers and three sisters who could help on the two farms, and there was actually little to keep the oldest boy on the farm, especially as times grew hard ... Eighteen-fifty-seven was such a hard time, a year of economic downturn ... and the Appersons endured some privations; unlike slaveowners of their region, they could not raise money by selling off their human property ...[238]*

The old house, which no longer exists, is labeled Hopkins House in the upper left corner of the map of 1951.[239] The Alfred Apperson house is shown on many of the Civil War maps of Orange County. A cemetery is located near the location of that house in which Alfred and Malinda are buried along with two others. There is a possibility that Alfred's father Peter is buried there. There is an estate inventory on file in the Orange County Clerk's Office of a Peter Apperson recorded November 14, 1834. That inventory lists farm animals and equipment, and household items and books.[240] Alfred's father received a pension for service during the Revolutionary War.[241]

The Henry D. Roach Family

Charles Payne and wife Lucy Jones sold Henry D. Roach the tract assigned to Charles Payne by the Commissioners in the division of land estate of Francis Jones.[242]

Henry had married their daughter Elizabeth Ann the previous year.[243] The parcel is described as 125 acres adjoining Harrison Gordon, Robert Roach, Roddy Hawkins, and Wild Cat Road, and the deed is signed by Robert Roach and Armistead C. Gordon, Justice of the Peace.[244] This was originally part of the John Spotswood plantation.[245] The property near Flat Run lies on Route 601, about five miles from Locust Grove. The house was built in circa 1845 and passed from him to his son Absalom Roach in 1885. It was a plain, eight-room frame house with two chimneys - one at each end.[246] All of this property and the adjacent land would, 100 years later, become part of Lake of the Woods.

Henry D. Roach was married to the sister of John Payne. Their daughter-in-law's report in the WPA of Virginia Historical Inventory does not match with the record of the deed discussed above.

> *Visited Mrs. Dolly Roach and her two sons, William and Lindsay ... The house she lives in is about eighty years old. (circa 1860) The farm was inherited from Mr. John Payne, who was a brother of the mother of Mr. Ab Roach, husband of the informant*

... She stressed these things. The present generation pays little attention to things, which happened in the past or to stories or happenings, which have been related to them.[247]

The Reynolds Family

The Reynolds house is located between the Roach families and Alfred Apperson's house and on the west side of Flat Run Road, just west of the junction of two branches of Flat Run. John Samuel Apperson makes reference to the Reynolds family in his diary. The 1850 U.S. Census lists Daniel G. Reynolds as a neighbor of the Henry and Robert Roach families. He was a millwright and had a sizable estate valued at $3,820.

"At home (Alfred Apperson's house) to dinner after which I started to visit Mr. H. Roach ... Mr. R and myself walked over to his brother's a short distance across the fields ... After this was over Mrs. Reynolds & lady came in and we spent a pleasant evening ... The old Squire came in ... His daughter Ann is a very handsome clever girl. Near two o'clock, I left ... From there to my father's I had a dark muddy lonesome walk." – John Samuel Apperson.[248]

Antebellum Houses at Germanna

UPPER: Gordon House at Germanna. Photo provided from the files of The Memorial Foundation of the Germanna Colonies in Virginia, Inc. Built on the site of the Enchanted Castle on the south side of Flat Run near its mouth on Rapidan River.

LOWER: Somerset (Flat Run), recently restored. Photo by Dan McFarland. Built on land on the north side of Flat Run across from the old Gordon property and near Skinner's Ford.

Robinson's Tavern Relic and Restored

Photos by Dan McFarland.

UPPER: Painting created circa 1936. On display in the main dining room of the new Robinson's Tavern & Grill, Locust Grove, Virginia.

LOWER: Original Tavern restored and occupied as a residence at Locust Grove, Virginia.

Homes, Still Standing, that Saw Action May 1864

Photos by Dan McFarland.

UPPER: Widow Willis house located on the Meadows Farms Golf Course. The house is abandoned. Historic markers are posted in front and rear.

LOWER: Ellwood, the Lacy House, located at Wilderness Battlefield, Fredericksburg and Spotsylvania National Military Park. The house has been fully restored to its appearance May 1864 and is open to visitors.

Homes, No Longer Standing, That Saw Action May 1864

These two homes had withstood the battles of 1863 and 1864 but no longer remain standing in Lake of the Woods due to subsequent fires.

UPPER: The antebellum Spotswood house pictured in a sketch by Alfred Waud drawn May 5, 1864 and annotated "Spotswood house." Library of Congress Prints and Photographs Division Washington, D.C. The sketch was made while standing on Germanna Plank Road facing east, near the current location of LOW front gate. This home was burned down circa 1870 and little was saved of its historic items.[249]

LOWER: The antebellum Roach family farm. *The Evening Star,* April 21, 1967. This home occupied the "Life Estate" at Lake of the Woods until set afire in 1972.

An 1800 Log Cabin on Apperson Land

UPPER LEFT: Image of Alfred and Malinda Jones Apperson circa 1860.

UPPER RIGHT: Photo by Dan McFarland. Exterior of the log cabin portion, circa 1800, of the Clarence Apperson house. Clarence was the great-grandson of Alfred and Matilda Apperson.

LOWER: Photo by Dan McFarland. Interior restoration of the log cabin with fireplace room.

Chapter 5   Time (Almost) Stands Still

For a hundred years, little changed along Germanna Road. The survivors of war never recovered. Their children eventually established the battlefield memorial, which was the biggest change in the area, but it was little more than a few acres acquired by the Federal government and a road sign. The only asset of any value was the land, and many sold what they could. With only family labor, the tilled acreage was replaced by timberland. The population of Orange County in 1860 was 10,851. The demographics were 4,407 white, 6,111 slaves and 188 free Negroes. A hundred years later, it was 7,052 whites and 5,519 Negroes for a total of 12,571.[250]

> There were 6,111 slaves in Orange in 1860, constituting an asset of quite a million and a half dollars, nearly double the value of all other personal property, which was wiped out as with a sponge.[251]

No Area of the County Saw as Much nor Endured as Much

> I have been a resident of Lake of the Woods since 1979. For the past six years I have become active in searching for relics from the Civil War. Here at the lake I have been fortunate to have found bullets, buttons, knapsack hooks, pie server, a knife and other types of memorabilia believed to be used during the civil war and possibly as far back as the Revolutionary War. I have searched several locations here at the lake including properties off of Westover Parkway, Confederate Circle, Monticello and Wilderness Drive. I was fortunate to find relics on my own property first on Happy Creek then on Birchside Circle. I belong to the Civil War Preservation Trust, and am a member of The Rappahannock Civil War Round Table ... also belong to the Orange County Historical Society. – Dan Hartwick, Member LOWA

From the opening of the Civil War until its end, no area of the county saw as much nor endured as much as the lower end of Orange County. Most of the men volunteered early on. The farms were either totally deserted, as was the Lacy farm, Ellwood, or run by the women and old men as was the Spotswood farm, Orange Grove. Company C, 7th Virginia Infantry, the Culpeper Rifles, listed two sons from the Apperson family, four from the Dempsey family, four from the Webb family, and three of the Willis boys. Many of the families within and surrounding the future Lake of the Woods also had sons join Company C, commanded by J. W. Almond of Orange, including Bledsoe, Cook, Coleman, Hawkins, Johnson, Morris, and Richards. James Roach joined the Orange Rangers, 6th Cavalry, along with two from the Almond family, two from the Reynolds family and a Mason and a Richards. The Reynolds and Sanders families added two each to the Peyton Battery along with a Mason.[252] Two of the Spotswood sons served in the 30th Virginia Infantry.

Even before this land saw actual combat, the adverse economic impact was felt by all. John Samuel Apperson wrote the following in his diary.

> *Nov. 30, 1862, "I pushed on and took the old road at Roache's and went to my father's. I saw F. Johnson at his Tanyard and The Old Grove looks very lonesome to what it used to. I found sister and mother both in bed but better than I expected. Eli has a running sore on his leg, which I do not like - he will never be healthy. Father was on the road looking at the army." – John Samuel Apperson[253]*

> *Dec. 1, 1862, "This morning H. D. Roach came over to see me ... I leave for the Reg't tomorrow ... Salt is an object with all persons in the country now. 2 oz. to each member of each family at 8 cts per pound distributed by committees appointed for the purpose. Speculators are selling salt for 1$ per pound. - John Samuel Apperson[254]*

The day before the Union Army of the Potomac crossed the Rappahannock for the first time, Major Lacy was to see the contrast between harsh life in the Confederate Army of Northern Virginia and fine life in the prosperous town of Fredericksburg. The next day was the end of prosperity for a hundred years in the original tracts of Lt. Gov. Alexander Spotswood.

> *On the 10th of December, 1862, ... "I informed General Lee that I had leave of absence for several days, and he kindly invited me to remain as his guest at his headquarters. I felt highly honored by the invitation, but the experience of one meal was enough. Rye coffee, heavy biscuits, and poor, tough beef I thought would hardly compensate for the honor of dining with the commander-in-chief. The night of the 10th I spent in Fredericksburg with my brother, the Rev. B. T. Lacy, D.D. ... where a company of young ladies had gathered to listen to my brother, a noted raconteur. It was very late before we retired." – Major J. Horace Lacy[255]*

Ellwood was left in the care of a manager with several black slaves. Major Lacy was captured June 10, 1862, while visiting his wife and five children at Greenwood, two miles east of the Orange-Spotsylvania County line. In the fall, he was released from Ft. Delaware and the family moved to a safe haven in Lexington, Virginia. The estate was deserted by May of 1863. The condition of the Virginia economy at that time was witnessed by E. A. Paul, a reporter for *The New York Times*.

> *The fear of famine was everywhere expressed; the government seizes upon everything that can go to sustain the army, leaving those who are not in the army to shift as best they can....In the counties visited there were but few rebels found at home, except the very old and the very young. In the nine days' travel did not see fifty able-bodied men who were not in some way connected with the army. Nearly every branch of business is at a stand-still. The shelves in stores are almost everywhere empty; the shop of the artisan is abandoned and in ruins.[256]*

Little is known about how most of Lacy's former slaves fared.

> *In 1863 one Chatham slave, Charles Henry Sprout, enlisted in the United States Colored Troops, African-American regiments that fought with the Northern armies. When Sprout was discharged in 1866 in Texas, he returned to Fredericksburg to live. He died in 1926 and was buried in the Fredericksburg National Cemetery. Another Lacy slave, Charlie Weedon, served as a guide for Confederate troops during military operations in the Chancellorsville and Wilderness campaigns. It is uncertain if he survived the war.*[257]

A year later during the Mine Run Campaign, the tanyard near Locust Grove was set afire by some Union Army soldiers. Other places in the area were vandalized, including Ellwood, but fortunately were not put to the torch.

> *… tanyard was operated by Eugene Morris' grandfather probably twenty years prior to the War Between the States, then by his father until 1910. It is related to him that the Northern Army took six hundred half tanned steer hides from the yard during the war. They were probably worth at that time about $9.00 each. When the hides were stolen, all buildings were burned and machinery destroyed. The total loss was estimated at about $10,000.*[258]

At the Henry D. Roach house, two miles south of Flat Run on Route 601, Absalom Roach, a young boy, stood on the porch and watched a battle. The Union troops raided the place and took nearly everything they had.[259] Absalom Roach lies buried at Zoar Cemetery at Burr Hill. He seems to have been only ten at the time of raid of his father's farm.[260] This probably occurred in November 1863 during the Mine Run Campaign battle of Payne Farm. As the Union Army retreated to Culpeper County, they ransacked and foraged the farms and mills of the lower end of Orange County.

Robinson's Tavern was used briefly as headquarters for General Meade in the Mine Run Campaign and as a field hospital after the Mine Run Campaign and during the Battle of the Wilderness. It was a prominent feature on Civil War maps of the area.[261] Thomas Almond, son of the owner of Robinson's Tavern, served as a private in Co. I, 6th Virginia Cavalry, having enlisted in April 1862. He was wounded twice during the war. His remarried widow, Lucy Almond Johnson, resided at Locust Grove, Orange County.[262] At the start of the Wilderness Campaign, Confederate Second Corps commander, Lt. Gen. Richard S. Ewell, stayed at the Robinson's Tavern on May 4, 1864.

During the Battle of Chancellorsville, John Samuel Apperson, a neighbor who was serving as a hospital steward in the Stonewall Brigade wrote the following in his diary on May 7, 1863.

> *"This morning by light I was up and off to my post (at field hospital … on Plank Road in Wilderness, Orange Co.) … Henry D. Roach was down in the evening … N. Jones invited me over to meet him … the old fields as I went along were familiar to me. Today I performed my first important operation, took off a Yankee's leg below the knee."*
> – John Samuel Apperson.[263]

The Spotswood farm remained inhabited by the owners throughout the battles of Chancellorsville, Mine Run and the Wilderness. During the Battle of Chancellorsville, "after ten or fifteen shots were fired at the house," John R. Spotswood, Jr., of Company E the 9th Cavalry was captured while convalescing at his home, Orange Grove. He died in a prisoner-of-war hospital a few weeks later.[264]

In Alfred Waud's sketch "Spotswood house", the white smoke is from the battle in the Wilderness visible in the distant background. Elements of the Army of the Potomac, VI Corps bivouacked here on May 4, 1864. From the vicinity of the Spotswood home, General Horatio Wright's division of the VI Corps entered into the fighting on May 5, rushing down the Spotswood Road to reinforce the V Corps. Gordon Rhea described the scene as a harrowing crawl.

> *Advancing up the woods road from Spotswood Plantation, Wright's Federals had wound along a narrow ridge. Wilderness Run lay to their south and the Flat Run to their north. Countless tributaries fed each of these creeks and cut steep-banked gullies that knifed off to all points of the compass. Hills popped up unexpectedly, separated by dark little swamps and streams. Obscure depressions and ridges, clogged with choking second growth, offered irresistible opportunities for ambush. A Union soldier described the countryside as the "awfullest brush, briars, grapevine, etc., I was ever in."*[265]

A Union hospital was temporarily established at the Spotswood House until Confederate shelling caused it to be moved. Rev. John Adams, the chaplain of the 5th Maine (a VI Corps unit), refers to the Spotswood Hospital during the phase of the battle that must have been Gordon's Flank Attack. He wrote on June 9, 1864:[266]

> *"At Spotswood Hospital, I came near being cut off from the army. The enemy had turned enough to cut off one road [obviously the Spotswood a.k.a. Culpeper Mine Road], which connected the hospital with the army; there was another road not a half-mile from it [probably the Germanna Plank Road]; if the enemy had pushed for that I should have been in Richmond before this, with a bevy of surgeons."*

Traces of the Spotswood Road, also known as the Culpeper Mine Road, are still visible even though a large part of it was obliterated by construction of the Lake of the Woods golf course and roads.[267]

> *Ina and Bob Hartwell owned the house on the corner of Lakeview Parkway and Mt. Pleasant. One day after an especially heavy rain, Ina found many old glass bottles, etc., in the yard. They were identified by someone at a museum as being from the Civil War era. Further research showed that there had been a Yankee hospital on the site.*[268]

The Union hospital at Spotswood's house must have covered several acres with its ambulance wagons, tents and wounded. The Union army crossed the Rapidan River with more than 500 ambulances, 294 hospital tents and 433 medical officers.[269] At least one third of those resources were in the Lake of the Woods area near Spotswood Park.

Confederate hospitals also were in the area for several weeks after the battle.

"We are about starting to "Wilderness" with a force of contrabands to bury the many dead who have been lying as they fell in those furious battles of May 5, 6, 7, 8, &c. We came from there about one week ago, where our brigade had been sent to bring in some wounded said to be in the rebel hospitals in the Wilderness ... The poor fellows that were rescued were the "worst wounded cases'" and their joy and surprise when our cavalry dashed up to their hospital tents was extreme. They assured us that they had received as kind treatment from the rebel attendants as had their own wounded, many of whom were still there in the hospitals. They only complained of an insufficiency of food -- but were anxious to get away toward our lines, even if they died in the ambulances, (some of whom did)." - J.A.M. MCPHERSON.[270]

"My total loss at the Wilderness was 1,250 killed and wounded. The burial parties from two divisions reported interring over 1,100 of the enemy. The third and largest made no report. When we moved probably one-third or more were still unburied of those who were within reach of our lines ..." - R. S. EWELL[271]

One of the earliest encounters in the Battle of the Wilderness occurred at the Widow Willis' house. On the morning of May 5, 1864, the 1st North Carolina Cavalry was patrolling just off the downriver crossings, led by the intrepid Major William H. H. Cowles. At 9 a. m., Cowles discovered Union pickets at Mrs. Willis' house on Flat Run Road, two miles below Germanna Ford.[272]

Before daylight of May 5 the reveille sounded, and as soon as it was light enough to see the road we were on our way to Germanna Ford of the Rapidan ... and soon after noon we crossed the Rapidan on the pontoon bridges, and, passing through the old Confederate bridge-head fortifications, we advanced about southeast along the Germanna Plank Road, toward Wilderness Tavern. This region was well named "the Wilderness." The country, which is rough in aspect, is generally covered with old forest with only narrow and obscure by-roads penetrating it, while clearings are few and far between. It was then in the fullest sense a wilderness. We kept on down the "plank road" — most of the plank worn out and gone — and about two and one-half or three miles from the bridge, we turned off to the right, following a private road, the main part of which ran southwest to "Widow Willis' place" - Colonel Cutcheon of the 20th Michigan Infantry.[273]

The Willis home still stands, but it is abandoned; it remained in the Willis family until 1944. Next to the house is the family cemetery where Mary Gordon and Larkin Willis lie. It was owned and preserved by Kube Dairy Farm in the 1960s and is currently on the Meadows Farm Golf Course on Flat Run Road.

Families in Orange County had every able male child serve and many either killed or wounded by the end of the war. The Larkin Willis family memory of H. Willis, recorded in 1936, while more myth than fact, is indicative of the local posture.[274] From the day after to several years after the Battle of the Wilderness, bodies were removed and properly buried.[275,276]

Mr. Larkin Willis, who lived near Germanna, had ten sons in the War Between the

States 1861-1865. Five of them were killed and the others were wounded. "What more can a nation ask than a father give all his sons to fight its battles."[277]

Alexander D. Spotswood served four years in Company C of the 30th Virginia Infantry. James T. Todd, former Orange County Treasurer, as a youngster visited in the Spotswood house. He recalls a story of the old Rebel soldier who refused to fight lying down. "Preferring to stand in a trench," Todd said, "Alec, as he was known by everyone, would fire his musket at the enemy, always shouting: 'Take that, you damn Yankee, you!'"[278] After the war, it took a while before life returned to anything that could be called normal. When Alexander Spotswood returned from the service, his 66-year-old father, John R. Spotswood, his mother and two sisters were living at the home. The property was completely run down. There was nobody there who was physically able to operate the farm.

…the mansion house at "Orange Grove," the home of the Governor's grandson, Captain John Spotswood, of Revolutionary fame, … through successive generations until some years ago (circa 1870s), when the house was burned. The fireback was then removed from the tall chimney left standing above the ruins of the mansion and placed in a capacious fireplace of a cottage on the grounds, which after several rooms had been added, was fitted up as a residence and used by the Spotswood (family) in the hard years following the war Between the States.[279]

Anna Townsend Willis reported the post-war history of Orange Grove.[280]

Like many other soldiers, Uncle Alex never quite got over his war-time experiences. That period seemed more real to him than the remaining years of his long life … It was a quiet life for the most part there at "Orange Grove". … After the Civil war, poverty was more a badge of patriotism than a disgrace in the South … in cousin Lelia's generation, the Spotswood's remained aristocratically hard up – a phase meaning being poor but never admitting it, even to themselves!

"I shall not attempt to describe the dreary and disheartening struggle of reconstruction days. My older children remember that time that tried men's souls even more severally than the four long years of conflict, and to the younger ones it has become familiar by frequent repetition. I sincerely hope that none of them may ever be called upon to pass through the fiery ordeal to which their parents were subjected, and that never again will our dear old State be so bowed in the dust with trouble and humiliation as in those dark days, and with this hope for the future I shall bring to a close these rambling memories of the past," – Elizabeth Churchill Jones Lacy.[281]

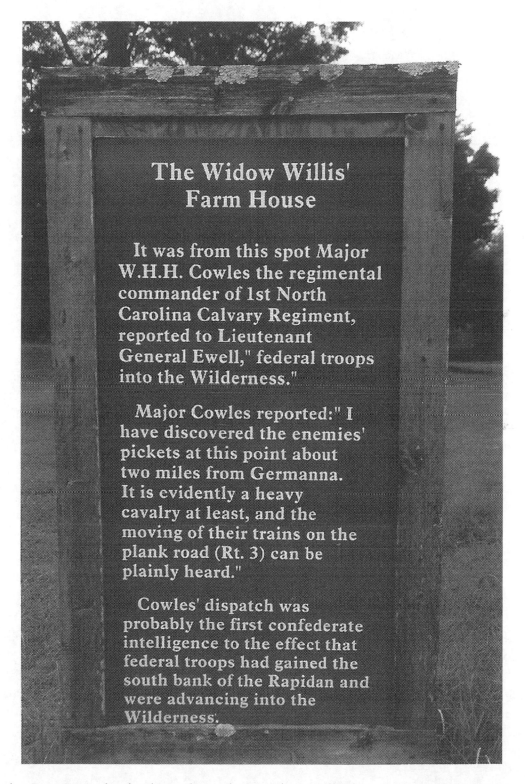

The Widow Willis'
Farm House

It was from this spot Major
W.H.H. Cowles the regimental
commander of 1st North
Carolina Calvary Regiment,
reported to Lieutenant
General Ewell," federal troops
into the Wilderness."

Major Cowles reported:" I
have discovered the enemies'
pickets at this point about
two miles from Germanna.
It is evidently a heavy
cavalry at least, and the
moving of their trains on the
plank road (Rt. 3) can be
plainly heard."

Cowles' dispatch was
probably the first confederate
intelligence to the effect that
federal troops had gained the
south bank of the Rapidan and
were advancing into the
Wilderness.

Photo by Dan McFarland. Plaque located at Widow Willis house on Meadows Farms Golf
Course.

Robert Roach to son James, 1866

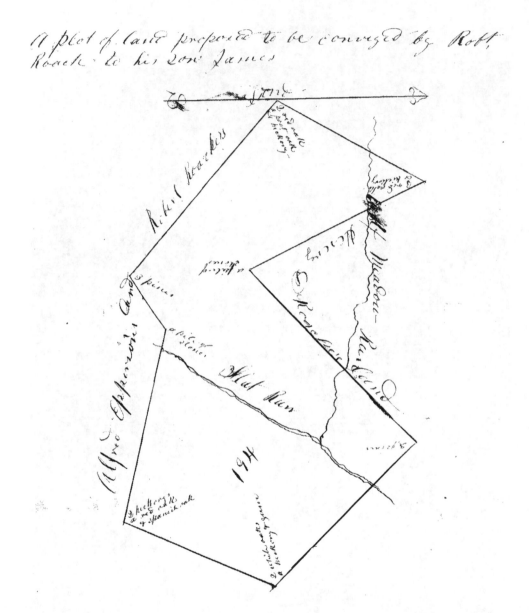

Land transfer continued in 1866 as before, irrespective of the status of statehood of the Commonwealth of Virginia. Robert Roach transferred his property on Route 601 (Flat Run Road) to his son James Roach.[282] The survey recorded is shown above. James was deputy sheriff of Orange County at age 26 when he married Adalade E. Row in 1859. He was sheriff when he married Henrietta J. Henderson soon after the Battle of Chancellorsville. He was still sheriff in 1867 when he married Jane G. Willis, daughter of James Willis and Elizabeth Gordon.[283]

Gordon Magisterial District

In 1870, the new constitution of the State became effective and the State was "readmitted into the Union." Each county had to be laid off into townships, and the Governor appointed Garrett Scott, R. L. Gordon, Ferdinand Jones, and William F. Brooking to perform that duty in Orange. Their report is recorded in the County Deed Book for 1870. The townships were named Barbour, Madison, Taylor, and Gordon, in memory of four eminent citizens of the county.[284]

From the creation of Orange County in 1734 until the adoption of the Constitution of 1870, the county was governed by the County Court consisting of "Gentlemen Justices" appointed by the Governor until 1852 and elected thereafter. In 1870, the legislative powers of the County Court were transferred to a Board of Supervisors elected from four magisterial districts.[285]

The original Alexandria Tract was the eastern part of the Gordon Magisterial District. The map of the area circa 1870 has several interesting features.[286] Germanna Road is labeled Culpeper Plank Road. The only structures shown near the road are the Willis Mill, Orange Grove (J. R. Spotswood farm), Flat Run Church, School House (W) and Vaucluse Gold Mine. The Spottswood Road along the high ground, which divides the Flat Run and Keaton Run watersheds, is clearly shown connecting to current Route 3 and Route 20. Little changed and by 1888 Burr Hill and Indiantown were the local centers of commerce with the Tinsley's Mill and the Willis' Mills respectively. Within the original Alexandria Tract, in 1888, only eight farmers were listed among the over two hundred principal farmers of the county.[287]

Some Families Stayed, Some Moved Away

After the sale of their mansion, Chatham, the Lacy family moved back to Ellwood in 1872.[288]

> ... there with my children and grandchildren life was again joyous – Elizabeth Churchill Jones Lacy.[289]

In July 1875, William Jones Lacy, eldest son of Horace and Betty Lacy, married Nora Willis in her home at Indiantown. After the birth of a son in May 1876, the couple moved to William's inherited Woodville. He buried Nora there in 1878. In December 1879, William married Sally Byrd Goodwin and they had three sons. William died of typhoid fever at Woodville on January 6, 1884.[290] Sally died the fall of the same year. The Lacy family left Ellwood in 1892 and put the estate under tenant management. In 1907 when Ellwood was sold, the tenant family, Mr. and Mrs. Robert Duval and twelve children moved to a 150-acre farm near Wilderness Post Office, Orange County. A son of a Union veteran, Mr. Hugh Willis purchased Ellwood, 1,520 acres, for a $5,000 note. The house was modernized with indoor plumbing, heat and electricity.

Two unmarried daughters of Benjamin Grymes, Hannah and Sallie, kept up the old house at Vaucluse after the rest of the family had scattered, and were true Virginia gentlewomen of the olden type. Hannah Grymes died and left a will dated February 28, 1876. Her estate was appraised at $276.[291] Peyton Grymes deeded 100 acres, including the mansion, to his son Benjamin A. Grymes, July 25, 1878.[292] Today, there is no evidence of Vaucluse, the home of the Benjamin Grymes family; neither was it listed in the WPA survey of this area taken in 1936.

Eli Apperson divided the Apperson land on Flat Run and conveyed to his twin sons, Alphonzo and Alonzo, born February 28, 1875.[293,294,295]

Thomas Almond had served in the 6th Virginia Calvary in the Civil War. His father had owned Robinson's Tavern valued in 1860 at $5,110. The tavern ceased operations in the latter part of the 19th Century and was used as a store and the Locust Grove post office. Thomas' remarried widow, Lucy Almond Johnson, still resided 60 years later at Locust Grove.[296]

William Churchill Spotswood, eldest son of the Spotswood family, had served in the 30th Virginia Infantry and died in 1870. His brother, Alexander D. Spottswood, also served in the 30th Virginia Infantry. Alexander married Lucy Harrison Gordon on December 15, 1869. She was the niece of Mary Gordon and Larkin Willis and great-granddaughter of James Gordon of Germanna.[297] Lucy and Alexander had their first child, Lelia, in 1871.[298] Lucy's father, John Addison Gordon died in Virginia in 1883 and was buried in Gordon House Cemetery at Germanna.[299] At his death, Germanna tract consisted of only 294 acres. The unmarried daughters sold the land to their cousin, J. M. Harris.[300] He was the last owner-occupant.[301]

John Rowzie Spotswood died at the age of 90; his obituary was published in the Fredericksburg Star on March 14, 1888. He was the owner of Orange Grove, and his name appears on several Civil War era maps marking his main house. Although he never put on a uniform due to his age at the start of the war, he witnessed firsthand the terror of war including the loss of a son and brief imprisonment during the Battle of Chancellorsville. During his life, the Orange Grove estate was reduced from thousands of acres and dozens of slaves to 500 acres farmed by the hands of the immediate family.

The conditions of the roads during the late 19th century were so bad that lower Orange County was at times isolated from the town of Orange, the location of the courthouse. Although John Rowzie Spotswood had been magistrate of the district, there never was a copy of a will entered into the courthouse records. The land was referred to as the J. R. Spottswood (successors) property 60 years after his death.[302] This caused his granddaughter Lelia great difficulty in establishing her right to sell the land. His son, Alexander D. Spottswood, assigned a trust to Charles Payne duly recorded on April 22, 1889.[303]

Alexander Gordon Spottswood was the only son of A. D. and Lucy. He never married. A businessman, he also operated the farm for his father when his father's health failed. He preceded his parents in death and is buried in the family cemetery located on Spottswood Road. His obituary appears in the Fredericksburg *Free Lance* on February 17, 1917. The photograph of his tombstone was provided by James C. Foote.

On February 1, 1923, Lelia's mother died at Orange Grove. Lucy Harrison Gordon Spottswood was buried in the family cemetery. Her obituary states, "Mrs. Spottswood was a woman of noble Chistian character, for more than fifty years a member of Flat Run Baptist Church."[304]

Alexander D. Spottswood was the last male descendant of Lt. Gov. Alexander Spotswood living on his great-great-great grandfather's grant in Orange County. A Virginian gentleman of the old school, he served as magistrate of the Gordon District. His obituary was printed in *The Free Lance* on December 11, 1924. It incorrectly stated that he died in the house he was born; he actually was born in the Spotswood house shown in the Waud sketch of 1864.

His will was written "____" day of May 1923. It stated, "devise all ... my property ... to my daughter ... Lelia Spottswood Willis, the wife of E. O. Willis ..." The will was probated December 1, 1925.[305] Lelia and her husband Edgar Willis moved to "the big, white house on Jamison Hill in the town of Culpeper."

With her amazing memory and a natural talent for writing, she fortunately realized the importance of recording memories of special events in the family. Her collection of letters, papers and pictures is a rich and lasting monument to her instinct for what was of value ... Lelia's heart still yearned back to Orange Grove, her childhood home. In the tender letter of goodbye she left us, she said that she had wanted to be buried at Orange Grove ... [306]

Betty Churchill Lacy died on May 3, 1907, at age 81. She was described in her obituary in the Fredericksburg *Free Lance* as "a woman of the highest Christian character, universally loved by all who knew her." That same year, their children sold Ellwood to Hugh Willis for $5,000. When Willis deeded the estate to his sister Blanche Jones and her son Gordon Willis Jones in 1933, it consisted of Ellwood Manor and 1,423 acres of land. Eventually Gordon Jones sold some of the property and donated the rest to the National Park Service, which took possession of the property upon the death of Jones' father, Leo Jones, in 1977.[307]

A. D. Spottswood, Wife and Son Buried at Orange Grove

MRS. A. D. SPOTTSWOOD

Passed Away At Home In Orange County At Advanced Age.

Mrs. Lucy Harrison Gordon Spottswood, wife of Mr. Alexander D. Spottswood, died at her home near Flat Run, Orange county, Thursday, aged 86 years. Mrs. Spottswood had been in bad health for several years and while her death was not unexpected it was a shock to a large number of relatives and friends.

She was a daughter of the late John Addison Gordon, of Orange Co., one of a family of thirteen children. Besides her husband she is survived by one daughter, Mrs. E. O. Willis, of Culpeper; one sister, Miss Fannie Gordon, of Raleigh, N. C., formerly of this city; one brother, Dr. William A. Gordon, of Orange county. She also had a number of relatives in this city.

Mrs. Spottswood was a woman of noble Christian character, for more than fifty years a member of Flat Run Baptist Church.

The funeral was held Friday afternoon at 3 o'clock, interment in the family burying ground on the home place, services conducted by Rev. E. O. Barnum, of Spotsylvania, pastor of Flat Run church.

ALEXANDER D. SPOTTSWOOD

Oldest Direct Descendant of One of Last Colonial Governors is Dead.

BELOVED IN HIS COMMUNITY

Mr. Alexander D. Spottswood, the oldest and one of the last direct descendants of Governor Alexander D. Spottswood, famous as one of best known of the Colonial governors of Virginia and leader of the Knights of the Golden Horseshoe, died at his home near Flat Run, Orange County, Va., Monday afternoon in the eighty-eighth year of his life. Mr. Spottswood died in the house in which he was born, built by a son of Governor Spottswood, not far from the famed residence of his ancestor at Germanna, where Virginia hospitality was lavishly dispensed in the early days of the country and where the Governor established one of the first iron foundries in America, colonizing it entirely with Germans. The ruins of the old residence of Governor Spottswood and some of the foundations of the buildings erected by the colonists are still to be seen.

A Virginia gentleman of the old school, Mr. Spottswood never for a moment in the course of his long life, thought of leaving the section of his nativity though he often was tempted to take up his residence elsewhere, and all of his days were spent among the people he knew and loved and for whom he always was willing to sacrifice and offer his services.

For many years he was a magistrate of the district in which he lived and his decisions in the interest of truth and justice are still remembered in his section. He was a member of the Flat Run Baptist church from which the funeral took place Tuesday afternoon at 2 o'clock, attended by a large number of sorrowing friends.

Last Spottswood House

"I remember a time when along about right here was the old Spotswood place. A narrow, shady road led off from the main road and through a gate to a small house, once the "quarters" of the large family home of John Spotswood grandson of Governor Alexander Spotswood." – Anna Townsend Willis[308]

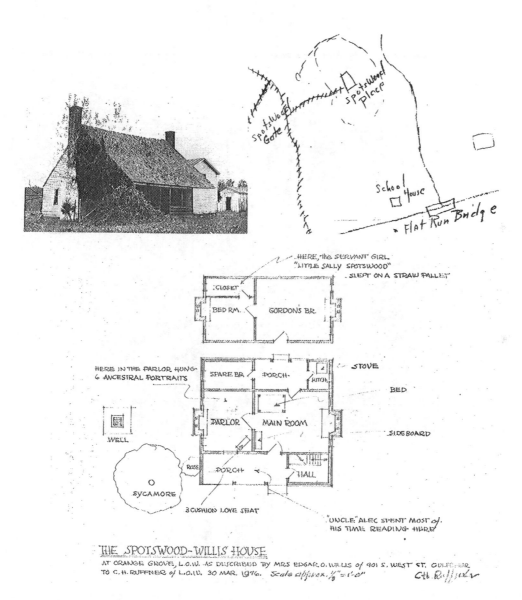

UPPER LEFT: Relic of the Spottswood cottage abandoned circa 1926. Photo taken in 1936.

UPPER RIGHT: Section of Frank Chenawith map circa 1951 locating the Spotswood place relic.

LOWER: Ruffner, Clifford H Jr. "The Spotswood- Willis House at Orange Grove," a 1976 architectural study in the historic file at the LOWA office.

Lelia Spottswood, the Last Resident of Orange Grove

John Partridge conveys to Edward Woodman

John A. Partridge of Washington, D.C., bought 100 to 200 acre parcels in the Flat Run Germanna Road area over a period from 1875 to 1890.[309] He paid from $2.50 to $9.75 an acre for land adjacent to Melville Mining Company and Greenwood Mining Company. On March 15, 1890, he sold 636 acres to Edward Woodman of Portland, Maine, for $2,000.[310] This was the last recorded land transaction by John Partridge in Orange County. The land is described as south side of Germanna Road, "the same tract conveyed in March 1841 by John H. Gordon and wife except three acres on Germanna road conveyed in January 1881 to the trustees of public schools of Gordon district."[311,312] Edward Woodman of Maine may have been buying for timberland or mineral rights or both. In 1918, he sold some of his land along Flat Run and Germanna Plank Road to J. W. Masters, "subject to the reservation of the mineral rights". It eventually became part of Lake of the Woods.

R. S. Knighton

The Virginia Historic Inventory 1936 map of Orange County clearly shows that Route 601 was named Knighton Road. It was named for R. S. Knighton. He was the Gordon District County Supervisor in 1928.[313] In that year, he sold to the County School Board of Orange County three acres for a school. The deed places the land adjacent to T. D. Reynolds and the Allen tract.[314] The school and the Knighton house are shown on the circa 1951 map. William Ray Apperson and neighbor children attended that school. John Mason recalls that Mr. Knighton died circa 1958. The "one-sty frm. House" on the Ayers property shown on Plat Book 1 page 3(a) was formerly the Knighton house.[315] It has since been remodeled and is still standing in Lake of the Woods, near to the back gate.

Knighton bought the land in September 1922 from Willie, and his wife Frances, Apperson for $6,310.[316] His neighbors at that time were Ab Roach, Alonzo Apperson and J. T. Payne. The land had at one time been owned by Eli Apperson. Eli's home was on this land as the deed states where he "now lives."[317] Eli had obtained the land from the James Roach estate and divided it. Eighty acres was given to his son Alfonso, 78 acres to his son Alonzo and the remaining 142 acres eventually became the Ayers property.

By comparing the 1866 survey of the land Robert Roach conveyed to his son James, it is obvious that at some time after 1866 James received an additional 106 acres from his father's estate. The land that the Knighton house stands on what was once the Robert Roach farm shown in many Civil War maps.

Memorialize the Battlefields

Fredericksburg & Spotsylvania National Military Park Administrative History written in 1955 by Frank Happel, former park historian, is summarized below.[318]

With the passing of those that had sent their sons to war, their descendants that still resided in this area became interested in memorializing these battlefields. In 1896, a National Battlefield Park Association was formed in Fredericksburg. It was composed of many prominent citizens of Fredericksburg and Spotsylvania and Orange counties. On April 16, a meeting was held in Fredericksburg; "To unite in regard to establishing Parks, to commemorate the great military battles of Fredericksburg, Chancellorsville, the Wilderness, and Spotsylvania C. H., in order to perpetuate the heroic valor of the American soldier of both armies, in the late Civil War."[319]

In 1924, the Secretary of War appointed a commission to inspect battlefields, report the feasibility of preserving them, place markers, construct roads, acquire sites where trenches on the main battle line are sufficiently well preserved to warrant retaining in their present condition. The concept was modeled on the Antietam system, ownership of little or no land other than roads. The Wilderness Battle was confined largely to the vicinity of roads; very few recognizable remains of trenches existed, and the commission recommended that markers be placed near public roads. A fiscal year 1929 report took issue with the Antietam model, but the tragedy was that there was not enough money to ensure adequate holdings.

The enabling act of February 14, 1927, established a national military park at and near Fredericksburg, Virginia, to mark and preserve historical points connected with the battles of Fredericksburg, Spotsylvania Court House, Wilderness, and Chancellorsville, including Salem Church, Virginia. The absence of Mine Run Campaign, also known as the Battle at Payne's Farm, is noted. The Secretary of War was authorized to condemn land where necessary and to accept donations. The Fredericksburg and Spotsylvania National Military Park was officially dedicated on October 19, 1928. Five years later, President Franklin D. Roosevelt transferred the park to the Department of the Interior.

> *In the 1920's there was a move to create a battlefield park administered by the War Dept. Hugh Willis, a graduate of the Univ. of Minnesota, fought legally but lost. He was forced to "cut up the property" (Ellwood) by selling three separate strips of earthworks on his land, totaling 96 acres. Thereafter, he and his wife, Esther, only vacationed at Ellwood for two weeks each August.[320]*

Wilderness Battlefield 1930 - 1950

UPPER: Civilian Conservation Corps Wilderness Camp, November 1934.[321]

LOWER LEFT: Close up of Virginia Historic Marker JJ 20, Virginia Department of Historic Resources.

LOWER RIGHT: Wilderness Battlefield along Route 20, circa 1942. Virginia State Chamber of Commerce Photographs at the Library of Virginia.[322]

The Next Thirty Years

A Civilian Conservation Corps (CCC) Camp was established October 14, 1933, at Wilderness.[323] In April 1941 the Wilderness CCC Camp closed, moving to Chancellorsville and then in 1942 to the A. P. Hill Military Reservation. On March 5, 1942, the Department of Interior accepted title to 20.789 acres of Wilderness Battlefield, commemorating the gallant action of the 12th New Jersey Regiment. A bronze plaque was erected on the Plank Road.

> *Where it crossed the road leading from the Route 20 to Flat Run there is evidence of several roads extending over a distance of approximately two hundred feet, this point is about one fourth mile north of present road leading to homes of W. R. Almond and James Herndon. It continues east in the same direction across the farm of Alonzo Apperson and emerges (where the) Wilderness Civilian Conservation Corps Camp is now located. There are large trees along this section of the road, and it probably has not been used at all for at least fifty years.*[324]

In 1933, David Bushell conducted a survey for the Smithsonian Institution on the land formerly a part of Spotswood's Germanna. Artifacts recovered were prehistoric in nature. The location of and relics of the Enchanted Castle were not found until 1960, by a group that included Atwell Somerville.[325]

The Orange County Bicentennial Committee produced a complementary report in 1934.

> *Orange County got through the reconstruction period in a very satisfactory manner, and from the seventies (1870s) to the present time (1934) the county has made constructive advances. The county agricultural achievement has been noticeable; free schools have moved forward in a progessive way; a fine system of roads has been well constructed, and new industries have from time to time been established in the county. Altogether, the people of Orange County remain a homogeneous group. Many of them are direct descendants of the first settlers, and possess the qualities of progress, sturdiness, thrift and integrity characteristic of their forebears. They have long been noted for their hospitality and social charm, and are worthy of their illustrious heritage.*[326]

In 1936, a group of Orange County citizens formed an association to acquire land in the Mine Run area for donation to the park, but they never acquired the land. Sixty-seven years later, Bill (Farmer) Meadows who had earlier purchased the Payne farm sold 685 acres of the battlefield to the Civil War Preservation Trust and Piedmont Environmental Council.

> *There are not many opportunities to buy a whole battlefield.*[327]

Action to upgrade Route 20 in Orange County was initiated in the late 1940s. The work actually began in 1952 to create a "24 ft. thoroughfare" that would eventually connect the town of Orange to Germanna Road. Completion of the project past Mine Run was delayed into the late 1960s.[328]

James Lindsay Almond, Jr., was elected governor of Virginia in 1957 for the term ending January 1962. He was born in Charlottesville, Virginia on June 15, 1898. As a youth, he attended the graded school in Locust Grove. In 1919, he taught school there. He was principal of Zoar High School from 1921 to 1922.[329,330] His father lies buried at Zoar Cemetery, Burr Hill, Orange County, Virginia.

The Somervilles returned to Orange County after World War II when Atwell Somerville took up residence in the town of Orange. After serving under General Henry H. Arnold throughout the Pacific, he applied for and was selected to attend University of Virginia law school. Upon graduation, he joined his uncle's law firm in Orange. He subsequently has served as attorney for the county, for Boise Cascade, and as attorney for Lake of the Woods.[331]

The Memorial Foundation of the Germanna Colonies in Virgina, Inc.

The First Fifty Years, a history of the Foundation, written by Dr. Katherine L. Brown, is summarized below.[332]

As part of the Orange County bicentennial celebration, on September 25, 1934, nearly 1,000 persons gathered at Germanna and left a marker to the birth place of the first congregation of the Reformed Church of the United States. This marker was the forerunner of a granite marker monument erected two decades later. A tradition of picnics started officially on Sunday, April 24, 1949, with the "First public basket picnic party in commemoration of the German settlements of 1714-1717 and 1719." The Society of Germanna Colonies followed with annual picnics in 1950, 1951, 1952, 1953, and 1954. There was no picnic held in 1955.

A new organization emerged. The Memorial Foundation was chartered by the state of Virginia as a non-profit corporation on March 12, 1956. The picnic of 1957 was held on the 270 acres purchased on Route 3 across the road from the site of Governor Spotswood's castle. The foundation had cleared land, built roads and a picnic area and erected a sign that read, "Siegen Forest" honoring the locality from which many of the early settlers came.

A new granite marker to the Second Colony was unveiled at the 1961 reunion. More than 200 people from eight states attended. The memorial at that time consisted of a small pentagon-shape covered picnic area, the 1953 granite marker, the new marker and the old millstones. In 1968, the trustees offered 100 acres for the proposed Germanna Community College. In 1971, Atwell Somerville, chairman of the Board of Directors of Germanna Community College was elected to the board of the Foundation.

In 1984, the Foundation considered purchase of the land across State Route 3. In 1985, they donated $2,500 toward the Historic Gordonsville organization for the purchase of 62.5 acres, at a price of $250,000 that included the Germanna Fort, Spotswood Castle and Gordon house area. The University of Maryland Center for Historic Preservation conducted an archaeological investigation of the 62-acre property from 1987 to 1999. Their project was titled Enchanted Castle site (44OR3) at Germanna.

The master plan showing the College, the future development of trails and monuments in the Memorial area and across Route 3 was presented at the 1994 Reunion. In 1998, construction started on the new visitor center. John Spotswood, son of the Lt. Gov., was re-interred in the Memorial on June 20, 2002.

Summer of 1964

The Germanna Road area traveling east from the Germanna Memorial was little changed from any other summer. The Germanna Ford Bridge was 30 years old and two lanes wide. Most of the land was forested and owned by timber companies, some locally as by the Goodwin brothers and others from Fredericksburg to Maine. Most of the few houses still standing pre-dated the Civil War. Only Routes 3 and 20 were paved, all the other roads were gravel, at best.

The turkeys ran wild and the area was a principal hunting region. The Apperson cousins had pastureland with cattle on both sides of Flat Run, itself no more than a small creek except where it got truly flat, and there it was a swamp. Ms. Roach still cooked and heated from the same wood fireplace. In a home with no utilities at all, she subsisted on her 125-acre farm. The Masons had the only convenience store within several miles, located next to the National Battlefield Park. The park itself was little more than a few cleared acres alongside Route 20 where battle trenches had been restored and a marker placed alongside the road. Only a few houses existed in the battlefield area including the Middlebrook and Apperson homes built in the 1950s. Along Germanna Road stood the old Flat Run Baptist Church and the Ferris house.

By the summer of 1964, James C. Foote was traveling the East coast looking for a stream surrounded by cheap land he could change into a vacation community.

When the word got out that Foote was buying up enough land to build a 500-acre lake no one took him seriously.[333]

Germanna Memorial, Then and Now

UPPER: Photo taken 1961. From the historic files of Memorial Foundation of the Germanna Colonies in Virginia Inc.

LOWER: Photo by Dan McFarland, November 2009.

Maps   1863 to 1951

Map of April 1863 by Lt. Izard

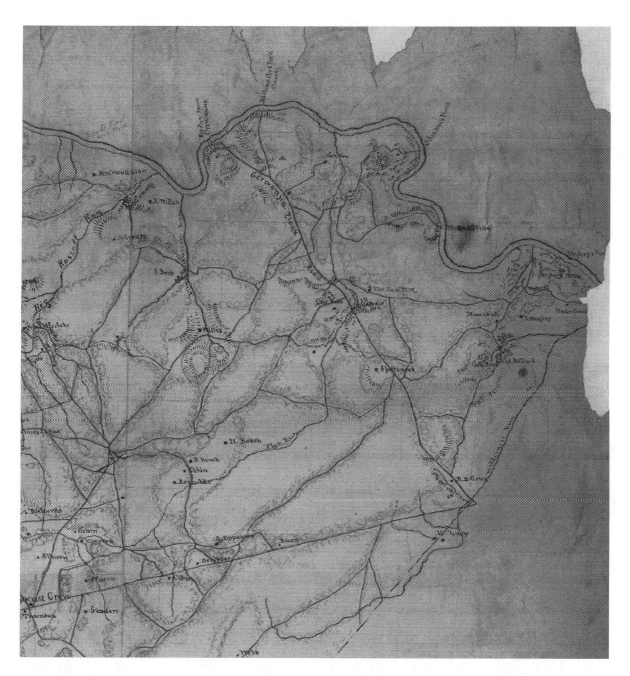

Part of a survey of Orange County, Virginia. From surveys and reconnaissance's by Walter Izard 1st Lt. Engrs. P.A.C.S.; approved April 8th 1863 by Albert H. Campbell, Capt. Prov. Engr., Chief Top. Dep. On left margin: Loaned to the War Records Office by Maj. Jed. Hotchkiss, Sept. 17, 1892. Library of Congress Geography and Map Division Washington, D.C. [334]

Map of May 6, 1864 by Jed Hotchkiss

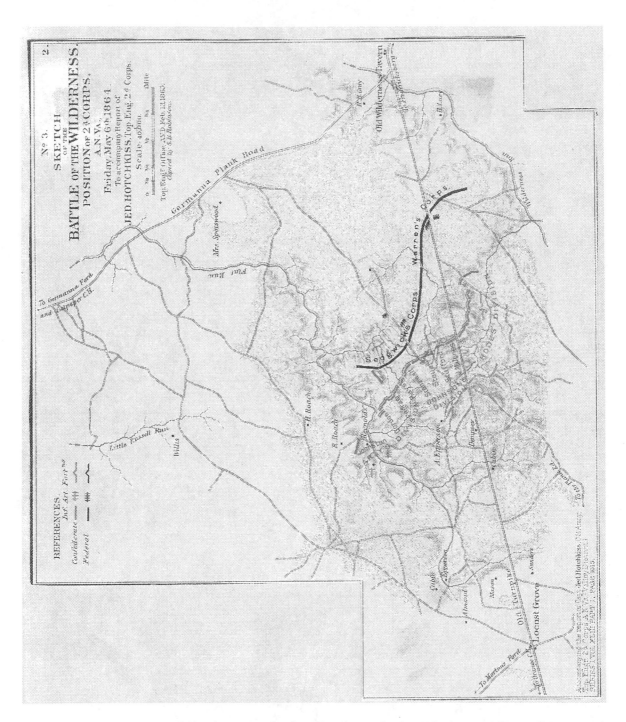

Hotchkiss map courtesy of Carolyn Nowakoski. Clearly marked are the homes of Mrs. Spotswood, H. Roach, R. Roach, Reynolds, A. Epperson (sic), Dempsey, Almond, Mason, Sanders, and Lacy.

Map of 1870

Part of Orange County Magisterial and School district map displayed in the County Clerk's office and published in W. W. Scott's History of Orange County, Virginia.

Map of 1936, Virginia Historical Inventory

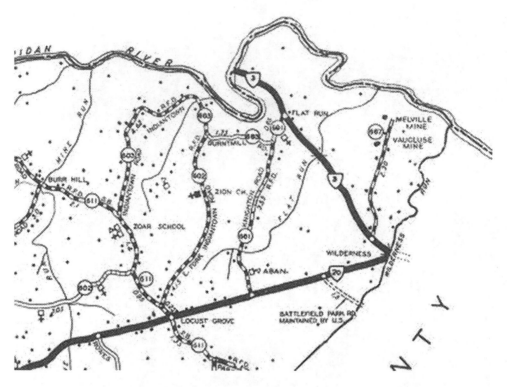

Part of the Map of Orange County showing Primary and Secondary Highways, Commonwealth of Virginia, Department of Highways, Division of Survey and Plans, revised July 1, 1936. Annotated, Virginia Historical Inventory Maps, the Library of Virginia. Elmer Vivian Johnson of Burr Hill and John C. Hendricks conducted surveys in 1936 under the WPA of Virginia Historic Inventory program. Their records reside in the Library of Virginia. The map above is taken from those surveys. Each dot represents a building in the area, mainly farmhouses, some of which had been abandoned.

Map of Circa 1951

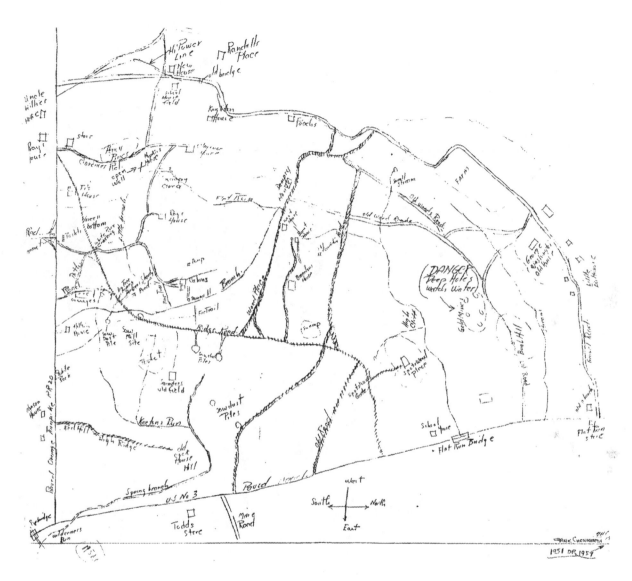

A map drawn by Frank Chenawith that shows the area that is currently Lake of the Woods, as it was in the 1950s. It does not contain a scale and is not of survey quality, but it is full of historic content. The Spotswood place is connected by Spotswood Gate to "Ridge Road", which is also known as Culpeper Mine Road and Spotswood Road on Civil War maps. The map was drawn for visitors to the Apperson family; such labels as Uncle Willies, Ray's place and Clarence House all refer to Appersons. Mr. Chenawith and his friends from Baltimore would come down to hunt.

1965 - 2010   *Lake of the Woods*

Aerial view annotated with the planned Lake of the Woods sub-division, 1965. Photo provided by James C. Foote.

Chapter 6   Virginia Wildlife Club, Inc.

In the past 10 to 12 weeks, buyers have contracted to pay more than $1.5 million for lots in ... An area of woodlands and farms and until recently, low land values.[335]

The 1960 census in Orange County listed 3,588 occupied houses. A sizable number of these homes still heated with firewood. Two thirds of these houses had telephones and televisions, typical of rural Virginia but far less than urban Northern Virginia. All this was about to change. Land that had been valued at $5 to $30 per acre for the last hundred years would increase 1000% in a few months.[336] It would increase another factor of ten when developed with lakes, roads and parks.

Lake of the Woods soon became 39% of the property valuation of the entire county. For a county that had seen nothing but decline in value for over a hundred years, Lake of the Woods was a major achievement. This had a profound and lasting impact on the land value of all of Orange County. The impact on the population of the county would take longer, but by the end of the century Lake of the Woods would exceed the population of the towns of Gordonville and Orange combined.[337]

The Goodwin Brothers

The Goodwin brothers had purchased for $13,125 the Spotswood property from Lelia Spotswood Willis in 1954. It now includes all of Lake of the Woods section 14 and parts of the surrounding sections and the main lake. Lelia had to make extraordinary efforts to obtain a clear title to her land.[338] In 1965, the Goodwins purchased the Roach property, which had access to Route 601. That year the road was improved with a hard surface from Flat Run (intersection of Route 601 and Route 3) to Route 20.[339]

The Goodwin brothers sold a total of 482 acres to Virginia Wildlife Clubs, Inc., (VWCI) in 1966.[340] William T. Goodwin, the surviving Goodwin brother, recalled that he and three other families were approached by James C. Foote to sell collectively at the price of $400 per acre. Billy Goodwin recalls later paying $4,000 for each of two lots in Lake of the Woods. He stated that the initial few lots went for $1,500, and then the price was raised to several thousand when they sold so well. He recalled that the entire development of over 4000 lots was sold out in less than 6 months.[341]

Anne M. Roach, First Resident of Lake of the Woods

Anne M. Roach shall have the right to peacefully reside on a portion of said ground for the remainder of her life ... [342]

Anne M. Roach, unmarried, sold to the Goodwin brothers 125 acres on Route 601, the same tract conveyed to Absalom Roach by deed of James W. Roach in 1895.[343,344] Absalom died intestate in or about 1924, leaving as his sole heirs his widow, Lelia M. Roach, and children, W.D. and A. L. The children subsequently died unmarried, vesting the fee simple title to the land to Anne M. Roach. When she sold her property to Goodwin, they agreed to a life estate of about three acres that contained a dwelling house, garden, out-house and access road.

Miss Ann Roach, an elderly woman, lives alone on a small farm on a corner of the development. Her house pre-dates the Civil War and has been the family homestead since. She was a young girl, she recalled, when her father told her stories of how the Battle of the Wilderness raged back and forth, in the vicinity of the house. A few minnie-balls are still embedded in her farm buildings. She plans to keep living in the home. This is part of her agreement in selling the land to the project.[345]

"When we moved here (November 1971), I remember seeing the old buildings still standing on the Life Estate. They preceded the Civil War by many years. A fire destroyed all in late 1971 or early 1972.[346] They say that there had been many antiques in the house, but all were lost. The ruins were left as was for a short time, but they began to be considered a hazard." - Carolyn Nowakoski.

"All I know is, things are changing. No, it's not what it used to be, anymore." - Miss Anne Roach, 1967 [347]

Miss Roach died October 9, 1973.[348] The life estate was a topic at the 6th Annual LOWA Meeting in September 1976. Soon thereafter, the Association had Fire and Rescue burn the place down.[349]

Miss Anne Roach and her Farmhouse, 1967

Picture from *The Evening Star,* April 21, 1967. Provided by James c. Foote.

Farm Families along Flat Run Sell

We conducted all the acquisition closings with the farmers right in the Orange County Courthouse. We borrowed office space and made it very convenient for the sellers – C. Daniel Clemente, LOWA Director 1967. [350,351]

Thirteen properties totaling 2,170 acres were sold to VWCI. The deeds were recorded on November 18, 1966.[352] When combined with the Goodwin's property it became the 2,652-acre Lake of the Woods.[353]

Family name	Acres sold
Wm. Ray & Pauline L. Apperson	75
Clarence G. & Alice P. Apperson	75
Patricia & Paul W. Ayres	145
Anne L. De Jarnette & Thorton Berry	102
Eva M. Brooks	24
Ann M. & M.H. Browning	248
Robert S. & Dorothy H. Coleman	189
J. Lee, Jr. & Fontaine B. Cooke	230
Ada M. & Edwin A. Gibson	568
John W. & Mabel J. Braswell	234
Orzal M. & Lucille S. Johnson	189
Warren W. Middlebrook	24
James T. & Orene D. Todd/ Broadus	67

Two parcels were owned by Edwin A. Gibson and his wife Ada Masters Gibson. One parcel of 352 acres she had inherited. Her father had owned more than the 352 acres.[354] His other land was conveyed to the U. S. for parkland in February 1932 and to J. M. Duval in the 1920s.[355,356] He had purchased the land from E. H. De Jarnette and Ed Woodman in 1918.[357] The Gibson property contains the road that went from Route 20 through the Mason parcel to the C. Apperson farm. Alongside that road is a cemetery marked as containing four graves. It is the Alfred Apperson family cemetery. Buried there are Alfred and his wife Malinda Jones Apperson, a Hopkins and an unknown, possibly Alfred's father, Peter.[358]

Robert S. Coleman obtained the land from A. B. Young of Fredericksburg on February 12, 1948.[359] In 1901, it was purchased from Chas. Kuper by the Wilderness Mining and Milling Co. of Washington, Pennsylvania. The plot for that sale contains the location of a gold mine shaft. The parcel was described as 189 acres situated near Wilderness Post Office, adjacent to Orange Grove Mining Co., Edward Woodman, Ralph Brooks, R. A. Jennings and J. R. Spottswood (successors).[360] Mabel J. Braswell was the descendant and sole heir of Robert A. Jennings. She acquired part of the 234 acres he had owned in 1883.[361]

The Coleman family operated a sawmill. Mr. Coleman bought the land and sold the lumber from the trees. The cut-over area was ideal for birds and deer.[362]

Orzal Johnson only held his land a couple of years when he sold it to VCWI. In 1905, D. A. Dempsey of Spotsylvania County bought that land at auction for $210.[363] It was not uncommon for parcels within the future LOW to be abandoned and placed on auction.

Many of these family names have very deep roots in Orange County. The Colemans, Cookes, Gibsons, Jennings and Johnsons first appear in Orange County records in the 1740s. The census of circa 1782 by Benjamin Grymes lists a John Jennings with ten white and no slaves. The census of 1850 lists the Brooke, Cooke, Jennings and Johnson families as neighbors of the Spotswoods. The roster of Company C, 7th Virginia Infantry, lists sons of the Apperson, Cook, Coleman and Johnson families.[364]

The Oldest House at LOW

While the construction of LOW was underway, at least three homes were allowed to remain standing, those of Ms. Roach and the Apperson cousins. Today both of the Apperson homes are on LOW numbered lots, owned by members of the Association.

The Clarence Apperson farm is shown as it looked while the small creek that passes by, Flat Run, is being dammed to create the Main Lake in the background. The lake would fill about two years after this picture was taken. The original portion of the Apperson house is circa 1800, as recorded in Orange County tax parcels detailed information. This is decades before Alfred, great-grandfather of Clarence first appears in any Orange County records.[365] When Clarence sold to VWCI, he did not want to keep back an acre or two, as had Miss Roach. The house was relocated from Ramsey Beach to 402 Harrison Circle prior to 1974.[366] There is a cemetery at Ramsey Beach that is probably an Apperson family cemetery. The county plat map lists it as holding one grave.

The Other Apperson cousin, the White House

The William Ray Apperson house, known today as White House at Lake of the Woods, was built in 1929 according to the Orange County tax records. William Ray, as a youth, saw the previous home burn down. The school teacher who taught at the local one-room school house was a border in their house. One day while cleaning a stain with gasoline she managed to start the fire that nearly killed her and consumed the house.[367]

The White House was being restored in the winter of 1972 when it caught fire and the interior was gutted. The newspaper article claimed the house was 75 years old.[368] The White House was one of two house fires and three woods fires allegedly set by the assistant fire chief of Lake of the Woods Volunteer Fire Department.

> *A spokesman for the fire company at Lake of the Woods said yesterday that Landes is no longer assistant fire chief.*[369]

John Mason, who played on and worked on the farm as a youth, stated that, "It looks the same today as before 1960." "There was a clear line of sight from William Apperson's to his cousin's house." William Apperson had built a wild turkey hunting lodge that is still standing on LOW Church property.

> *"I'd heard that people in Orange resented Virginia Wildlife because development here meant that the hunting of wild turkey would be ruined. For years, though, wild turkey tracks could often be seen ... Because of "no hunting" later, perhaps they, as well as many deer, felt that this was a safe refuge?"* - Carolyn Nowakoski [370]

Mason, the Family that Didn't Sell

The only road in LOW named for a local family other than Spottswood Road was Mason Street. Granville Mason owned twelve acres adjacent to Lake of the Woods but he only sold a 0.25 acre sliver, right of way of record, to VWCI.[371] The Masons owned the general store and barber shop on Route 20 near the battlefield. The trace of the road from there to the Apperson farms can still be seen. Mrs. Mason served breakfast to Jim Foote's workmen.[372] The addition of this parcel to the development would have allowed an entrance from Route 20. That did not happen, but Jim did reward the Granville Masons by naming a road Mason Street. It is located in Section 7. The Masons did sell a few years later to Patricia & Paul W. Ayres.[373]

The Apperson Farmhouses

UPPER: Clarence Apperson farm, 1967. Courtesy of James C. Foote.

MIDDLE: The oldest home at LOW, i.e. the Clarence Apperson farmhouse, restored. Photo by Dan McFarland.

LOWER: The White House at LOW, i.e. the William Ray Apperson farmhouse, restored. Photo by Dan McFarland.

Plat of Lake of the Woods near the Front Gate, October 1966

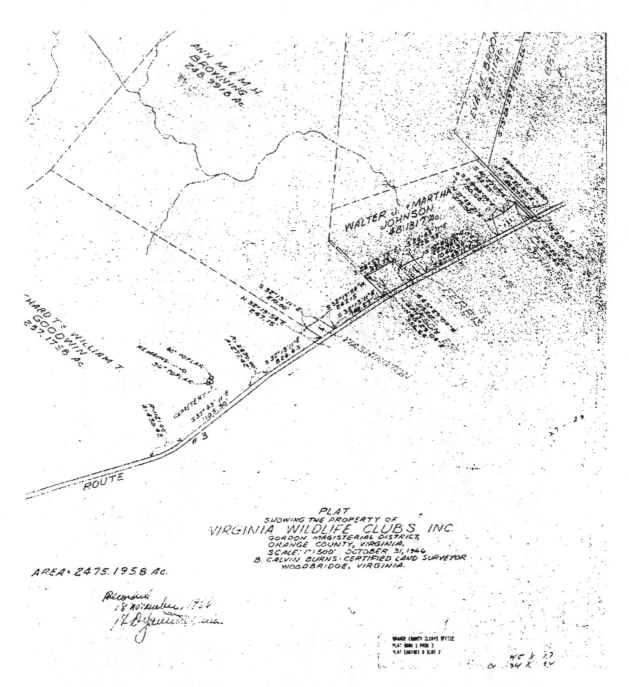

Plat Book 1, page 7, Orange County Clerk's Office.

Plat of Lake of the Woods near the Back Gate, October 1966

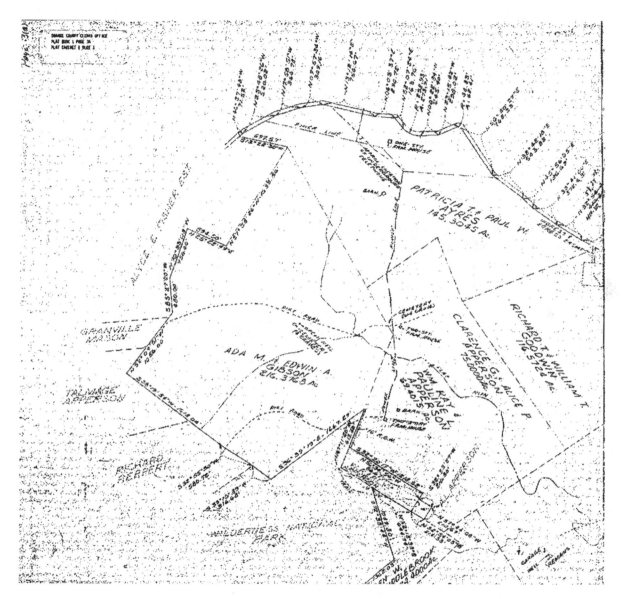

Plat Book 1, page 34, Orange County Clerk's Office.

Fisher's farm gets added to LOWA Section 6

William G. Fisher at the time of his death, August 23, 1964, owned a parcel of land adjacent to Granville Mason and Edwin Gibson. That land filled the "notch" shown in Plat Virginia Wildlife Club, Area of LOW Back Gate. Mr. Fisher had purchased from C. L. Young and his wife Ruby 315 acres on the north side of Old Turnpike Road, Route 20, adjacent to C. Apperson and Mr. Mason on February 28, 1951.[374] The Youngs had purchased it in 1945 for $3,600 from J. P. Dempsey, trustee for H. C. Lewis, widow, of New Jersey.[375] This land was part of the Allen tract, also known as the Somerville tract of 419 acres surveyed by E. J. Woodville in 1929. At that time, the adjacent owners were W. R. Almond and Mrs. Apperson.[376]

Three and a half years after his death, the heirs of the Fisher estate sold part of the land, 105 acres, to the VWCI.[377] Other parts were sold to the state and utility companies; their land included part of Route 601. As part of the transaction, VCWI paid $20,000 for 70 acres.[378]

The maps, Map Book 1 pages 1-3, show the location of cemeteries; the few structures still standing in 1966 and the remains of older structures including the Spotswood brick relic, now seen in Spotswood Park, the Apperson farms, the Apperson cemetery on the dirt road on Gibson property, and the Roach life estate.

1969: Two new Sections Added

In the future, proposals for a motel and town house sites overlooking the lake are shaping up,[379]

Lake of the Woods grew by adding 17 large lots and dedicating them as Section 16, and by adding 209 standard size lots and dedicating them as Section 14.[380,381] Section 14 was originally conceived to be used for the building of accommodations for visiting lot owners and guests. Jim Foote also had ideas for the building of a memorial to the Spotswoods. He had no idea that lot owners would want to build homes, especially primary residences, as soon as they did.[382] There may have been other reasons for the change of plans related to Boise's reluctance to further invest in this development. Within a few months after Section 14 was recorded, it was nearly sold-out. A lakefront lot was sold for $17,000.[383] Section 16 lies across Germanna Highway from the Main Lake at Lake of the Woods. It is unique; the lots are large enough for the boarding of horses. It is not gated.

Sections 15, 17 & 19

… In the future, proposals for a motel and town house sites overlooking the lake are shaping up, as well as a commercial area to be located somewhere in the $5 million development … The area … may also have an airport, grass strip long enough to accommodate … a DC-3.[384]

Only one of these future proposals ever materialized, the commercial area. A strip of land along Route 3 was declared Section 15 and 17 in November 1969 for exclusive commercial use.[385] The covenants for these sections empower the ECC to control the building on these lots. The lot owners are not assessed and they have no vote.

In open forum, John Nolan presented to the Board of Directors a petition of approximately 500 names rejecting the proposed annexing of Section 19.[386]

> *We the undersigned members of the Lake of the Woods Association request that the Board of Directors reject the proposal to enlarge our subdivision by the annexation of a Section 19 adjacent to Section 2.*
>
> *Motion to withdraw from the table action on adding proposed Section 19 to LOWA and accept Mr. Potter's letter of February 6, 1989 withdrawing from further consideration said proposal.*

There are only two properties adjacent to Section 2, 135 acres now owned by U.S. government, description Apperson, DB456 001 and 40 acres owned by Warren Middlebrook, description Embry, DB 176 219, 222. Jim Foote had planned to buy more land from Mr. Middlebrook, which would have provided access to Route 20, but Mr. Middlebrook refused.[387]

Jim Foote had an option, at about $50 per acre, on a few thousand acres on the southeast side of Route 20, which he wanted to add to the LOW property. Tom Perine vetoed the idea and would not commit the funding.

Ferris Building

Eugene F. Ferris, Jr., and Linda Brooks Ferris his wife, conveyed one acre fronting Route No. 3 to Lake of the Woods, Inc., recorded August 18, 1997.[388] Mr. Ferris and his first wife, Betty, bought the acre in August 22, 1963, from Hubert Ashby Weakley and wife. The county tax records indicate the house was built in 1964. In May 1998, it was proposed to be deeded to the LOW Fire and Rescue along with some adjoining land. By July of that year it was refurbished and became the Teen Center. Eugene Ferris worked for Jim Foote as a maintenance man and continued on the maintenance staff of LOWA.

9.9 & Goodwin Property

The Association procured a total of 40.6 acres adjoining section 12. 9.9 acres, described as DB 399 812, may have access to Flat Run Road.[389] The remaining three parcels were acquired from Billy Goodwin. Two parcels which total 18 acres are described as DB 646 449. The remaining parcel of 12.7 acres was acquired June 7, 2001, by Quit Claim deed.

For the sum of $12,731, W.T. (Billy) Goodwin conveyed 12.731 acres adjoining property of Lake of the Woods Association. The 12.731-acre parcel is a portion of the Woodman tract acquired by Ada Masters Gibson in OCDB 195 at page 233. Adjoining surveys of conveyed parcels from Howard Masters referred to this tract as being in the name of Daniel and Edith Ward; however, no recorded conveyance was found. The land had been acquired by Goodwin Brothers Lumber Company and recorded in OCDB 301 at page 242.

Ever since this land was acquired, the Association has studied how it could be used. Most of the studies have focused on other than single-family housing, similar to the initial plans for section 14. Some of the land is used for member and maintenance leaf-dump and mulch-pickup.

> *Mr. Hollenbach appointed an Ad hoc Land Use Committee to address land use associated with the 9.9 acres and Shoosmith area and to investigate possible future locations for Maintenance, Golf Maintenance, and Fire & Rescue. Members will be Mike Mishkin (Chairman), Ed McCarthy, a representative of the Planning and Maint & Ecol Committees, a representative from Staff, and any prior Planning Committee members.*[390]

Ten years later, another study was authorized.

> *Motion by Elliott, second by Embrey, passed unanimously, to direct the Planning Committee to proceed with the Land Use Update Study and the Senior Housing Study.*[391]

Chapter 7   The Founders of Lake of the Woods

Thomas Perine the Lakebuilder

The September 1966 *Time Magazine* featured an article about Thomas Perine, the chairman of U.S. Land, Inc.[392] The 500 acre lake in Virginia mentioned in the article would become Lake of the Woods which was established in 1967 by Virginia Wildlife Clubs, Inc., a subsidiary of U.S. Land, Inc.[393]

People, says Lakebuilder Thomas J. Perine, chairman of Indianapolis' U.S. Land, Inc., have the same motivation to go to water as birds have to fly south in the winter. Perine, 34, is capitalizing on that motivation all across the country by building lakes … Perine has already finished lakes of similar size outside Cleveland and Chicago, is now building others … and a 500-acre lake in Virginia, 45 minutes south of Washington, D.C.

Perine starts with a rural valley near a metropolitan center that is fed by a fresh water stream, which can be readily dammed. He makes his lakes in one swell swoop that takes less than a year and keeps speculators from driving up the prices. In that time, he puts in the roads and services and, as a fillip, adds country clubs, tennis courts and swimming pools … lake, golf course or park—within a few hundred feet of every lot. To protect property values, deed restrictions are tight … only one single-family home may be erected on any one lot.

Perine apparently only visited Virginia once, in February 1967.[394] In an interview with the *Washington Post*, he explained some of the details of his operation.[395]

"Obviously, we cannot afford to pay outlandish sums for land if the lot prices are to remain within reach. Our development costs are high because what we do to the land is our basic contribution. We must have a site that is right, where natural valleys can be filled from natural streams after a dam is built … We are determined to save every tree that we can. A man can lose a job by cutting down the wrong tree."

Officials of Virginia Wildlife Clubs, Inc., said they wanted to become an accepted part of the community and planned to be permanent residents.[396] By July 1967, Thomas Perine's company, U.S. Land Inc., had been bought by Boise Cascade. Thomas A. Perine at age 37 founded a new company in the Bahamas to develop a resort complex.[397] Jim Foote reported that Tom Perine died shortly thereafter.

The developer continued to operate as Virginia Wildlife Clubs into the 1970s. The earliest deed recorded in Orange County by Boise Cascade Recreation Communities Corporation was in 1971.[398] The last record of Virginia Wildlife Clubs was on Nov 26, 1972.[399]

> *In a stock swap, Boise Cascade acquired Indianapolis' U.S. Land Inc., which thrives by building artificial lakes in northern Virginia or California's Mother Lode country, then selling the land around them for residential and resort use. With the purchase, Boise Cascade became the nation's most thoroughly integrated company in the housing field.[400]*

Jim Foote described U. S. Land officials as men "who like to roll up their sleeves, work in the dirt and are interested in getting the job done."[401] He recalls that, "Boise wanted to change everything; they insisted on shined shoes, coat and tie; it wasn't much fun anymore."

Boise Cascade introduced a change to the financing of purchases. In order to facilitate the sale, Boise Cascade agreed to handle the financing with the buyer, since a bank would be concerned about the buyer defaulting. Boise Cascade contacted General Electric Credit Corporation (GECC, now called GE Capital), about GECC buying its "paper." After the initial loan, GECC continued to buy new loans from Boise Cascade.[402]

James C. Foote, at Age 29, Created Lake of the Woods

James, prefers to be called Jim, C. Foote was the developer of Lake of the Woods. Jim was an experienced developer of lake property when he met Mr. Perine who appointed him Vice President of Virginia Wildlife Clubs, Inc., a division of U. S. Land Inc. This is Jim's story of how he built Lake of the Woods.[403] Tom Perine and Jim Foote were working on three sites, one near Atlanta, one near Boston and one near Washington D.C. Jim would get topographic maps of the area of interest and spread them all over the dining room. He would then locate the streams and design the future lakes. Jim was interested in the Wilderness Run area on the Spotsylvania and Orange counties line. He had designed a dam twice as big as the dam at Lake of the Woods to create a very large Wilderness Run Lake. He would call on the farmers, take them up in a helicopter for a ride, and try to buy options on their land. He had most of the future Wilderness Run Lake property committed, except for one farm. He flew to New York to negotiate with the owner of that farm. When things did not seem to be working out, he moved west to Flat Run and proceeded to design a lake community totally within Orange County.

The next thirty days "were fun as hell." Jim remembers taking Mrs. Roach on her first helicopter ride, and cutting her firewood. In 1965, there were no restrictions on planned community development in Orange County. Jim Foote needed no government review or approval to put together the land purchases and in one day recorded the deeds of the future Lake of the Woods.[404]

> *"I do not recall how long I was on the (LOWA) Board of Directors. At the time we recorded the subdivision plats there was no subdivision control ordinance in Orange*

County. We were able to record almost 3,000 lots at one time without any county review process. We did not interface with the Board of Supervisors." – C. Daniel Clemente. [405]

Almost three years later, September 9, 1969, the zoning ordinance of Orange County was amended by adding clarification entitled "Planned Residential Communities, (R-3)."[406]

The Dedication and Plat of Lake of the Woods Subdivision

We wanted to get the lots recorded in one day, to avoid the county supervisors from changing the regulations; it went on to near midnight – James C. Foote.

The Dedication and Plat of Lake of the Woods Subdivision was recorded on February 3, 1967.[407] Each section, 1 through 13 was recorded separately. While today, there is no distinction in restrictive covenants among the sections, that has not always been true. The Dedication and Plat lists the owner rights, which include: to control and use all of the streets ... all of the said streets shall remain and be private thoroughfares, and to control and use all the area shown ... as Lakes, Beach areas, Access areas and Park areas and each of the said Lakes and the ground underlying each of the said lakes shall remain private property.

As for financing most of the construction costs, it went as follows: A lot would be sold and the company would take back a purchase money note secured by a first trust on the lot. The note would then be sold to Guaranty Bank & Trust in Springfield, VA. Earnest Carter was the President of that bank. The proceeds from the sale of the notes provided the liquidity for construction of improvements so there would not be a construction loan per se. It was a very smooth operation and we were creating a new kind of consumer paper. Turned out to be very good paper. Payment defaults were few - C. Daniel Clemente.

VWCI obtained a 36-month note for $5,000,000 on the LOW property from Guaranty Bank and Trust Company of Fairfax, Virginia, recorded on November 30, 1966.[408] As the lots were sold, VWCI would partially repay the note and lots would be released.[409] The developed land was mortgaged at over $2,500 an acre. The very first half-acre lots went for $1,500, but soon afterwards the going price was $4,000 and up. There are recorded a few instances of buy-back by VWCI from lot owners in 1969 to 1971. The annotations on the deeds indicate the prices of lots in that time period were $6,000 to $8,995.

Lake of the Woods, a Virginia Non-Stock Corporation

Lake of the Woods was approved for incorporation by Virginia on April 21, 1967, and given charter number 111895. The incorporators of Lake of the Woods were James C. Foote of Springfield, VA, John S. Keating, Jr., of Hinsdale, IL and Wesley T. Butler of Springfield, VA. The original three directors where Mr. Butler, Mr. Keating and C. Daniel Clemente of Falls Church, Virginia.

VWCI established policies and procedures that have served the community well and set the standard for similar communities.[410] The Restrictive Covenants were recorded on March 1, 1967.[411] Many of the restrictions of lot owners in Lake of the Woods have remained essentially unchanged. These include the general prohibitions of having trailers and tents, signs of any kind, junk cars, or exposed fuel tanks on a lot; parking on any street, overnight parking of trucks, and the infamous "no tree over six inches in diameter shall be removed ... without written consent of the ECC."

The Declaration of Restrictions of 1967 included section 12 that stated, "no person shall acquire such title (to any lot in the Subdivision) until he has been approved for membership in the association nor shall the owner of a lot ... convey the title to any person who has not been approved in writing for membership in the Association." This covenant enforced the concept of a "private association." A letter written in August 1967 clearly indicates that acceptance for membership preceded transfer of property.[412]

> *"Please accept my personal congratulations on your having been accepted for membership in the Lake of the Woods association ... I am enclosing your permanent membership card and auto decal ... Very shortly, you will be receiving your Warranty Deed to Lot ... which transfers title of the property to your name."* – John S. Keating, Jr., President U.S. Land, Inc.

Article V paragraph 1 of the Articles of Incorporation specified a membership committee. The membership committee met many times.[413] There are today other lake communities, in other states, which were established by U.S. Land, Inc., that continue to require Board of Director approval for membership.[414]

James C. Foote

Photo courtesy of James C. Foote.

Construction and Sales

In finding a site for such a project, the builders claim that 82 factors have to be considered. Most involve topography and soil, but others concern items as availability and even ... whether a cemetery is on the site, since it is against the law to flood a cemetery. They plan their own hard surfaced roads, central water distribution system, fire and police protection in their area.[415]

The Flat Run site was selected June 1965 by Jim Foote. Professional consultants and engineers started looking at the area in October 1965. All of the land for the project was acquired locally through broker Ernie Welsh, Pates Realty and Insurance Co. and Shaw Realty Co. of Alexandria. Welsh said that it was hoped work could begin on the project later in the fall of 1966 with the construction of the dam the first order of business. The go-ahead for the project came Monday, September 26, 1966, when Orange County Circuit Judge Harold H. Purcell gave approval for the construction of a dam near the junction of Flat Run and Route 3 at a cost of $325,000.[416] The matter was brought before Circuit Judge Purcell as a legal technicality required before impounding of water was permitted. Robert S. Washburn of Indianapolis, attorney for Virginia Wildlife Clubs, Inc., showed engineers' sketches and testified that the flow below the proposed dam to be located on Flat Run was in accordance with legislation. He told the court that legal title would belong to property owners while equitable title will belong to Virginia Wildlife Clubs, Inc., which will assume all costs.[417]

Within a few weeks after court approval, workmen and heavy equipment had cleared more than 30 acres of the 2,600-acre tract, making way for a 1,500-foot dam just off Route 3. The next week construction began on the 60-foot-high dam, requiring some 300,000 cubic yards of earth. Clearing of the heavily wooded area was done by a contractor from Aurora, Ill., hiring local workmen. Both timber and pulpwood were hauled from the site. Construction of the dam was done by Shoosmith Bros., Chester, Chesterfield County, Virginia. One year later, the workforce grew to some 300 men.[418] By October 1967, the lake was filling at a rate of eight inches a week and a second smaller lake was being bulldozed out of the land. About 32 miles of roads had been cut through the timberland and another eight miles was to be cut. Forty miles of water piping for a central water system was being installed.[419] Among items turned up by bulldozers and workmen of the Lake of the Woods tract, are portions of muskets, bayonets, federal belt buckles and bullets. Many undoubtedly relics of Gordon's strategic attack.[420]

... by April of next year, 200 acres of the big lake will be under water, a large club house overlooking 2 ½ miles of lake, will be nearing completion; one of the two proposed swimming pools will be nearly completed, an 18-hole golf course will be underway ... in the $5 million development ... the company wants to keep the landscape as rustic as possible ... There will be one main entrance to the area on Virginia 3 ... possibly another entrance. [421]

The back nine holes were opened to play in 1969. The golf course was built to PGA standards by VWCI at an estimated cost of $200,000.[422]

Tom Perine had given Jim Foote a sales target of 560 lots the first year. By the end of April 1967, 114 lots worth more than $1.5 million already had been sold at Lake of the Woods, even though the grand opening was scheduled for May 20.[423] In the next month they sold another 165 lots. Lake of the Woods held the official opening on Saturday June 17, 1967.[424] By the end of September, sales topped $10 million.[425] The lot prices ranged from $3,195 to $12,000. They sold another million dollars the following month.[426] After one year, over 1,650 lots had been sold for total revenue of over $16 million. Lake of the Woods was a huge financial success and "made the Perine company". Jim Foote's top salesman had an annual income of $6,000 before joining Jim, and $85,000 in his first year of sales. Jim also had a salesman who was not satisfied with his income; he was arrested for robbing the bank in the town of Orange.[427]

> *The hay-riders were having fun; so were the salesmen. And back down at the big circus tent where people were really getting down to the business with paper and pencils, buyers seemed to be having fun, too ... We saw cars there from Maryland, West Virginia and New York, parked near ours. Maybe the people from far away had dream houses in their hearts, too.*[428]

One of the many sales techniques employed was completing the 16th hole of the golf course before any others because it ran alongside of the highway; visitors could see it before they entered. It cost $6,000 to construct. Another was to do all roads and park construction on Thursday to Monday, while potential customers were visiting. One of the original octagon buildings was the sales office.[429] Jim told his people, sell from your car or take our customers to the picnic tables, but never into the office.[430]

> *Don and "first heard about LOW the summer of 1968 or '69 when a salesman from here called to say that one of Don's co-workers ... had given our name as people who might be interested. The salesman went on to say that there was a pool here with a lifeguard, so we should bring the children who would be safe while we looked around ... Prices sounded high ..."* – Carolyn Nowakoski [431]

Open Today

UPPER: Original sales office, 1967. Photo courtesy of James C. Foote.

LOWER: Original front entrance. Photo on display in the LOWA General Manager's office.

The Lake of the Woods Golf and Country Club

This is a private operation for property owners and their guests. That's the name of the game. All roads and parks will be owned and maintained by an association of which each owner must become a member before he may purchase property. Minimum annual membership charge is $30 a lot. The golf course, clubhouses, pools, campgrounds, etc., will be owned by Lake of the Woods Golf and Country Club, Inc., for which property owners are eligible for membership. Dues will be about $7.50 a month.[432]

The recreational amenities are defined in the Restrictive Covenants, dated March 1, 1967, as lakes, dams, marinas, beaches, lake access tracts, golf courses, tennis courts, swimming pools, clubhouse and adjacent clubhouse grounds and campgrounds. The list omits parks, which are clearly in the Dedication and Plat of February 3, 1967, but does include lakes and beaches, which also are in the D and P. Neither mentions the stables. The stables were included along with all the other amenities listed above in a sales brochure circa 1967.

Ride! Here's an added bonus. Saddle up at Lake of the Woods' private stables, and explore the interesting bridle paths of lovely Wilderness Battlefield Park.

The heart and soul of the amenities was the clubhouse complex with the clubhouse, "a focal point for family fun," picnic and beach area, tennis courts and pool and all with a magnificent lake view. The developer located the golf course some distance from this complex and built a "starters house" which became the Pro Shop.

A very important amenity was the campgrounds. VWCI controlled many aspects of home design but was not in the business of homebuilding. Their concept was to have the amenities constructed and access available to a lot owner as soon as they purchased a lot. VWCI wrote Restrictive Covenants that prohibited trailers or tents on these lots but did provide a large campground for the members. Their business model assumed their customers would use the amenities on the weekends and summers vacations but not build residences until much later. They planned for a lodge, a 250 room private motel, in addition to the campground.[433] They never built the lodge, possibly due to the rapid sales of lots and the start of home construction.

One interesting thing is that a lot owner if he chooses to camp can do so only in a designed area. The trouble seems to be that people will pitch a tent and then just leave it there for the rest of the year. Also banned are trailers.[434]

As part of its policy, VWCI planned to remain permanently at the helm of the project, unlike most other developers.[435] There was no intention to ever pass ownership of Lake of the Woods Golf and Country Club to the members. That changed when Boise Cascade bought out U.S. Land, Inc. The transfer of ownership became effective November 30, 1972.[436]

Clubhouse

We get ... people in the same business from all over the country. They want to know how we've been able to do so well. The answer is simple. We don't punch a stake in the ground and announce, this will be the clubhouse. We build the clubhouse - James C. Foote. [437]

The project master plan was created by B. Calvin Burns of Prince William Engineering of Woodbridge, Virginia. Shoosmith Excavation Co. cleared the lakebeds and opened the roads. Its headquarters were where the LOW Shoosmith Building now stands.[438] The consulting landscape architect for the project was the prominent architect Edward Durrell Stone, Jr., of Ft. Lauderdale, Florida. His drawing board turned out the design for the 145-foot clubhouse, the community entrance and surrounding landscaping. Cost was budgeted at about $500,000.[439,440] The complex was nearly complete by October 1967, with tennis courts, pool with attached bath building, clubhouse with patios, and a white shady beach toward which the water was slowly rising.[441] A grand party was hosted by Jim and Shirley Foote in February 1968. Anna Townsend Willis attended and wrote her impressions.[442]

Mrs. Shirley Foote did the planning and supervision of the decor of the Lodge (Clubhouse) ... "What I really want is for it to look intimate and homelike." It was her idea, since it is real country with woods all around, to bring the outdoor look inside, using autumn shades of brown, yellow, and green. The wide chimney breast adds to the country look, also, And on the crisp, winter night of the party, huge logs from "the Spotswood woods" burned in the big fireplace. Food and drink, music and firelight and people, it had all of the ingredients of a good party ... And, last but by no means least, was Barney Duggan, the Ambassador of Good Will for the town-by-the-lake! Resplendent in white brocade, buckles and bows and silver wig, Barney stood near the framed portrait of the colonial governor, Alexander Spotswood, whom he was impersonating for the evening.[443]

The framed portrait of the colonial governor was made by the Goad Studio of Culpeper, from a small black and white copy of a portrait, found in the belongings of the late Mrs. Lelia Spotswood Willis of Culpeper. The picture, which is of much interest to historians, and Virginias in particular, was mounted on the Clubhouse wall above a glass-topped case housing a collection of memorabilia found around the grounds of Orange Grove.[444,445]

"Just inside the front doors (of the Clubhouse) were two large display cases, which held relics from the Civil War, found when the roads, etc., were put in. I especially remember a large, leather saddlebag ... The Clubhouse was rather small with a Great Hall and small dining room, and two offices ... Downstairs, an independent "bottle club" was established early on." – Carolyn Nowakoski

"Spotswood picture was in clubhouse with display cases of civil war artifacts plus a bunch of other stuff which has disappeared over time." – Ruthan O'Toole

Newspaper Photos Circa 1967

Reproduced from newspaper clippings in James C. Foote's collection of Lake of the Woods memorabilia.

UPPER: Clubhouses complex circa 1967.

LOWER: James C. Foote pointing to the distant waterline during construction of the main dam.

Chapter 8   The Forefathers of Lake of the Woods

Boise Cascade CEO Departs

The venture into recreational communities was a financial failure; Boise cut its losses wherever it could, including the career of their CEO, Mr. Hansberger.

> *Robert V. Hansberger ... proceeded to turn the enterprise into one of the most glamorous conglomerates of the conglomerate-mad 1960s ... he also moved the company into real estate, leisure homes, Latin American bonds and utilities, and urban renewal ... But in 1972, the company found itself in deep trouble with its Latin American investments and its domestic real estate operations. Hansberger walked the plank ... and Boise Cascade took a $200 million write-off ...* [446]

The initial seven LOWA officers who were all property owners were appointed in March, 1969 by the Board of Directors, who were all employees of the developer.

> *The President of LOWA was also named to the Board of Directors, pursuant to the Articles of Incorporation, after this requirement was called to the Board's attention.* [447]

The LOWA Board of Directors elected in September 1971 were members James H. Stewart, Ernest J. Holcomb and William A. Newman, Jr., and four Boise officials. At the special Board of Directors meeting of January 29, 1972, the Boise officials submitted their resignations and were replaced by members.

> *Mr. Holcomb then moved the appointment of Arnold E. Chase, Richard C. Wilbur, Mrs. Ruth F. Dugan and John R. Henry to fill the four vacancies - terms to expire April 21, 1972. Seconded and carried unanimously.* [448]

The first Board of Directors of Lake of the Woods that included only lot owners showed great initiative and steadfastness in their negotiation of the turnover from the developer. The histories of the negotiations were written by past presidents Ernest Holcomb, Arnold Chase and Jack Eckel. [449,450,451]

> *Boise Cascade ... wished to sell the recreational facilities at Lake of the Woods to the Association for ... two and one-half million dollars ... the first Board of Directors that*

include only lot owners ... made a counter offer to accept ... free of charge, but to pay Boise Cascade $212,500 for certain non-recreational properties and ... equipment ... owned by the Corporation.[452]

However, clearly, Boise Cascade was eager to cut their losses and run. John R. Henry, surviving LOWA director from that time, has the rest of the story. James Stewart, president of LOWA, had visited Boise Cascade headquarters and knew that their lawyers and representatives at the negotiations with LOW were instructed to settle.[453] At that time Boise Cascade was defending a series of lawsuits from the California Attorney General pertaining to their recreational communities in California. Those suits were eventually settled at a cost of $59 million.[454]

At the 6th Annual Meeting, the President made the following introductions:

The first President of the Association was Mr. Ernest Holcomb. Mr. Holcomb picked up our Association when it was truly an infant and he cared for it and he guarded it with all that he had to offer.

Our second President was Mr. Jim Stewart and he saw this awkward child through many trying states.[455]

Mr. Arnold Chase, our third president, with Mr. Holcomb, was instrumental in the acquisition of Lake of the Woods Association from Boise Cascade in its entirety.[456]

Mr. Jack Eckel, our fourth president, a very strong, definite individual, brought to this position 35 years of industrial management background.

Mr. Glen Barton, the fifth president who served just prior to the current President's term, still contributes as an ongoing Director of the Board and will continue to do so until September 1977.

These past presidents who started the history of Lake of the Woods Association and still contribute a great deal of experience and volunteer service to our Association and the community as a whole. Gentlemen, our heartfelt thanks to you, the forefathers of Lake of the Woods.

Another gentleman most valuable to Lake of the Woods who has seen several years of growth with us is our Corporation Attorney, Mr. Atwell Somerville.[457]

Ernie Holcomb was one of the first lot owners. He had retired as Hearing Officer for the U. S. Department of Agriculture, a position similar to a Federal judge.

James H. Stewart, served after World War II as an officer and civilian capacity in Austria and Germany. He was reassigned from Germany to Washington, D. C. area in 1957 and served with the Department of Defense both as an Electrical Engineer and as a Senior Analyst. He built his home in the Tara section of Lake of the Woods in 1968. James Stewart, although President of the Wilderness Club, does not appear in any of the pictures in the O'Toole's Wilderness Club photograph collection. As many former government agency employees who have retired to LOW, he kept a "low profile."

Arnold Chase moved into his newly built house in 1970 after retiring from the U. S. Labor Department's Bureau of Labor Statistics, where he was an Assistant Commissioner.

Jack Eckel was a retired Vice President of U.S. Steel and a pretty smart cookie – Atwell Somerville.[458]

The First Five Presidents

LEFT UPPER to LOWER: Ernest J. and Erin Holcomb, Wilderness Club Photo Collection circa 1970, courtesy of Ruthan O'Toole. James H. Stewart, reproduced from the LOWA Newsletter 1968. Arnold and Ferne Chase, Wilderness Club Photo Collection circa 1970, courtesy of Ruthan O'Toole

RIGHT UPPER to LOWER: Jack Eckel, courtesy of his daughter, Jan Eckel Griffin. Glen & Doris Barton, Wilderness Club Photo Collection circa 1970, courtesy of Ruthan O'Toole

Staffing the Association

With the Boise management departing, the Association established the following key positions, solicited candidates and selected staff.[459]

- General Manager and a Comptroller each of whom will report to the Board through the President.
- Comptroller responsible for payroll, accounting, budget and inventory controls in addition to maintaining proper internal fiscal accountability and procedural controls. He will operate independent of the manager.
- General Manager responsible for supervision and coordination of all other activities.
- Superintendent of Maintenance under direction of the General Manager, responsible for maintaining all facilities - roads, parks, lakes, golf course, buildings and equipment and supervising the employees involved, including the greens keeper.
- Club Manager under the General Manager's direction will be responsible for all food service, all recreational activities, youth activities and the operation of the swimming pools.
- Golf Professional will report to the General Manager and have the usual responsibilities of a Pro; sponsor golf course activities, operate the Pro Shop, and give golf lessons.

The first personnel action by the Board of Directors was to terminate Mr. Glenn A. Marburger as Manager of LOWA effective August 31, 1972, with an additional month's pay; appoint Mr. Edward E. Lane, as Acting General Manager effective August 1, 1972, and appointment of Mr. C. Boyd Pierson as Controller under the new organization.[460,461] By September 1, 1973, B. C. Nelson, Jr., was appointed General Manager.

> *... one of the strong points in employing Bud Nelson as our General Manager was his assurance that he had the competence and experience to provide (1) good security, (2) fire and rescue protection, and (3) much better road maintenance. Within weeks after he reported, all but two or three of the security force resigned, and it became necessary to contract with the Dodson Agency for our security. Fire protection became even worse and a total reorganization became necessary. Road Maintenance continued "in house" through the good efforts of the Maintenance Superintendent and his staff with no change as a result of our employing Nelson as our General Manager – Ernest J. Holcomb.*

Within a year, it was agreed that additional help was needed at the Club, as well as a Club Manager, to allow Mr. Nelson to devote his time to being General Manager.[462] Within three years, he was gone.

> *"... the General Manger either was fired or quit ... We have had so many GM's and clubhouse managers over the years that I can not tell you how many. One GM was escorted out the gate by security and told never to enter the property again. I have forgotten why." – Carolyn Nowakoski.*

President Lee Bauer served without pay as General Manager until a new one was hired. She announced at the June 12, 1976, meeting that a new General Manager had been selected. At the 6th Annual Meeting, the President stated, "Another new acquisition to the Lake of the Woods management staff is the General Manager, Mr. Art Warren. Mr. Warren is a 3-year resident of Lake of the Woods and brings to the management forces a background of planning and budget control."[463]

> *Mr. Warren stated that over the past year the community has moved through a unique period in its history. In doing so, we have tested our values, attitudes and beliefs in our community and ourselves. We have in many instances redefined and re-evaluated the very goals and objectives we have set for Lake of the Woods and this process of re-examination has been somewhat painful and confusing to many, not only to our citizens and our elected officials, but also to our staff -- to those who are charged with the day by day responsibility of managing Lake of the Woods...But through it all, we have learned that our faith in our community is strong. We have learned that we are more than a collection of strangers occupying the same geographical territory. For history has placed all of us within a common border and under a common law. All of us share one precious possession -- a sense of pride in our community.*

Arthur S. Warren served as manager for three years and resigned in September 1979.[464] Col. Warren J. Lodge was hired by President Alan Potter to be the next General Manager.[465] Warren Lodge (GM) lived at the 'Lake' and served until his death in 1992, the longest term for any General Manager before or since.

> *"I knew Warren … Warren told it like it was."* – Carolyn Nowakoski.

> *"Warren Lodge (GM) talked them out of it." (Referring to the state mandating a multi-million dollar upgrade to the main dam circa 1987).* –Alan Polk, President LOWA, 1991 and 2000

Environmental Control Committee (ECC)

> *"It's a true beauty spot – natural Virginia countryside with lots of trees. This asset is also a problem because we are determined to save every tree we can."* – Thomas A. Perine.[466]

Many of the members were used to the bureaucracy of city building permits, codes and inspectors. At the time the first house was built at LOW, Orange County had no zoning ordinance or any building code.[467]

The ECC was created by the developers by Section 5 of the Restrictive Covenants. The restrictions and rules on residences are included in Sections 4 through 9 of the Restrictive Covenants. In 1970, the developer transferred responsibility for appointment of the ECC members to the Board of Directors of the LOWA, Inc. Until 1972, this was a superficial change since the developer controlled the Board of Directors. In 1972, the ECC began a building inspection program for construction within LOW utilizing standards promulgated by the FHA. The ECC employed its own building inspectors, Wylie Via and Bob Elliott. In April 1974, to comply with Virginia statutes, Orange County initiated a building inspection program in accordance with a statewide building code. The ECC and its inspectors were included in this program.[468]

For several years, the Chairman of the ECC served as an Assistant Zoning Administrator for Orange County responsible for all construction within the LOW development. Similarly, our inspectors, served as Assistant Building Inspectors for Orange County, assigned to LOW. The ECC collected fees (based on the value of construction) for issuance of Orange County Building Permits; they remitted these fees to Orange County and in return, received back from the County 90% of the amount collected to cover the salaries and expenses of the two LOW building inspectors. On May 10, 1977, six families from LOW asked the Orange County Board of Supervisors to require stricter enforcement of building codes.[469] At a LOWA Board of Directors meeting four days later:

> *The President stated that another item discussed during Executive Session was the establishment of a Temporary Committee for the purpose of studying the relationship between Orange County Building Inspectors and the Environmental Control Committee program. This Committee will be chaired by Mr. John Nolan. Mr. Glen Barton will serve on the Committee and Mr. Bill Adrian and Mr. Cliff Ruffner will also be asked to serve on this Committee.*[470]

> *Mr. Eckel reported that the ECC had recommended ... that Cliff Ruffner be appointed as chairman.*[471]

Mr. Clifford H. Ruffner, Jr., was appointed to the ECC on October 7, 1971. Col. Ruffner received a Bachelors of Architecture from Cornell in 1939 and served a distinguished career in the US Army.[472,473] He apparently was very interested in the history of the LOW area and wrote two documents on file at the LOWA administration office. One is an architect's study of the Spotswood house that had stood on, what is now, Spotswood Park.[474] The other was the infamous "The Legend of Trail Rock."

> *The legend of Trail Rock is a joke/story that Cliff Ruffner told several times at community gatherings such as the annual variety show that the O'Tooles used to produce in the 70's – Jeff Flynn.*[475]

Legend of Trail Rock

The Legend of Trail Rock
(Indian Rocke)

Indian Rocke or Trail Rock, located on the Lake of the Woods' clubhouse grounds, is richly interwoven in the fabric of the early history of Virginia. The rock was originally on Flat Run at the crossing of the Mattaponi Trail and a branch trail to the West.

It was a convenient landmark, both for the Indians and white settlers, marking a one day journey from the settlement at Falmouth on the trail west, and a two days' journey south from the Indian village below Quantico.

Earliest mention of the rock was made by Captain John Smith in his Chronicle of 1651: "We spent ye first nyghte at ye Trayle Rocke whiche abounds in deere and raccoon". There is little evidence to support the oft' repeated tale that Pocahontas guided Captain Smith on this journey. An "R" carved on the rock, (Now unfortunately, on the underside) is thought to have been scratched by John Rolfe while on a beaver trapping expedition.

Governor Spotswood, ever conscious of trade possibilities, established a small trading post near the rock. The post was supervised by Spotswood's son who showed more interest in gaming and hunting. The trading post burned in 1738, and was never rebuilt. In 1720, Ebenezer Elliston the notorious highwayman of Colonial times, was apprehended by King George's marshals while in camp at trayle rock.

As plank roads were pushed through the wilderness 1500 yards to the east, Trail Rock lost its prominence as a landmark.

Governor Spotswood, and avid gardener in his retirement, desired to move the rock to his house as a part of a "Wylde garden in ye Oriental style"; but after spending three days and the labor of four stalwart iron miners, he noted in his journal: "It is amply evident that the Almighty has no wish to grace my terrace with this most obstinate of stones".

The rock became a trysting place for lovers and a meeting place for hunters. The records show that Church picnics were held there.

During the War Between the States, General Hooker met here with his staff. His adjutant, sitting on the rock, narrowly missed death as the rock was struck by a Southern cannon ball. It is said that he found it extremely painful to sit a horse for the next three days and that his fellow officers derived considerable amusement from his plight.

(Contributed by Cliff Ruffner)

NOTE: The rock referred to above is located at the Clubhouse on the side toward the Lake.)

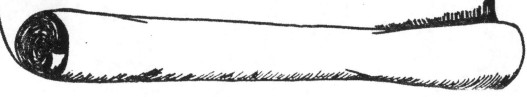

Reproduced from LOWA historic files. Cliff Ruffner's humor is so subtle as to confuse some that this is fact and not fiction.

The ECC collects a filing fee for every plan submitted for review and one-time fee for the construction of a home, the road maintenance fee, which marks the transition from a lot owner to a resident. These fees have been in existence since before 1976. The fee was consumed for operational expenses, mainly to reduce the annual assessment, for over 25 years until the Board of Directors established a policy to fund the Road Reserve from this fee.

As reported at the 6th Annual Meeting, the ECC consisted of three volunteer voting members and two alternates, supported by one staff secretary.

> *The ECC is presently (1976) comprised of three members: Lavina Lundwall, Paul Kilduff and Mr. Stoebe as Chairman. In the past year, from last September up to now, the ECC has approved and issued 60 building permits for single-family dwellings within the LOW development … Since its inception, the ECC has issued buildings permits for a total of 575 homes.*

An issue that has plagued the ECC to this day is resolution of disputes between owner and builder.

> *The ECC is not, and I repeat not, a referee between the owner and the builder. The owner must deal directly with his builder. We do not handle complaints from an owner against his builder. Neither do we recommend any specific builder over others who also build within the LOW area.*[476]

In the Association's twentieth year, the Board established the new position of Environmental Control Inspector to inspect member's lots and buildings for compliance with the regulations.[477]

Security and Fire Protection

The first responsibility that Boise Cascade transferred to the Association was security and fire protection. The Association assumed responsibility in summer of 1969.

> *We took over the developer's security force and its two patrol cars, both of which were in very poor condition and had to be replaced in 1970.*[478]

The Board of Directors on August 30, 1971, established the Security and Safety Committee and the Rules and Regulations, which state in part that the Traffic Laws of the Commonwealth of Virginia shall apply in general on all roads and streets in Lake of the Woods.[479] At the 4th Annual meeting, President Arnold Chase touched briefly on the duties of the Dodson Security Agency who had provided security and fire and rescue services to the Association since December 1972. He started with a couple of the people who had worked for Boise.[480] George Dodson became a member in April 1975. At that time, there were about 500 homes within LOW.

> *Mr. Dodson's contract was not a sole-source, but a follow-on contract. He had been hired on a previous contract with competitive bidding. We were satisfied with his services … In addition, we have heard no evidence of the failure to perform on the part of the*

petitioners nor have we heard any numbers cited that we are not getting a good value for our dollar.[481]

Mr. Gordon Gay pointed out that radar is now (1976) in effect and 17 people have been stopped for speeding. In talking with Mr. Dodson, he believes this is doing a good job in bringing the speed down, especially on Lakeview Parkway … Mr. Gay stated that we try to enforce the rules as best as we can.[482]

During the summer of 1976, the lake was patrolled about 30 hours a week and about 20 hours of this was on weekends. The Lake patrol issued 27 citations that year. Most of it was speeding in the coves.[483] At the end of that summer, Mr. George Dodson provided the membership a report at the 6th Annual Meeting.

… the Association pays him an annual fee. He furnishes the automobile, the red lights, all maintenance, all gasoline and oil, everything pertaining to that automobile. He also owns the Security Boat, furnishes the fuel, repairs, and insurance on both of the vehicles. He also has to furnish his men with uniforms and equipment. He has to get his personnel sworn in by the Orange County Circuit Court, which is for a 4-year period. He must obtain insurance for this 4-year period.

The security structure at the main gate was built in 1978. This simple structure was anything but simple to build as the contractor defaulted and had unpaid sub-contractor bills.484 The General Manager became the general contractor and completed the new Security building at the main gate before the 8th Annual Meeting. At that meeting, Jeff Flynn spoke for the Civic League in the general question and answer session. His three questions would be asked over and again for the next thirty years. The Security Force contract is presently before the Board for renewal. There are numerous reports of vendors/contractors and their employees and families fishing, swimming, picnicking, and in general just using the facilities.

Question: 1 - Are there any new instructions in the contract to increase the effectiveness of the Security Force? 2 - Would you spell out the services that we can expect from the Security Force? 3 - Would you inform us of the new contract cost?[485]

Over his 36 years of service, George Dodson has seen the size of the security force at Lake of the Woods grow, the creation of a "truly gated" community with front entrance guard house and recently the creation of an automatic gated back entrance.[486]

Fire Chief Bruce Willets, a volunteer fireman for 60 years, thanked George Dodson, now head of Dodson Security at Lake of the Woods. "He set up the first course to be taught to LOW fire and rescue volunteers," he said. "It was a first-aid course back when Lake of the Woods was just a greasy spot on the ground." According to Public Relations Director Hank Altman, the LOW Fire and Rescue Company was first chartered in August 1971. "Our first ambulance was a station wagon," he laughed. The original building, still in use, was a double-wide trailer.[487]

LOW Front Entrance Security 1967. Photo on display in the LOWA General Manager's Office.

LOW Fire and Rescue is composed of volunteer and paid fire and rescue staff. Its first-due area is the entire Route 3 corridor in northeastern Orange County and the west side of Route 20 from Route 3 to Locust Grove Town Center at Route 611.

> *(LOW has) its own fire and rescue teams, which (General Manager Warren J.) Lodge called "as good as any in the state of Virginia – fabulous." His wife, Jean, is on the rescue squad, working 12 hours every fourth day.*[488]

The Lake of the Woods Volunteer Fire and Rescue Department was created under the Laws of the Commonwealth of Virginia on August 23, 1971. It started with two fire trucks, one 1938 model and one 1946 model with a 1942 engine. Mr. Holcomb proposed the purchase of two used Class A fire trucks from the Oxon Hill, Md., Fire Company. He stated that the two Oxon Hill trucks could be purchased at a cost of $11,500 (for the two), that their original cost was about $52,000 each, that they were being made available since Maryland regulations do not permit first line equipment in excess of fifteen years in age. At that time, in Orange County none of the four fire companies or the one rescue squad was formally supported by the County. Lake of the Woods Association purchased the two Oxon Hill fire trucks at a cost not to exceed $12,000.[489] Lease-Purchase and Management Agreements between the LOWA and the LOW Volunteer Fire & Rescue Company were established in 1972.[490] That year the association began annual donations to the Fire and Rescue Department.[491] In 1973, Mr. Holcomb reported that the new Fire Chief, Mr. Natto, was doing an outstanding job in organizing and training the Fire & Rescue Co.; they had 25-35 members participating and 18 of those attended a first aid class.

Mr. Eckel reported the F&R Co. had 2 old fire trucks that weren't of any value to them *and they believed they could get someone to pick them up as antiques for $200 to $300 … Mr. Holcomb then brought up the subject of the fire trucks to be housed in a new building … He also had a sketch prepared by Cliff Ruffner of the proposed building which would be at the rear of the Fire Dept.*[492]

Three years later, the Fire and Rescue Squad attended the 6th Annual Meeting with its new fire truck and new ambulance. In addition to the annual donation, the Association supports the LOW Fire and Rescue fund raising during the annual Fourth of July event. In 1979, the Association granted a long-term lease to the Fire & Rescue to allow them to make an addition to the existing firehouse.

… expressed his thanks for the cooperation of the Board, management and Security Force … Because of additional new equipment coming in and eventual loss of space in the Holcomb Building, an addition to the firehouse will be necessary and the backing of the Association is necessary for this. – Bob Kitchen, President of the LOW Fire and Rescue Company [493]

Chapter 9   Volunteers, the Heart of Lake of the Woods

The President ... announced that a committee of volunteers headed by Mrs. Ferne Chase was prepared to provide hot and cold drinks and doughnuts at a nominal charge for the benefit of the LOW Volunteer Fire and Rescue Company. – 3rd Annual Meeting

While many purchased lots as an investment, those that did so for the social value, those that came most weekends and built the first few hundred homes, established a tradition of volunteerism that is seldom seen elsewhere.

Ten Lake of the Woods residents have received honor awards from the Lake of the Woods Association for leadership and service to the community. Ernest J. Holcomb was given a plaque and certificate for his work in planning and development of facilities and services in the early stages of the community. Ruth Dugan received the same Distinguished Service award, for setting up fiscal and management programs for the association. A group award was given to seven association members who successfully negotiated with Boise-Cascade, the developer, for acquisition of its holdings, including the clubhouse, golf course and other recreational amenities, these members were John R. Henry, Arnold Chase, Ruth Dugan, Ernest Holcomb, William A. Newman, Richard Wilbur and James Stewart. ... Five outstanding service awards were given to William H. Adrain, for voluntary service as an architect and engineer; Richard H. Bayless, for setting up social activities; Barbara-Sue O'Toole, for organizing social and civic activities; Clifford H. Ruffner, for work on environmental control, revenue, and fire and rescue programs; and Edward E. Lane, for planning and directing maintenance and improvement of roads, buildings and recreational facilities. The awards were presented Monday (September 1, 1975) by Lake of the Woods Association President Glen T. Barton in a ceremony attended by some 200 persons. The association plans to make this an annual event.[494]

"A major problem for the Board and committees was that almost every volunteer was a leader and not a follower." – John R. Henry, Director 1971-1974.[495]

"We have about 180 people who are volunteers who serve on committees and really make this place go. I can find you one of anything you want here. That makes for a lot of free advice." – General Manager Warren Lodge (GM), 1986.

"LOW has fantastic resources amongst its population from which we can do just about

anything - time and money plays a very important role, however." – General Manager Richard Wade, 1995.[496]

Typical of the professional services provided by members as volunteers were the architects William Adrian and Lou Potter. Both of them provided their services at no cost, Mr. Adrian for the Association office, later named the Holcomb Building and Ms. Potter for the Clubhouse restoration after the 1980 fire.

> *"Mr. Adrian served as our supervising architect and did an outstanding job. He generously prepared the plans and supervised construction at no cost whatsoever to the Association."* – Ernest J. Holcomb [497]

> *"His (LOWA President Al Potter) wife, Lou Potter was also a big asset. She was an architect and an enormous help in designing the building and over-seeing the construction. I wish we had a building at the Lake named for them."* – Fran Harding, Director 1979-1980 [498]

Golf Course "Rock Parties"

The farmers in Orange County knew that the land in the Flat Run area was not fit for much more than oaks and pines. VWCI had promised an eighteen-hole professional golf course at Lake of the Woods. The first truly unstructured volunteers were the LOW rock-pickers. Boise sponsored several "Rock Picking Parties", which meant that free beer and soft drinks were provided to the several dozen families that participated.

> *About the time that we moved here (November 1971), only nine holes were finished on the golf course. Someone organized a "Rock-Pickers" club to clear the area for the remaining nine holes. My husband participated for several Saturdays* – Carolyn Nowakoski [499]

> *It was reported that the dump trucks moved more than forty tons of rock per day during the several weekend parties.*[500]

1975 Honor Awards Winners for Leadership and Service

Wilderness Club Photo Collection circa 1970, courtesy of Ruthan O'Toole.

LEFT UPPER to LOWER: Barbara-Sue O'Toole, John R. Henry

RIGHT UPPER to LOWER: John and Ruth Dugan, Cliff and Yvonne Ruffner
Ernie Holcomb, James Stewart and Arnold Chase previously shown. No photographs were found for the others.

Lake Of The Woods
Newsletter

EDITORIAL OFFICES:
P.O. BOX 66510, CHICAGO, ILLINOIS 60666   JULY 1969

rock pickers party a great success!

113 "Rock Pickers" cleared away 53 tons of rubble from the Lake of the Woods golf course last April 18th. Even tho the weather was rainy, the volunteers were loyal, and braved the elements with no complaints.

The day began with a continental breakfast served at the Pro Shop. The group started picking rocks at 9:30 and worked thru until 5:00. A trailer furnished by Pepsi-Cola followed the group thru-out their day's labors serving Pepsi and beer. A buffet luncheon was served to the men at the clubhouse.

After the rock picking, a steak dinner and cocktail party were in order. Citations of merit signed by Bob Yoxall, Vice President of Boise Cascade Properties, Inc., were presented to each of the participants.

Club manager, Jack Rosemond, announced plans for another rock pickers party, to include both husband and wife, on July 12.

Here is part of the 53 tons of rocks collected.

Loyal rock pickers, hard at work.

Rock pickers enjoy a Pepsi break.

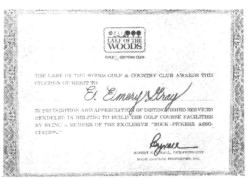

A certificate was presented to each rock picker.

Time out for lunch.

114

The Wilderness Bottle Club

Boise Cascade was eager to set up a bar at the Clubhouse, an enhancement for the sales of lots. Orange County was a dry county at the time, and selling liquor by the drink was illegal. An obvious solution was to form a bottle club. They set up the facility in the Clubhouse, furnished it and accepted John R. Henry's offer to take on a job at Lake of the Woods on a voluntary basis. Thus, the Wilderness Bottle Club was the first of the many major volunteer organizations. In order to get a liquor license, a non-profit company was chartered November 7, 1968, with a governing board that excluded Boise Cascade. The president of the Club, James Stewart, and the Treasurer, John R. Henry, would later be members of the first all volunteer Board of Directors of Lake of the Woods. The Club became the social center of the community. Many of the social activities at the Lake have their roots in the Wilderness Bottle Club.

> *When Boise left, (the) Board … immediately shut down the Wilderness Club. They would not have the club competing with the Assn.* - John R. Henry [501,502]

> *Be sure to come to the authentic Irish wake for the Wilderness Club on June 30th. We will open at 3:00 PM on that day and close at midnight when both our liquor license and lease expire.* [503]

> *A few more Wilderness Club Wake comments. As bottles were emptied the pinebox coffin that Sonny Weedon made was filled. Just before midnight Dick Carter delivered the eulogy: Sistern & Brethren. The procession was from the club to the clubhouse dock where the box was thrown in & expected to sink. It was discovered the next morning having floated down to Al Whittaker's dock and my brothers Buzzy & Geri were dispatched to fetch it out of the lake.* – Ruthan O'Toole [504]

The Association managed the Bottle Club as part of the Clubhouse until Orange County went from dry to liquor by the drink in 1975, hence not the need for a bottle club any longer.

Courtesy of Ruthan O'Toole, the Wilderness Club Photo Album.

UPPER: Sonny Weedon & Barbara-Sue O'Toole, circa 1970.

LOWER: John O'Toole circa 1970.

Civic League

President M. Lee Bauer welcomes all new people who wish to serve on any of these committees. Until you get into the operational part of the whole Association, you can probably question sometimes what is done and why. Once you are in the middle, you have no doubt in your minds as to why something is done.[505,506]

You do not have to be "part of" the operation of the Association to question "what is done and why;" many members prefer to gather in opposition to current policy and/or the Board of Directors. This is normal in any homeowners' association. At times, members will form a formal organization, separate from any control by the Association, to exercise their rights.

The first such organization at Lake of the Woods was the Civic League. While principally a political organization, it also served a social function, sponsoring activities that eventually became Association supported activities.[507]

Mrs. Barbara O'Toole requested permission from the Board to use the facilities of the Country Club the four Sundays in August, the night before Labor Day and Labor Day to produce the Variety Show, which will be sponsored by the Civic League.[508]

The Board thanked Mr. Nowakoski for his interest and asked him to give further consideration to recommending to the Board upon the desirability of stocking fishable size trout in the fall and having a trout fishing derby sponsored by the Civic League …[509]

Several of the changes requested by the League have become standard practice, 30 years later.

Mr. Bob Kitchen, President of the Civic League, brought up the question again of permitting property owners to speak up at the time a pertinent subject is being discussed, as suggested by the Civic League to the Board at previous meetings.[510,511]

Mr. Bob Kitchen, President of the Civic League, stressed the importance of well functioning standing committees and felt it should be a responsibility shared by the Board, the committee chairmen and members. The Civic League recommended that one member of the Board be appointed to serve as an ex-officio member of each standing committee in order to improve communications and to insure board consideration of committee recommendations.[512]

The League published a newsletter that provided an outlet for dialogue to other members outside of the control of the Association. While the records are sketchy at best, it appears that accusations were made impugning their fairness.

In answer to comments made about the Civic League Newsletter, Mr. Kitchen stated the Newsletter stands on its own and is not biased toward any of the candidates running for office.[513]

The political agenda of this group was stated at the January 26, 1974, Board of Directors meeting.

> *Mr. Kitchen … felt that assessments should be established to take care of the basic maintenance cost of all lots and that those who use the facilities should pay an additional assessment similar to what Boise had, i.e., $60 for lot assessment and $120 for Country Club dues. An additional assessment could be obtained through taxing people, based upon the distance they lived from LOW, e.g., tax those living within a radius of 70 miles. He also recommended that those who own several lots should only have to pay the pro-rated maintenance costs per lot rather than the $135 per lot as now required.*

All of the above is contrary to the Restrictive Covenants; even if the Board of Directors wanted to oblige, they could not legally do so.

The Civic League eventually dissolved. The last mention of this organization, in the available Board of Directors minutes, was the 8th Annual Meeting where Jeff Flynn spoke for the Civic League. Thirty years later, he was chosen by the other Directors to be Vice-President of the Association.

The LOW Phonebook & the Civic Club

The LOW phone book has always been a volunteer publication; the net proceeds from sales are contributed to Fire and Rescue. The first LOW Directory was produced in 1971. Carolyn Nowakoski helped with the second directory in the spring of 1972. At the same time as collecting information from neighbors, she also collected funds for Fire and Rescue. Marion Durben prepared the directory for many years.

While Ed McCarthy was President, Jim McCullough added an editorial page to the phone book. The Directors banned the phone book sale on Association property, and Jim reacted by establishing a forum, oral and print, for any LOWA member to express their point of view, the Civic Club.

"Be Concerned, Be Informed, Be Involved" is the motto of the LOW Civic Club, which hosts monthly speakers and provides an open forum where property owners can learn about issues that affect their lives, interests and investment in the LOW community. Members are invited to submit articles on community matters for publication in the club's monthly newsletter, *Lakeviews*.

Marion Durben, 2005, courtesy of Dan McFarland.

AN OPEN LETTER
From this directory's publisher

As Lake of the Woods matures, we continue to build about a hundred new homes each year. Most are attractive and add to the ambiance of the community, but alas, some don't, and others that are beginning to show their age are contributing to a gradual but steady erosion of property values. It is incumbent on every property owner to _act_ . Here is what must be done. I think all items are important.

1. Tighten down on compliance with provisions of the restrictive covenants. If a house or yard or lot is unsightly, you and your neighbors jointly bring it to the attention of the ECC. Business vehicles (cars and trucks with signs, or with tools and equipment mounted) are not legally parked outdoors in LOW overnight, except in public parking areas with LOWA permission. This is a residential area.

2. Stop questioning the responsibility of the ECC to determine and enforce color schemes; it is assigned by the restrictive covenants. White garage doors _stand out_. Encourage the ECC to be fair but firm in making LOW look better. Why not _paint your door_?

3. Enforce restrictive covenants on house occupancy. It is not reasonable to regularly see four or more cars at a single family dwelling. Some of our homes look like boarding houses. . . are they?

4. We've had a rash of transients who occupy, then _trash_ rental homes. It seems to be a national problem, but there has to be a way to stop this problem in a _secure gated_ community. When a home has been _trashed_ it must be denied an occupancy permit as hazardous to health. If water, sewer, or electric service is disconnected, the occupants should be required to vacate the home immediately. It is hard on an owner who must rent out a home temporarily for economic reasons, but it is incumbent on him to demand serious security deposits to prevent a house from becoming an eyesore, or public nuisance, and lowering nearby property values.

5. Let us stop _nickel and diming_. The amount of our annual assessment is laughable when you consider that this is 1998 and people are paying over $15,000 for a modest automobile. Ask what it costs to live at Aquia Harbor or any other homeowner association-managed property in the area. Our fees are less than most condo fees and yet we are blessed with a beautiful, well planned community with extensive amenities. We should be adding to them, but we are not; we are letting what we have run down. The Board of Directors should increase the annual assessment by about $360 per lot, and _then_ adopt an annual increase at the rate of the CPI. How much is this? People complain about high prices and then spend 50¢ for a can of soda pop. What do cigarettes cost? Yes, it takes money to live. The current assessment per property works out to $1.28 a day. An increase to $2.28 is not going to break anyone who consciously bought into a resort–like residential community.

6. Build the year round swimming and exercise facility NOW. Taking surveys of who would use such a facility is counter productive. It would be used by hundreds of LOWites who now drive to Culpeper or Fredericksburg too often. Swimming is not a summer-only sport, and our citizens deserve the facilities to keep themselves healthy. If we do not need all of the new assessment income, return some of it in the form of restaurant credits to help keep our food facility viable. Form a committee to investigate ways of aiding long-time residents who might be hurt by increased fees, or helping young people who _actively serve_ the community by working as firemen or EMTs. But don't keep LOW _cheap_.

7. Stop complaining if some new amenity is not _your cup of tea_. We've been subsidizing golf, the stables, pools, tennis, youth activities, and the clubhouse. THIS IS RIGHT - but it is selfish if some try to promote their preferences while attempting to defeat those of other LOWites.

8. Keep volunteering - and support others who do. Help publicize activities. We've had a fine volunteer Board of Directors for the 17 years I've been here, but often they become too focused on pinching pennies. Economy is important, but not at the expense of keeping up our community. Do you know we had a board that lowered assessments on two occasions? Yes; $2 a year! That cost LOWA $8400 each time, money that could have meant much more to it than $2 did to a property owner.

9. Talk to your friends and neighbors. It seems the only persons being heard are those who say the fees are high instead of too low. Tell the Board what you think.

This editorial is not sanctioned by LOWA or LOW F&R. It reflects the opinions of Jim McCullough, association member, and volunteer Directory Publisher 1992- to date.

DIRECTORY INDEX

1.

Reproduced from Civic Club historic files.

Louise and James McCullough are credited with having originated the Civic Club.[514] They are the only couple to have twice received the Association's Distinguished Service Award, in 1993 and again in 2003.

More than One Hundred Clubs

More than 100 clubs and associations have been formed at LOW. Activities and Clubs are open to all residents and tenants of LOW, although some national organizations may have specific selective requirements for membership.[515] The clubs vary greatly on their level of social activity, fund raising, service and charity. The following is illustrative of the diversity and development of these clubs.

> *"When I first moved here, I was invited to join a group of women who met in each other's homes. We drank coffee, did handwork such as knitting, and complained about our builders ... (we) became know as the Stitch and Bitch group."* – Carolyn Nowakoski

At that time, fall of 1971, there were no more than 150 homes built and most were secondary homes. Out of this group grew many of the major clubs and activities at Lake of the Woods. As the community of primary residences grew, the group persuaded the Clubhouse manager, an employee of Boise Cascade, to make every Wednesday, "Ladies Day".[516] They held the first Fire and Rescue bazaar in the fall of 1973. When the group spent some of its money for flowers and planted them at the gate and front of the Holcomb Building, they informally started the Garden Club.

When the square-dance club started in October 1972, it helped keep the LOW clubhouse in business by providing entertainment for dinner guests. The club, which is the oldest social club at LOW, now has 59 members.

> *"It was great seeing the former dancers renewing friendships and talking over old times,"* said Anne Boyd, chairperson of the club's anniversary committee ... Betty Evans joined the club in 1986 ..."It brought back a lot of memories of dances my husband and I had enjoyed," she said.[517]

> *There was a big party at the Clubhouse Friday night, May 8. Everyone had fun dining and dancing, but it was a bittersweet event. After 18 years as our club caller and over 40 years of calling in all, Jesse Shackelford has retired. We will miss his great voice and gentle nature. More than 120 current and former dancers from all around our region (as far south as Richmond and beyond) came to wish Jesse and his "taw," Lillian, a happy, healthy retirement. There were testimonials to Jesse and an elegant speech from the man of the hour.* - Anne Boyd, Secretary, LOW Square Dance Club

The LOW Garden Club is a non-profit group that joined in 1978 with the Virginia Federation of Garden Clubs. Their objective is to serve LOW through civic and beautification endeavors. Annual fundraising activities enable continuation of these projects. The Club is responsible for the Memorial Garden adjacent to the ECC building, holiday decorations at the Clubhouse and the monthly "Keep LOW Beautiful" program, among other projects.

Since its inception and organization in 1982, the LOW Players have been contributing to the cultural enrichment of the Lake of the Woods community. From its initial production, *The Curious Savage*, some 25 years ago, 45 shows have been presented to supportive and appreciative audiences. This dedicated group has continued to grow and flourish. Growth involved having to construct a stage twice a year in the very busy clubhouse to finally getting their own stage in 2006 in the newly-built Community Center.

The LOW Lions Club received its charter in 1982. The time seemed ripe to move forward promptly as the population had reached the size that could support a large and active service club. There were no clubs designed for the men at LOW although there were several for the women, and there were many opportunities for providing assistance to some unfortunate individuals here at LOW and to those in surrounding parts of eastern Orange County.

I would like to dedicate this history (of the Lake of the Woods Lions Club 1982-2000) to the person who inspired it: District Governor Barbara Story. – Lion Ralph E. Cook, author and President of LOW Lions 1999.[518]

Daniel (Danny) Schafer, a member of LOWA and Past District Governor and member of the Orange Lions Club, initiated the effort to establish a Lions Club. Lion Danny moved into LOW in 1983 and served in an advisory capacity, "Guiding Lion," for the Club over the next eleven years.

There were 109 charter members. Membership has varied little, ranging from a high of 132 in 1986 to a low of 97 in 1997. In 1987, the Lions International Convention removed "male" as one of the criteria for joining. In August 1989, the LOW Lions Club inducted Nan Taylor. Two months later, Barbara Story became the second woman to be inducted. The Lions Club is the only service organization that has both built facilities in LOW, the Lions Pavilion in 1985, the bus stop shelter in 1987, and the Velona-Long Building in 1994, and been given a LOWA facility, initially the marina building and recently the Ferris Building for the eyeglass program.

Lion Tom Walker screened the eyes of 300 children[519]

Committees

We expect to involve the membership in the various committees ... With the help of such committees we hope to read as accurately as possible what the membership interests are in both scope and depth. - E.J. Holcomb

Few committees are specified in the Articles of Incorporation: the Environmental Control Committee, a Finance Committee, a Legal and Compliance Committee and a Maintenance and Ecology Committee. By the summer of 1972, the number of committees had grown to seven. Most committees were chaired by one of the elected directors of the Association and staffed with volunteers. Several of the future community leaders served on these committees before seeking election to the Board of Directors. The names and functions of various committees evolved as the Association matured.

> *Mr. Newman commented that each committee should have responsibility for determination of policy recommendations to the Board, user charges to be levied, development of a budget for committee activities ... Mr. Chase made the point that the committees are really of two classes, functional such as Environmental Control, Membership, Disciplinary and Compliance, and those advisory in nature such as Conservation and Ecology, Maintenance, Golf, Utilities, Campground ... Mr. Holcomb suggested that Inventory Committee be absorbed by Budget and Accounting; Club Activities include Teen Club; Marina and Lakes Committee be included in Security and Safety Committee; and Golf Course under Maintenance Committee.[520]*

> *The Acting General Manager proposed that the present Ecology Committee be consolidated as a subcommittee with the Roads and Parks Committee and that the new committee be renamed Maintenance and Ecology Committee.[521]*

An interesting assessment of volunteerism was made by Director Dugan. "Committees will not accept responsibility -- that they will work when they want to work". An example of this was provided at the September 22, 1973, Board of Directors meeting.

> *Mr. Kitchen... questioned the absence of Notices of Board Meetings in the Newsletter and at the mail boxes ... Mr. Chase answered that the Newsletter has been somewhat irregular as the committee has fallen apart, but the Association would try to get the notices out in the future.*

At the 6th Annual Meeting, the chairpersons or their representative of five standing committees and six "temporary" committees presented their reports to the membership.[522,523] The President stated, "The Board is in the process of trying to form a Stables Committee to help promote and utilize the fine stable facilities. It is also hoped to reactivate a Recreation Committee with a chairman and a representative from the respective recreational facilities and round out all of the committees here at Lake of the Woods."

At the 8th Annual Meeting, on September 4, 1978, chairpersons or their representative of seven standing committees and five "temporary" committees presented their reports to the membership.[524] At that time, there were 15 committees supported by 108 volunteers. It is indicative of how much has changed that the second largest committee was Campgrounds with ten members, the smallest was Rules with only two.[525] Thirteen years later, October 5, 1991, there were 18 committees supported by 147 volunteers. During the interval, the Recreation committee evolved to the Clubhouse and Youth Activities committees. The Lake committee was split off from Maintenance and Ecology.

Today more than 200 members serve on 19 standing committees. That is approximately one volunteer for every 12 homes built. In 1972, at least 50 members served, or approximately one volunteer for every five homes. In the early years, everyone participated at one time or another that had built a home. Today the members who houses are secondary residences, tend to be very active users of the amenities, especially during the summer months, but with a few notable exceptions do not participate on the LOWA committees.

Chapter 10   A Different Kind of Golf and Country Club

This is a private operation for property owners and their guests. That's the name of the game … The golf course, clubhouses, pools, campgrounds, etc., will be owned by property owners … eligible for membership.[526]

The club venue, clubhouse, beach and pool complex overlooking a large lake is magnificent. The golf course is a regulation eighteen-hole course through the woods and between the main and small lakes. The golf-pro is a PGA member.

Once the Association bought the Golf and Country Club from Boise Cascade, the distinction between Club employee and Club member vanished.[527] Even prior to 1972, when the Bottle Club opened in November 1968 as independent of Boise Cascade, but with membership limited to LOW Golf and Country Club members, a different kind of country club came into being. For the members, the Club became the social center of the community as soon as the salesmen left for the day.

Boise used the Clubhouse for selling property, but it had no meal service, no service at all. John and Barbara-Sue O'Toole acted as volunteer host and hostess of the club, making newcomers feel welcome. If somebody came in for the first time, they did not let them sit down until they had met everybody in the club. They took them around and introduced them to every single person there. Jeff Flynn, who performed in many of the community variety shows agrees. "Barbara-Sue was a very special person. She got things done."[528]

The Barbara-Sue O'Toole variety shows became an institution. Levin Houston, a professor of music at Mary Washington College, who wrote much of the music for the productions, including his song, "At the Lake of the Woods," directed and brought his band to perform. His participation in the Labor Day weekend variety shows lasted for sixteen years.[529]

After the LOW Golf and Country Club was purchased by the Association, the LOW Board of Directors took control, and the distinction between Wilderness Bottle Club and the Lake of the Woods Clubhouse dissolved; it all became "the Club."

Mr. Chase announced that the General Manager has asked the members of the Board and their spouses to serve collectively as hosts and hostesses for the Club during the month of April, on the days when the Club is open, when we have Open House for the people of Orange, Fredericksburg and Culpeper. Schedules and a planned program of activities are to be arranged between the Board members.[530]

Club Manager

It was agreed that additional help was needed at the Club House as well as a Club manager to allow Mr. Nelson to devote his time to being General Manager.[531]

Duke Smiders was hired as Clubhouse manager, but Carla, his wife, did as much. They rented across from the round-house, thus as tenants in good standing they were both members and employees, and always on call. They managed the entire clubhouse facility, the restaurant at the Club and the snack bar at the Pro Shop.[532] Carla remembers having to enforce the rules of those days. It was especially difficult to tell a woman on the Board of Directors, she could not enter with rollers in your hair! The nearest stores were in Fredericksburg, and for a wedding, she would buy the wedding cakes there. It was always a stressful drive back on the old two-lane Germanna Road with a large cake in the car.

The highlight of the Smiders' service at the Lake was the surprise visit to the clubhouse by President Gerald R. Ford. He was the most distinguished of all the VIPs at the Lee Elder Golf Tournament. They had been planning the party for that evening, but were not prepared for the President's request that afternoon for a martini! She quickly, produced a bottle of Beefeater's gin, had the President sign the "corkage charge" book, and prepared his martini.[533] However, before he could drink it, the Secret Service agent required a second martini, which he sampled before the President could raise his elbow.

In 1976, the decision to provide a Club manager was reversed. Mrs. Anita Gayhart, the Club Chef and Mr. Rick Harty, the Assistant Chef were introduced at the 6th Annual Meeting.

There should be an additional amount of $13,000 added … in order to retain Mr. Michael Smider as Country Club Manager; and have the monies to cover his salary for that period of time until the new General Manager is selected and takes over the duties of General Manager and Country Club Manager, as stipulated on the page under the heading of General Administration. At the time the new General Manager assumes the responsibilities of the Club Manager, there will be hired a Dining Room Hostess.[534]

The food service continued for several years alongside the bottle club. The Club charged a corkage fee. In 1976, eight years after the state law permitted liquor by the drink, the Board of Directors approved a $50 donation toward legal fees by a group of Orange County businessmen to get Liquor by the Drink on the ballot in November. Two years later, the bottle club ceased and the Board of Directors established liquor service at the Club, an achievement recognized at the 8ᵗʰ Annual meeting as one of the year's most important.

The Board of Directors maintained direct control of the bar procedures for several more years.

Mr. Baratz asked the Board if they wished to readdress the clubhouse liquor policy, as he had learned that some members may not have had a full understanding of the issue. Mr. Goodier made a motion to rescind the policy prohibiting serving doubles and multi-

liquored drinks at the Clubhouse. Mr. Hollenbach seconded, and the motion passed unanimously.[535]

Richard Wallace was introduced at the 11th Annual LOWA Meeting as the recently hired Club Manager.[536] In 1996, he was elected to be the 5th District County Supervisor.[537]

President Sorte presented a plaque to former Clubhouse Manager Richard D. Wallace for his "devotion and commitment to outstanding service" as clubhouse manager during the period 1984-1990.[538]

Rich Wallace served longer than any other clubhouse manager did. He was preceded as Clubhouse Manager in July 1984 by Norman Howard. Mr. Howard was a longtime employee of Howard Johnsons; he was their food and beverage manager in Oklahoma City when he was invited by Warren Lodge (GM) for an interview and then selected for the job. Mr. Howard only served for a few months but he made a lasting impact.[539] In 1984, the Clubhouse was "still in the 60s." When a member was turned away because of lack of a suit jacket, Mr. Howard went to a thrift store and bought six jackets of various sizes so he never had to turn away a paying customer again. He gained the support of the Maintenance Department by serving them complimentary lunches when they were working at the clubhouse. Eugene F. (Frank) Ferris, who had been a Boise Cascade maintenance employee took care of the clubhouse and became Norm's friend.

We (Norm and Frank) discovered two drains in the kitchen we didn't know were there.
– Norman Howard

Wednesday Ladies Day had grown to be Wednesday Ladies Bridge; they filled the clubhouse. Norm charged $3.75 for lunch. The day he served roast beef with melted Swiss cheese and broccoli and cheese soup, Barbara Story told him, "Best lunch we have ever had." Norm recalls the ladies left the waitresses $240 in tips. He had a policy that all tip money went to the hourly employees. Norm had many more innovations that went counter to the prevailing attitude that the clubhouse was for formal dining: what he calls the Fort LOW Clubhouse, which followed the standard Army Officer Club policies of that era. The first time he served catfish and fries in the Sports Lounge; he filled it and sold out in 90 minutes while main dining had one table occupied.

Another practice that we do not see any more were the private parties, elegant affairs with guest chefs, special menus, even an ice sculpture. These grand affairs would cost several thousand dollars, and members would try to outdo the last party.

Would there ever be a profit?

In 1972, the Clubhouse was large enough to hold all the residents and weekend members. A large fraction of these members played golf. Within only a few years, the fact that all members' assessments supported the "County Club and Golf Course" caused friction and division in the community.

We thought we should acquire the recreational amenities even with a loss history to bring as much a possible under one entity and management; that when Lake of the Woods had 1,000 homes, more or less the facilities would operate at a profit and possibly result in reduced lot assessments. – Ernest J. Holcomb

Concern for perceived high costs of the food service at the Club was expressed as early as March 1974.

Mr. Chase emphasized that the Budget Committee had reduced the (1974) budget expenses for the Club House at anticipated revenues and that we are hoping to set up adequate controls to see that this is done.[540]

Substantial deficits are projected (in 1976) for most revenue producing activities of the Association. For example, for every dollar received from Club House activites the Association will spend almost twice this amount. – Charles Willner, Treasurer[541]

Mr. Nowakoski (LOWA Vice-President) stated that he had just explained that a complete P&L for the pools, the tennis courts and the other facilities is not available.[542] *The action of this Board in trying to resolve some of the problems that have been handed down over the past 5 years is dealing with that question. The prime rules that existed have existed for a large number of reasons. They led to this Board negotiating the departure of the previous General Manager for that reason ... This information is under active study and is being handled by the Finance Committee as fast as they can formulate them to alter, reconfigure the books in such a way as to present total visibility for all income cost centers.*[543]

When the Association was in its tenth year of the all-member Board of Directors, that Board set the objective that all amenities become self-sufficient. Almost 30 years later, this objective is as elusive as ever.[544] Mrs. Lundwall, chairperson of the Planning Committee, presented a five-year plan to the board August 9, 1982.

Presently, assessment revenues are being used to subsidize operation of the amenities. It is the objective and goal that eventually all amenities will become self-supporting. The Board agreed to the proposed change.

Two years later, the Board of Directors, under the presidency of Bill Carpenter, considered a motion to change the policy regarding fees charged for use of the clubhouse.[545]

As a Community Center, the Clubhouse facilities are to be available on a priority basis to all LOW community organizations and social/recreational groups... without room rental or cleaning charges. Outside LOW banquets and events shall be scheduled around these LOW community meetings. All food and beverage services should be provided on a break-even basis for the LOW groups.[546] *It is directed that the set-up and clean-up costs be covered by charging Committees and Community Services account.*

It is not clear whether the intent of "on a break-even basis" meant to cover the cost of the food and beverage and the servers' salaries or also included the kitchen staff, management salaries, repair, replacement, and utilities. It is clear that the "set-up and clean-up costs" were to be paid from the assessment. This motion illustrates two of the conflicts that have existed ever since the purchase from Boise Cascade; are all members to pay a share of the cost of the food and beverage service, and are there special LOW clubs that should receive favorable pricing consideration? After extensive discussion and motions to amend, the motion was tabled. No Board of Directors since has ever been successful in resolving these conflicts.

PGA Golf Pro

A PGA Golf-Pro has always been on the staff of the Association; Smith (Smitty) Beasley was the first. In December 1971, the Lake of the Woods Golf and Country Club golf team traveled to Castle Harbor, Bermuda.

> *Paced by pro Smith Beasley and John O'Toole, the Lake of the Woods Golf and Country Club golf team tied for second place in the eighth annual (Castle Harbor, Bermuda) Pro Golf Tournament.*[547]

While the course expanded from nine to eighteen holes and during the first few years thereafter, an unofficial bottle club existed at the weekend golf games. Various members would sponsor a hole, not for beautifying the tee box as today, but to host a bar at the tee. A different kind of Tee party!

> *Lake of the Woods lost the golf tournament it expected to host (May 1971) … pro Smitty Beasley was understandably disappointed…* [548]

The following summer Boise Cascade hired golf pro Bob Post.[549]

The Lake of the Woods golf course has achieved a distinction very few have, the honor to host a standing President of the United States. John R. Henry was in charge of arrangements for the tournament. It was his invitation that resulted in President Gerald R. Ford attending.

> *My letter went to The President, 1600 PA. Ave Washington, DC. – John R. Henry*[550]

In 1975, Robert Lee Elder purchased a lot in section 5 and became a member of LOWA.[551] Lee Elder is best remembered for becoming the first African-American to play in the Masters Tournament in 1975.[552,553] That May he hosted the Lee Elder golf professional tournament.[554] Over a hundred members participated, such as Mrs. Larkin Weedon who drove to National Airport to chauffer Greg Morris to LOW.[555]

> *… with President Gerald R. Ford, the comedian Flip Wilson, the great tennis star, Athena Gibson, the former heavyweight champion, Joe Louis, and Greg Morris from Mission Impossible – all in attendance and playing in the event … The secret service even had the squirrels wired for sound! – Jack Eckel*[556]

Bill Howard as a course marshal wore a "red shirt" and watched President Gerald R. Ford, Bob Murphy, Joe Louis, and Flip Wilson. The Secret Service required all the members working the course to wear the red shirt. He remembers that the Golf Pro, Bob Post, sued Lee Elder to pay for the rent of additional golf carts.[557] At a Board of Directors special meeting in January 19, 1976, the Association reimbursed Bob Post.

Bob's mother was the Pro Shop manager. One day she told Bill to "get out of here with those cigars." Bill took a grievance to the board and they agreed he could smoke his cigars.[558]

On August 7 to 10, 1975, LOW hosted the Virginia State Golf Association Open.

> *Lake of the Woods golf pro Bob Post admits most of the members were in "A state of shock" over the announcement.[559]*

By 1976, the earlier benevolent attitude of the members toward golf became stratified. A group of members petitioned the Board.[560]

> *… this petition really says, … fire the Golf Pro … You want us to agree to go to the general membership now and have them turn around on issues which they are unfamiliar with and direct us to fire the man we just hired. 30 folks signed the thing that said they want you to … 25 of them aren't even golfers. – Don Nowakoski, Director LOWA, July 1976*

Other members questioned the practice of allowing PGA card-carrying golfers, who were not LOW members, on the LOW golf course. The issue of guest privileges, reciprocal play and the like has been raised periodically ever since.

In the spring of 1981, the Board of Directors unanimously agreed not to renew Bob Post's contract. Post worked at LOW for eight years and during that time was one of the more successful players in the Middle Atlantic PGA Section, capturing the State Open in 1977 and playing on the pro tour in 1979.[561] Bob lived at LOW for many years after he resigned from the Golf Pro job.

> *"I'm not so good on public relations, I was more concerned about running a business than going to cocktail parties." – Bob Post, 1981*

Bruce Lehnhard became the Golf Pro at LOW on May 1, 1981. He was the 1982 match play champion of the Middle Atlantic PGA. In a tournament in 1987, he shot a one-under-par to win. The following year he placed third at the national Club Pro Championships at Pinehurst, N. C.[562]

> *"I have certainly had better single rounds, but I've never played that well at that level for four days." – Bruce Lehnhard, 1988*

In 1992, he entered the Kemper TPC at Avenel along with a former LOWA member, John Daly.

> *John Daly did in fact live here (LOW) and play golf here … My recollection is the late 70's … I do not know the exact year, but John did in fact play in this Club Championship and did in fact post a lower score than all the other players. There were no age restrictions at the time, and the only reason there is controversy is because several of the members*

didn't want to accept his victory. The Pro Shop and my staff all recognized it and he was rewarded for his play by most of the membership. John was a controversy then just as he is now. – Bob Post, LOW Head Pro 1972-1981.[563]

At the 25th Annual meeting, the president announced that Larry Yatchum was hired to fill the maintenance superintendent's position, Rea Hargraves was given responsibility for complete golf operations and Don Show had been promoted to golf course manager.

"I came to Lake of the Woods in April of 1990. Before I came to Lake of the Woods, I was a Head Golf Professional at White Lake Golf Course in Elizabethtown, N.C. I … met Bruce, John Broaddus was the MGA Chairman and Warren Lodge (GM) was LOWA General Manager. I worked for 2 years as Bruce's assistant. He made the tour qualifier and left Lake of the Woods. When I came, I remember Warren Lodge (GM) telling me, "you will be here 2 to 3 years then you're gone" Now I've been here for nearly 20 years. I would not change a thing." - Rea Hargraves, PGA Golf Professional, LOWGC [564]

One of the bizarre features of the VWCI designed golf course is its remoteness from the Clubhouse. A building, no more than a starter shack with locker rooms and grill was put by the first tee. It evolved with additions and fixes for almost forty years until torn down and replaced in 2008. The new facility is named the Woods Center in honor of Barbara Wood, past General Manager and long-time member of LOWA.

Bill Howard with 35 year old souvenir of the Lee Elder Tournament, photo by Dan McFarland.

President Gerald R. Ford, Flip Wilson and others at the Lee Elder Tournament, courtesy of Dan McFarland.

Lakes for Fishing and Skiing

That too (the small lake) was a mud hole- Carolyn Nowakoski

Once the main lake and small lake filled and were no longer mud holes, both the lakes' physical condition and their use by members became issues.

Lake of the Woods Skiers competed in state competition at Petersburg, Virginia in 1970.[565] The first Lake of the Woods ski tournament was held September 1972. Approximately 200 spectators attended to see the 94 entrants.[566] The 1977 Open water skiing tournament attracted 79 skiers from Maine to North Carolina. Julie Wilmot of Lake of the Woods and Gordon Gay of Falmouth were the big winners of that weekend in the Lake of the Woods Open.[567] A trick skiing event in June 1981 attracted a field of 81 skiers, including three former champions.[568] A decade later, the Ski Club membership had become one of the youngest in the nation with ages ranging from 5 to 20 and an average of just 10.[569]

Mr. Gordon Gay announced that the second round of the Ski Show would proceed at the termination of the (4th) Annual Meeting. He added that he also lived at LOW since 1968 and was very optimistic about it. Gordon and Sandy Gay and sons Russell and Chris, circa 1970, photo courtesy of Ruthan O'Toole.

The Fishing Club was formed prior to the 4th Annual Meeting. In January 1974, the Potomac Bassmasters were invited to use the lake.[570] The Fishing Club is a non-profit club that meets monthly to share creel reports and discuss issues affecting the quality of fishing in our lakes. By 1978, opposition to non-member use of the lakes became an issue.[571] A Bassmasters of Northern Virginia tournament was held in 1979.

At a special meeting on August 20, 1972, a Marina and Lakes committee was proposed and recommended to be included in the Security and Safety committee. At that same meeting proposed boat operating polices were tabled. Comments by members were heard concerning boats on the beaches and limiting high speeds only to the center of the lake.

> *Skier-fishermen co-existence is an issue, because we've grown so fast in the last two or three years. An equitable solution is needed.* – Lake Users Chairman Joe Kovach
>
> *(In response):* "*I don't think we have problems that reasonable people can't solve. Of course if the world was made up of only reasonable people, there wouldn't be any need for lawyers.*" – Gordon Gay, nationally ranked water skier, member LOWA and a lawyer[572]

Over the years, the rules have evolved for regulating boating. The regulations for the "Use of the Lakes" were first revised in May 1978. By 1987 a Lake Users Committee was established. A special meeting was held April 23, 1990, for the purpose of approving the proposed Lake Users Rules.

Boating has always had, by far, the greatest participation of any amenity. For the first two decades, the majority of homeowners registered one or more boats.[573] During the 1990s, the number of registered boats grew little. The popularity of ski-boats decreased while personal watercraft (a.k.a. jet-skis), pontoon boats and non-powered boats increased. By 1997, less than half the homeowners and a fifth of the unimproved lot owners registered one or more boats. During the 21st century, on average, for every six homes built there is one additional boat registered.[574]

Stables

The stables had a rough start. At the September 1973 board meeting it was announced that "The stables were becoming a nightmare and the stable manager has resigned." By August 1976, the board was very concerned about the amount of the assessment spent on this amenity. After they established a Stables Committee, the LOW stables became one of the most important hosts of horse shows in the region. For the next decade, the LOW stables enjoyed record turnouts at the various horse shows.[575] In November 1982, the board established a policy on stable barns and corrals on lots applicable to Section 16 only.[576]

> *The Lake of the Woods 1984 horse show season schedule will run from March 18 through Nov. 4. Division championships are offered …*[577]

> *The horse show season at Lake of the Woods is from May to November (1986) and the shows always are well attended … The closest competition was in pleasure pony … For the 1987 show season, Linda Dickenson, manager of the Lake of the Woods stables, has some plans for changes in the program …*[578]

The Lake of the Woods horse show continued for many years to put on the first hunter show for the season and it remained something special to a loyal following of competitors.[579] At the 25th Annual Membership Meeting, it was reported that 1995 was a good year at the stables. In 2007, Betsy Carter's column "Horse Scene" reported:

> *This Sunday is the start of the local summer show season with the Lake of the Woods show. LOW has been offering a show series for over 30 years and it has always been well attended. One of the reasons why LOW has always been a successful show is because the show ring is maintained. The jumps and the courses are very inviting and the show runs smoothly.*[580]

Chapter 11   Easter 1980, Fire and Faith

The clubhouse fire occurred before sunrise on Easter Sunday 1980. The LOW Church was meeting at the clubhouse in those days, and fire prevented the church goers from meeting. The church elders took them to Spotswood Park for a service. More than 250 attended, bringing their own chairs.[581] The rebuilt clubhouse opened on Thanksgiving Day, 1981. The LOW Church attendance that day exceeded 300 people.[582]

Clubhouse Restoration

The April 12, 1980, BOD minutes are quite brief but do indicate that the immediate response by the Board of Directors was to procure firefighting equipment, commit to rebuilding the clubhouse, and establish a temporary restaurant, the Flame.

> *Mr. Dick Burbank, LOW Fire Chief, gave a report on the Clubhouse fire the early morning of April 6. Following the report on the fire, Nowakoski made a motion that $3,000 be taken from current funds to purchase a "deluge pump" … passed unanimously.*

> *A clubhouse rebuilding committee was established with Ed Harn as Chairman.*

> *Nowakoski made a motion that $600 be appropriated for a dishwasher. The dishwasher would be installed in the Flame Restaurant and at a later date would be used in the Pro Shop.*

The story of the fire has been published many times over the years. A member across the lake from the clubhouse called in the fire a little after 4 a.m. The fire was on the back porch going up to the roof. The first fire truck arrived minutes later and fire engines from surrounding Fire & Rescue stations responded. They saved the main entrance and office wing. These are the common features in all the articles.

All members of the security force were also members of the fire and rescue companies. George Dodson, chief of security, provided the following report.[583]

> *A security patrol had checked the clubhouse building at 3:15 a. m. and things looked fine … the fire was discovered when a clubhouse alarm went off at 4:25 a.m. and by 6 a.m. 95 percent of the building was destroyed … by the time the first firemen from Lake of the Woods Department got to the scene much of the building was already in flames*

… Dodson called on the state arson investigator who examined the scene … arson was apparently not involved in the blaze … may have been caused by a lighted cigarette put into the trash.

The clubhouse will definitely be replaced. Lake of the Woods is definitely going to have a clubhouse. – General Manager Warren J. Lodge[584]

"I don't think clearing the site and rebuilding was considered, but the new clubhouse was very different from the old. As I recall, the new clubhouse cost a million dollars, and the insurance did not cover it all. I don't recall who the lending agent was, but we definitely had to borrow for the reconstruction." – Fran Harding, Director LOWA in 1980 [585]

General Manager Warren Lodge (GM) negotiated a $557,000 settlement with the insurance company, the biggest fire insurance claim in Orange County in 72 years.

… the directors … confer with the Farmers Home Administration … about a low interest loan to finance the new community center.[586]

During the rebuilding period, two buildings served as clubhouse facilities. One was a small LOWA-owned house on Lakeview Parkway dubbed "The Flame," which served dinners and where bridge was held on Wednesdays. The other was the larger Morton building in the parking lot of the Pro Shop.[587]

"The Flame Restaurant was set up by the Club manager, Warren Lodge (GM), in a small house across the street from the burned out clubhouse. Make-shift meals were served, but it really wasn't very satisfactory. The times John and I ate there, there was no air conditioning and the food was mediocre." – Fran Harding

"After the fire, the church met in Spotswood Park, the Teen Center, our Firehouse, and the Morton building (community center). After the clubhouse was rebuilt, the first event held there was our Thanksgiving Service in 1981." – Carolyn Nowakoski

The reconstructed Clubhouse differed markedly from the old one. The Wilderness Bar was brought up from the basement and became an informal dining room and bar, and a sprinkler system was installed in the new clubhouse.[588]

"To me the real hero of the rebuilding experience was the President of the Board of Directors, Al Potter. He was a lawyer and along with Atwell Somerville, the Association's lawyer, guided us through the legalities. However, his biggest contribution was his skill in holding the building contractor to the specifications, timetable, and assuring quality control throughout the rebuilding… I often marveled at his no-nonsense determination and ability to see that our Clubhouse was going to be well-built and within budget. He succeeded. His wife, Lou Potter was also a big asset. She was an architect and an enormous help in designing the building and over-seeing the construction. I wish we had a building at the Lake named for them." – Fran Harding[589]

The grand opening of the Clubhouse was held on Sunday, December 6, 1981, to provide an opportunity for all members, both resident and non-resident, to view the new facility.[590] Within a year after reopening, the Board of Directors passed unanimously a motion to eliminate the Clubhouse Committee as its task had been accomplished, particularly after completion of the Clubhouse and the appointment of a Clubhouse Manager.[591]

> *… (at the December 11, 1982, BOD meeting) during the Open Forum, Orlo Jackson had voiced his objection to the Board action at the November meeting in eliminating the Clubhouse Committee. He pointed out that volunteers are often difficult to find. Also, both President Law and Vice President Oertel stated their regrets at not expressing appreciation and thanks to the Clubhouse Committee for its excellent contributions to the Association. There was a motion by Walsh, seconded by Natoli, to reconsider the November 13 decision on the Clubhouse Committee … Natoli believed the Board had acted hastily and had mishandled the issue. Stoll said the Association was actually run by its committees and their influence is great … Ivey stated that the issue was more controversial than the Board members realized at the last meeting … He moved, seconded by Boheim, that the previous motion (to reconsider) be tabled until the January 8, 1983, meeting.*

The Clubhouse committee was reestablished and reconstituted by a 5 to 1 vote at the January 1983 BOD meeting.

Concurrent with motions pertaining to the Clubhouse Committee were motions dealing with holding funerals at the clubhouse.[592] The resulting Board of Directors ruling captures the apparent need to distinguish Lake of the Woods from a country club.

> *Mr. and Mrs. Bookbinder voiced their objections to holding funerals at the clubhouse, suggesting a vote of the entire membership on the question. President Law said the issue had been thoroughly debated by the Board, taking into consideration the fact that the clubhouse is not a clubhouse in the "country club" sense; it is actually a "Community Center." Walsh pointed out that a previous Board had called it a community center because of the wide variety of activities conducted there.*[593]

At the 19th annual meeting, the Chairman of the Awards Committee, Barbara Story, presented to the Association replacement plaques listing those members who have received Outstanding Service Awards and Distinguished Service Awards. The originals were destroyed in the 1980 Easter Sunday Fire at the Clubhouse.

> *President Pierce, accepting the plaques from Ms. Story, expressed his sincere appreciation and thanks to the Awards Committee for their efforts.*

By 1987, it was evident that upgrades were required to the kitchen and fire suppression system. The first of many subsequent Clubhouse expansion and/or upgrade A & E studies was authorized in 1989.[594] A major renovation was accomplished in the spring of 1996, which required closing the Clubhouse for a couple of months.[595]

Photos courtesy of Dan McFarland

UPPER: Clubhouse Fire

LOWER: Clubhouse at start of reconstruction

LOW Church

(In 1971) Pennsylvanians Jack and Ruth Eckel found their retirement home at Lake of the Woods that fit their needs; it was close to their daughter ... had a lake, pure drinking water and few mosquitos. But ... (not) long before they realized it lacked one important thing - a church.[596]

The church members had two goals, to have a permanent pastor and to have their own building. All that they wanted was a little chapel in the woods, but the growth in every way exceeded all dreams! - Carolyn Nowakoski

The first multi-denominational worship service at Lake of the Woods was held at the Clubhouse December 5, 1971.[597] Ione Brown was the Sunday school superintendent. She would bring her cupcakes and set up Sunday school at the Clubhouse. She found herself short a couple of cupcakes for the kids; that Sunday a couple of new employees at the clubhouse had cupcakes with their coffee.[598]

On April 28, 1974, a small group of community leaders founded the Lake of the Woods Church.

"Ten of us ...felt that every community should have a church. We wrote a Constitution that we and 29 others signed on April 28, 1974, thus formalizing the LOW multi-denominational Church. Of the ten founders, I was the youngest, and am now the only one left ... the others were (Ruth and John) Eckel, Bob and Ruby Clark, Ernie and Erin Holcomb, John Ostby and Borgny (Ostby) and my husband Don. We all became close friends." – Carolyn Nowakoski

Negotiations for property upon which to build a church were occurring by 1978 between the LOW Church Board of Elders and the Association. The first notice to the members was made at the February 11, 1978, Board of Directors Meeting.

The Board of Directors presented a counter-offer to the Church for a leasing agreement rather than a purchase and formed a committee of the Board of Directors consisting of Mr. Duell, Mr. Nowakoski and Mr. Law to discuss the lease arrangement with Church officials.[599] The committee presented the proposed leasing arrangement to the Board of Directors in August 1978. The "Questions and Answers" at the 8th Annual Meeting provides an interesting question concerning the definition of conflict of interest of LOWA Directors.

There has been a proposal made to lease LOW property to LOW Church for $1.00 a year for 30 years for the purpose of building a church within the Lake. Will ... property owners be able to vote on this? If this is done by board action, will members of the Board who are also members of the church abstain from voting because of conflict of interest? - Member Doris Barton

The response was given by Vice-President Nolan.

The Board has the authority to act. It will not be forwarded for a vote ... the legal definition of conflict of interest is, on a Board of this nature, the person does not vote if he is to receive some identifiable monetary benefit from the result thereof. If conflict of interest means something broader, then, on many occasions, no member of the Board could vote on issues.

More than 70 members attended the August 8, 1981, BOD meeting.

… the early church members encountered much opposition from a small but vocal group … That group did not want a church in LOW, period. That small group was anti almost everything. – Carolyn Nowakoski

Twenty motions to re-write sections of the lease were discussed and voted on that day, and finally the final vote to approve was taken. The Board of Directors election of September 1980 had swung the majority away from approval of the lease.

Vote then taken, as follows: In favor: Ivey, Stivers-Bauer and Nowakoski. Opposed: Oertel, Law, Natoli, with Potter voting against, so motion failed.

Rev. Roy Cosby of the newly formed parish of St. Patrick Catholic Church began holding mass at the LOW Clubhouse in May 1983.[600] The 8 a.m. Sunday mass continued at the clubhouse until the church was built in 1985. Sonny Weedon would come in a little early to set up the altar area.[601]

The LOW church purchased property from the Appersons, a few of the men from the church were standing in a circle on the property … One of (them) felt something touch him. It was "Daisy", the resident pet deer in the area. –Carolyn Nowakoski

The LOW church purchased four acres from Mr. Apperson on October 31, 1982, and, some years later, exercised their option to purchase four more acres. It is outside the LOW perimeter, but because of a "grandfather clause," church members are able to use the LOWA roads. The woodland had been mainly used for hunting wild turkey.

The initial church building was dedicated in September 1987 and was almost completely furnished by gifts.[602]

"… the day that the first part of the LOW Church building was dedicated, I saw Atwell Somerville in the narthex. He congratulated me and added that the people of Orange knew that we had encountered many obstacles … that we had coped with dignity had impressed everyone in Orange. … we all felt that coming from Atwell, they were really something." – Carolyn Nowakoski

At the June 1998 BOD meeting, President Ed McCarthy stated that representatives of the LOW Church met with the Board to discuss the purchase of a lot for an exit driveway from Church property to Lakeview Parkway. The Board is in favor of the Church's proposal, and a final agreement is to be worked out after consultation with legal counsel. In contrast to the three year negotiation and vocal opposition by some members 20 years earlier, the last time that the Association planned to transfer land to the LOW Church, this time the agreement was quickly settled and unanimously approved at the August 1998 BOD meeting.

Chapter 12   The Forty Year Problems

But if the last 20 years are any indication, Lake of the Woods will continue to take care of its problems on its own, without so much as a ripple.[603]

The basic infrastructure of Lake of the Woods, the roads, the dams that form the lakes, and the water and sewer systems have been chronic problems that have been treated for over forty years. They all appear to have attained a workable maturity and compliance with the state regulations.

The first effort to address these problems was at the June 18, 1972, BOD meeting. Mr. Holcomb discussed the findings in the report prepared by Martin, Clifford & Assoc. relative to possible acquisition of the recreational amenities from Boise Cascade.

He highlighted:

*Maintenance of roads will require more work at greater cost than originally estimated …

*Ditches, culverts, artificial drains, etc., met the requirements for storm drainage as included in the statement filed with HUD …

*Water system is good - quality of water is good …

*Sewer system is classed as experimental by State Water Control Board. <u>No</u> bond has been required by the Water Control Board for the installation of an acceptable system.

*Dam will meet the requirements for a 100-year storm. Computed by Martin, Clifford as 2 feet of water over the spillway crest and by Bauer Eng. at 2-1/2 feet

*Recommend that the crack in the (main lake dam) spillway be repaired.

The community has developed in spurts of buying followed by years of slow growth. The prices of lots have soared and fallen. By 1969, about 4,200 of the 4,271 lots had been sold for a total of $25 million. This resulted in a very large increase in the total assessed value of the county. Over the next ten years, lot prices declined, up to 20% of the assessments were delinquent, and foreclosures were common. Homes continued to be built at a rate that would have taken 100 years to build out the 'Lake.' Part of the problem was the general economy, part was the lack of a central developer to advertise nationally and part was the lack of progress in solving the infrastructure problems.

Rapidan Land Company entered the community in the 1980s and created a large increase in the value of Lake of the Woods.

> *Rapidan Land Co. recently bought about 416 of the unimproved lots at Lake of the Woods at bargain prices, launched an advertising blitz and resold them, often for 10 times as much, months later.*[604]

> *Even at the $14,000 ... his company has been getting for lots there, Lake of the Woods is still a bargain.* – John Chrisemer, Rapidan Land Co.[605]

By 1986, 18% of the county's real estate tax revenue came from the Lake of the Woods.[606] New homes were being built at LOW about five times as fast as they were at the beginning of the eighties. 146 building permits were issued in 1985, as compared to 40 in 1981. The shift from a few hundred homes occupied mainly during the weekends to over 1,000 homes mainly occupied all year placed an additional burden on the LOW infrastructure, which is mainly the responsibility of the Maintenance Superintendent.

> *According to Warren Lodge (GM), the General Manager of the Lake of the Woods Association, most of the development's 1980s boom is attributable to those people who were simply biding their time to build. Favorable interest rates help fuel the explosion.*[607]

Roads

> *The roads were in poor condition and they broke up badly in the winter of 1969-1970 ... The developer had argued that "dirt trails" were all that he was obligated to provide ... the road specifications under the Shoosmith contract required 5 inches of base, compared to Virginia Route requirements for subdivision streets of 6 inches. (A moot point since Orange County had no subdivision requirements.) We had a test made ... which shows ... the base ranged between zero inches to 5 inches.*[608]

The officers of LOWA filed a class action suit against the developer.[609] As the result of out-of-court settlement, the developer spent an additional $300,000 on road reconstruction. The work was performed by the Shoosmith Company, which according to rumors, put up $100,000 of the cost.

> *In answer to complaints about our roads, Mr. Lane stated that our roads cannot be compared to state roads as ours are not a macadam type road; we have surface type roads and they do get sinks which we have to keep building up as soon as we are able to. He stated that on two occasions, road technicians have rated our roads as excellent.*[610]

By 1976, the Association had a road program that repaired and resurfaced the roads on a three to four year cycle.

> *Mr. Reynolds, Maintenance Superintendent, stated that this year as in years past, they have budgeted for 10 miles of road resurfacing. So far to date, they have done 6 ½ miles*

which is more than they normally accomplish at this period because of new equipment ... and extra help ... [611]

Over the years, the Maintenance Department grew in manpower and equipment, becoming the largest road maintenance organization in the county. It is said that it even exceeds that of Fredericksburg. Twenty years after road construction, in 1987, the Board of Directors unanimously accepted in principle the Maintenance & Ecology (M&E) Committee Road Study and expressed appreciation for the fine work of the M&E Committee.[612] Special fees were levied from 1989 to 1992 to fund the paving and upgrading to Lakeview Parkway; the paving finally occurred in 1996. The Lakeview Parkway paving project had been reduced in scope and cost compared to the earlier concept. The initially planned widening was deleted and the extent of roadbed upgrading was reduced. The main road in LOW showed signs of damage within five years.

During this time, Flat Run Road was similarly upgraded by the State.

> *Mr. Hollenbach reported (May 1996) that he has ... written to our Board of Supervisors member, Richard Wallace, with copies to VDOT and Delegate "Butch Davies", to encourage support for paving of (Route) 601. The back entrance on 601 was opened during the time the hazardous chemical spill closed portions of Rt. 3 and 20. However, 601 eventually had to be closed because of the murky, muddy, road condition.*[613]

One of the signs that things were changing was the day "Master Sergeant" Elton Rupe reported to work at LOW in 2001.

> *"Nobody wants to know what I did, only what am I going to do. I was frequently asked to be a guest speaker during my tour as an Instructor at the Engineer School and my biography always sounded like a eulogy. This is a condensed version. Joined the Marine Corps in 1979 at the age of 18. Attended Marine Corps Drill Instructor School. Retired in 2001 as the Deputy Director of Facilities Maintenance from Marine Corps Base Quantico. Arrived at Lake of the Woods four days later as the new Maintenance Superintendent."*

A major upgrade occurred in the 21st century; it was titled the Lakeview Rehabilitation Project. Included in this rehabilitation project was the replacement of 55 existing culverts and a road shoulder to be surface treated with chip and seal. An engineering study of Lakeview Parkway was completed by CTI Consultants in July 2004. This study included pavement coring at 22 locations, sub-surface exploration, laboratory testing, evaluation, recommended remedial measures and the overlay thickness design. In May 2005, work began on the recommended remedial measures, which consisted of patching severely distressed areas and edge repair. In May 2006, work began on culvert pipe replacement and asphalt overlay. Work continued in 2007 and completed in 2008, for a total of 7 miles of roadway.

Drainage Easements and Culverts

While the dams are designed to handle epoch rainfalls, the LOW drainage system is designed for

10-year storms. Two of the largest upgrades to the drainage system were a result of the September 2002 drainage study of Flat Run and Harpers Ferry by Culpeper Engineering. In 2003, at a cost of over $1 million, twin Omega box culverts were installed at Flat Run and triple concrete elliptical pipes were installed at the Harpers Ferry Mail station, upgrading both to the capacity of a 25-year storm. In addition, LOWA Maintenance has recently completed a multi-year replacement of culverts in our roads. Lakeview Parkway had six upgrades.

There are approximately 16.2 miles of platted drainage easements, over 100 miles of roadside ditches and approximately 50 miles of roads that constitute the drainage system in LOW. The drainage system was not built to the state regulations adopted in 1992. The easements were established in the original plots, circa 1967, and have resulted in chronic problems on a small number of lots. The problems are usually associated with a failure to have an easement appear on the deed or the placing of the easement somewhere other than on the lot's natural watercourse. Lack of easement or improper placement does not hinder the flow of water from neighbor to neighbor to finally one of the lakes. These problems are handled one at a time, and over the years elaborate drainage systems have been built, and changes to easement lines have been recorded.

In August 1978, the BOD unanimously adopted the Drainage Policies and Procedures written jointly by the Chairmen of ECC and M&E.

> *The LOWA has no obligation to divert or improve any area of natural drainage flow ... on any privately owned lot within the Lake of the Woods.*

It is commonly misunderstood that the BOD can provide relief to lot owners, settle disputes between adjacent lot owners and disputes between lot owner and builder, or participate in any matters that involve the privacy rights of lot owners.

> *Private lot owners or LOWA have no authority to divert or change the drainage flow ... when such action affects the established drainage system.*

Ten years after the subdivision was platted, the problem of "natural drainage area with no easement" was recognized. Procedures were adopted that allowed lot owners to improve the drainage and to "relocate drainage flow as long as the influent and effluent points at his property boundaries remain the same." The state and county have established regulations and enforcement authority in the last 30 years that supersede the ECC. This has elevated the visibility of complaints about lot drainage to the regional newspapers.[614]

> *A drainage easement within LOW cannot be relocated without the formal written approval of LOWA, other affected property owners, and any affected utility company ...*

The procedures authorize approval by the Maintenance Superintendent. The rigor that was applied to the formality and thoroughness of the approval process has been largely dependent on the personality of the person holding that job.

> *The M&E committee will identify major erosion areas with the drainage system which contribute significant siltation of lakes and will recommend a planned course*

of action with estimated costs to correct the problem ... In the event the BOD accepts responsibility for correcting a drainage problem and provides necessary funding, the General Manager will ... correct the problem in accordance with the approved course of action.

The last part of the 1978 policy provides the exception to the rule that drainage problems between private properties, not affecting any LOWA property, are not a matter for the Board of Directors. They have the right to expend Association funds to correct drainage on private lots, and have in a few cases, exercised that right. The other part of this section of the policy establishes the objective to plan a course of action to correct the overall problem of major erosion and siltation of the lakes, and places the responsibility for that plan on a volunteer committee! Nine years later, August 1987, this responsibility was transferred to LOWA staff when the BOD added a new position to the maintenance staff, Erosion Control/Culvert/Bulkhead Inspector. Twenty years later, 2008, the Association hired Jesse Graves, a state certified Erosion and Sediment Control Inspector with a college degree and prior experience. Ms. Graves has completed an extensive analysis and published a report in 2009, on which the LOWA Board of Supervisors has acted.[615] Based on the inspections conducted, the "LOW drainage system has come a long way." There are 654 lots with drainage easements and approximately 14% of the drainage easements are impaired and require repairs to function properly. The average repair is estimated at $1,800. The effected lot owners have been notified by LOWA to correct the deficiencies.

Sewer and Water

The developer had planned to have individual septic tanks for every house. Orange County had a doctor, the head of the health department who was quite good. He went out to Lake of the Woods and looked the situation over and said, "No." For that reason, the developer had to go to a central sewer system. – Atwell Somerville

After ... a few owners decided to immediately build a home. They failed their percolation test. It was a close call, the newspapers spread the story and sales were cut in half! In ten days, we had a solution. – Jim Foote [616]

The Restrictive Covenants were changed in June 8, 1967, to add a sewer system to LOWA. The initial charge was $2 per month for each lot owner and a $585 connection fee when they built their residence.[617] That was increased to $785 in September 1967.[618] Problems persisted for many years.[619] The first documented complaint was filed in 1970; a couple complained of "hissing noises" loud enough to keep them up at night. By 1971, there were approximately 200 connections on the system designed for 2,125.[620] Between 1972 and 1977, the contractor and sub-contractors retained by Boise Cascade to install the sewer system argued a lawsuit in district and appellant courts over failure to pay and perform.[621]

(Ten years later) Ron Pierce was the man that resolved the sewer and water crisis.
– Alan Polk, President 1991 and 2000

Operations improved significantly in 1987. LOWA President Pierce worked with the State Water Control Board (SWCB) and the county supervisors and talked them into having the Rapidan Service Authority (RSA) take over from a California company. RSA issued bonds to finance the $2 million construction of a water treatment plant and replacement of the sewer plant.[622]

> *NOW, THEREFORE, BE IT RESOLVED, that the … Association does support RSA's acquisition of the assets of the Utility Company and RSA's operation of the water and sewer … and that the costs of operating the same shall be borne by the users of the system, as aforesaid, and*
>
> *IT IS FURTHER RESOLVED that this resolution be spread upon the record books of the Association and be binding upon this Board and all future Boards receiving service from RSA.[623]*

The concise history of the "sewer problem" was provided in the state's special order.[624]

1. When the septic systems quickly failed due to soil characteristics, the developer installed the Lake of the Woods sewage treatment plant and a closed-air vacuum sewerage collection system to collect and convey wastewater …

2. From the outset, the Lake of the Woods sewerage collection system experienced significant problems. … By the 1980s, raw sewage in the vacuum system was backing up onto private lots and into homes approximately 50 to 60 times per day …

3. RSA … voluntarily acquired the water and wastewater systems from the private owner on November 1, 1987.

4. Pursuant to a Consent Special Order issued by the Board in 1990 and amended in 1991, and a second Order issued in 1992, RSA made substantial capital improvements to the system … In addition, RSA has established and implemented an effective operation and maintenance program … RSA asserts that all of these measures have been accomplished at a significant financial cost to Lake of the Woods residents.

5. RSA has succeeded in reducing sewage overflows from an average of 50 or 60 per day to 1 to 2 per day.

6. … DEQ issued a Notice of Violation ("NOV") to RSA on June 4, 2003 … The NOV specifically alleges the Lake of the Woods sewerage collection system experienced at least 16 sanitary sewer overflows between April 6 and April 12, 2003, and that five of the overflows occurred on lakefront lots.

7. RSA asserts that it has no information that any of these overflows have reached state waters.

8. On July 10, 2003, RSA submitted to DEQ a plan and schedule for submitting an engineering study to evaluate alternatives for minimizing overflows from the collection system, including replacing or upgrading the collection system, and for implementing interim measures to reduce the number of overflows from the system.

Five years later, RSA and DEQ agreed on a new course of action, a plan for annual capital improvements in lieu of replacing the collection system. The RSA charge increased $7 per month per lot to fund $350,000 of annual improvements.[625]

Mr. Holcomb … presented the "As Built Plans" and stated that these plans showed that four or six inch pipe had been used in all locations except a few cul-de-sacs. Six inch lines service all fire hydrants. He noted … requesting the installation of additional fire hydrants where the distance between a lot and the nearest fire hydrant exceeded 1,000 feet.[626]

The water distribution system was designed and installed at a cost of $900,000.[627] The quality of the potable water has always been good, whether supplied by wells or, after 1991, supplied by drawing from the Rapidan River. The issues have been twofold, adequacy of the pressure and the impact of drought.

President Ed Law stated that the Maintenance and Ecology Committee study on potable water covered three main considerations: monitoring of water levels in capped wells … Association or Utility Company responsibility for the hydrant distribution system; and whether or not pressures in the hydrant system are sufficient for fire fighting.[628]

RSA has over the years upgraded the water system and solved local problems. The most recent problem was the discovery during construction of the Woods Center of inadequate water pressure at the Golf Pro Shop location. That problem was solved by the Association. The location of the Pro Shop was not relocated from the #1 tee to the #9 green in order for the Association to avoid the cost of installation of new utility lines and pipes; however, the inadequacy of the water service line was not known when that decision was made. The result was a costly charge to the Association to meet the county building inspector's requirements.

One issue that has not been solved is a contingency in case of drought. The entire county faces this issue.[629] In the last drought, 1998-2002, RSA and the county indicated their desire to tap the LOW main lake to serve potable water to this end of the county. LOWA was opposed to such action because it would result in prohibiting gas-powered boats on the lake!

Damn Dam

The dam inspection report has been received and concludes that the dam is in good shape except for some minor repairs. – Edwin Harn, President 1979

In the fall of 1966, the construction of the dam was the first order of business. A go-ahead for the project came Monday, September 26, 1966, when Orange County Circuit Judge Harold. H. Purcell gave approval for the construction of an eastern dam near the junction of Flat Run and

Route 3 at a cost of $325,000.[630] The matter was brought before Circuit Judge Harold Purcell as a legal technicality required before impounding of water is permitted. Robert S. Washburn of Indianapolis, attorney for Virginia Wildlife Clubs, Inc., showed engineers' sketches and testified that flow below the proposed dam to be located on Flat Run was in accordance with legislation. He told the court that legal title would belong to property owners while equitable title will belong to Virginia Wildlife Clubs, Inc., which will assume all costs.[631]

> *Our attorneys eased our worries about the main lake damn in advising us that in transferring the dams and lakes to us the developer could not transfer his torts. Moreover, the developer recognized this and assured us that the company would maintain for all their corporations a $250 million liability policy which would also provide coverage of any liabilities they might have with respect to Lake of the Woods including the dams.[632]*

> *A hurricane that swept through the area washed out a dam in another county ... Our unwillingness to accept these risks and the developer's determination reached a confrontation stage to the point that we were told that the developer would make the transfer whether we liked it or not. – Ernest Holcomb*

The dam survived Hurricane Camille in August 1969. There are various versions of when the lake filled to the spillway. Ernest Holcomb has written that the spillway first overflowed in February 1970. However, Bill Howard remembers the lake was twenty feet closer to his house in the midst of Camille; obviously, water must have been over the spillway. In any case, the lake encroaches on several lots during a heavy storm and will flood many homes upstream of the dam if the maximum probable flood ever occurs.[633]

> *The National Park Service reported 4.76 inches of rain here (on August 27, 1971, due to tropical storm Dora), compared to 4.62 inches during Camille.[634]*

Discussions continued for the next three years. In June 1972, a special meeting was held. Coincidently, Hurricane Agnes occurred that month.

> *Mr. Holcomb discussed the findings in the Engineering Report prepared by Martin, Clifford and Associates relative to possible acquisition of the recreational amenities from Boise Cascade.[635]*

> **Dam will meet the requirements for a 100-year storm. Computed by Martin, Clifford as 2 feet of water over the spillway crest and by Bauer Engineering at 2-1/2 feet over the crest.*

> **Recommend that the crack in the spillway be repaired.*

> *(Two years later), Mr. Eckel brought up the dam repair situation ... He noted that this project could result in an emergency condition that would cost considerable money if not*

corrected soon … After some discussion, Mr. Illch moved that the Board allocate the money to have the spillway repaired up to $3,700.[636]

The 1976 Virginia General Assembly authorized the Water Board to draw up the necessary rules and regulations for dam safety and inspection.

The state has neither the procedures nor money for professional inspection of the nonfederal dams in the state.[637]

Upon approval of the new state dam safety regulations, the General Manager provided recommendations that were unanimously accepted by the Board of Directors.[638] Subsequently, in 1979, a policy was established regarding lowering of the lake and the General Manager was tasked to develop an emergency procedure program for notification, particularly for those people who live below the dam.[639]

LOWA received a letter from the state dated January 15, 1987, that resulted in the General Manager obtaining a professional engineering firm to perform engineering studies of both dams at a cost not to exceed $18,000.

Such study is necessary in determining what must be done in order to meet State requirements for upgrading the Dams.[640]

A lengthy debate was heard at the March 1987 Board of Directors meeting. General Manager Lodge was directed to write an article for the Newsletter to inform all members of the discussion. Little evidence exists of how the planned upgrade to the dam was reconsidered.[641] The engineering work was completed by Dewberry and Davis. Their analysis indicated the spillway could only handle half the rainfall that the state required before the dam would be overtopped. The upgrade designed by Dewberry and Davis would have been very expensive. A meeting with the Soil Conservation Service in Richmond on June 30, 1987, resulted in success in having the main dam classification reconsidered.[642]

Our engineers will do further studies. We will then return to Richmond for discussion regarding the study results. - R. H. Pierce, President LOWA

The last action of the Board of Directors occurred at their October 1987 meeting wherein they approved, "Raise structure or purchase and raise/demolish structure." The details of the negotiation between LOWA and the state are not known. What is known is the result, a favorable discussion that avoided all further cost to LOWA. This result is attributed to General Manager Warren Lodge (GM) by Alan Polk.[643]

The last major flood in the LOW area, and the greatest flood recorded in a hundred years, was the unnamed storm of June 27, 1995. The people inside the 7-Eleven store at the intersection of Route 3 and Route 20 were evacuated via rooftop door and taken away by the Lake of the Woods Fire and Rescue Tele-SQRT fire truck. Some of the firemen in an inflatable water rescue boat were almost swept away on Wilderness Run.

A decade later, the same fight would be replayed, but this time with much more exposure and a different ending. Negotiations started in 1998 when LOWA was notified by DCR that due to increase in traffic on Route 3, a sunny-day break of the main dam would probably result in loss of life. In 2001, the main dam was reclassified as a Hazard Class 1. The Association officers, Dewberry the dam engineering firm and the Dam Safety Division Director negotiated an acceptable solution to all parties that would have affordably increased spillway capacity.[644] During these years, the LOW dam received awards by dam safety organizations. Former Gov. Mark Warner appointed Joseph Maroon director of the Virginia Department of Conservation and Recreation (DCR) in March 2002. Any former agreements became void, and the new DCR policy was that the main dam spillway must handle a full 38 inches of rain in 24 hours without exception.

A major event was the Virginia Soil Water Conservation Board meeting June 15, 2004.[645] At this meeting, LOWA asked the SWCB to grant a relaxation to the spillway upgrade based primarily on an aggressive Emergency Action Plan (EAP) to serve as a warning mechanism to reduce the probability of the loss of life. The DCR staff response was, "If granted, this would be the first – ever such relaxation and would establish a broad precedent for the Commonwealth." It was not granted. The result of the meeting was expressed in three motions.

> *MOTION: Board issue the Lake of the Woods Association a Regular Class I,*
>
> *Operation and Maintenance Certificate for Keaton's Run Dam, Inventory Number 13708, with an emergency spillway capacity reduction from the full PMF to the ½ PMF capacity, under Section 4VAC 50-20-130 of the 2004 Virginia Impounding Structure Regulations …*
>
> *MOTION: Board issue … Conditional Certificate (THAT) requires the LOWA to proceed with the engineering design, plans and specifications for an increased spillway capacity to safely pass the full PMF (38" rainfall in 24 hr).*
>
> *MOTION: Board establish an Ad Hoc Committee for the express purpose of studying the Classes of Impounding Structures, §4VAC 50-20-40 and Performance Standards Required for Impounding Structures, §4VAC 50-20-50 … The Committee shall complete its work by April 30, 2005.*

LOWA was disappointed when the Ad Hoc committee report did not support reducing the spillway requirement below a full PMF. The Association maintained a lobbying effort in Richmond with the result that the SWCB voted unanimously at their July 2005 meeting to begin the processes necessary to review and perhaps change the way the state regulates dams.

> *"This is what we've been trying to get them to do, to open up the regulations," said Lake of the Woods Association President Neil Buttimer, who attended the board meeting. "We've been opposed to the one-size-fits-all regulations. Obviously, we're pleased." The DCR's Maroon stressed that "there is no assurance that any given dam would benefit from regulatory change," but LOW's Buttimer is hoping for the best.[646]*

The Association expected to have at least a two-year respite before it had to expend any funds to upgrade the dam on its main lake, but it did expend nearly $1 million over the years to finish design work and accomplish other upgrades of the dam not associated with the spillway. After three years of review and revision, new regulations were put into effect September 26, 2008. The result of the new regulations was the Lake of the Woods main dam would have to be altered to accommodate a worst-case scenario.

> *DCR Public Relations Manager Gary Waugh explained, "… We told (LOWA) that the evacuation plan, while a very good step in the right direction, would not, in and of itself, be sufficient. They also … talked about … a dam that could handle the overflow from two-thirds of a PMF. We said that in our analysis to date, that is not sufficient. Everything we have seen still points towards the dam needing to handle a full PMF.*[647]

The technical analysis of the impact of an epoch rainfall on the risk of dam failure is extremely complex. For the case of the LOW main dam, the problem can be simply stated as VDOT culverts under Route 3 below the dam are designed to handle approximately 8.5 inches of rain in 24 hours. This is likely to occur once every hundred years, the 100-year storm. When that happens, the lake will be 5 feet below the top of the dam. The National Weather Service has published that the LOW area is expected to have 14 inches of rain in 24 hours once in a thousand years. The staff at Hydrometeorological Design Studies Center (HDSC) has estimated, when asked by President Buttimer, that the 38 inches in 24 hours is a one in a million-year event. The main dam is currently conservatively rated at handling 23 inches in 24 hours without overflowing the top of the dam. Without any doubt, in a half PMF storm Route 3 will be destroyed and the dam will be unaffected. In general, hundred year storms will shut down all of the surrounding roads, 3, 601 and 20. For at least 10 years, members, staff and Directors of LOWA have argued with the state officials and their elected representatives, "Why is it necessary to upgrade to one in a million storm when much more likely storms that have no effect on the dam will destroy all means of travel out of the area?" The statements that follow were made at the June 2004 SWCB meeting by LOWA members. All of the major points made would be repeated and reinforced over the next five years. It was a contest of wills, and DCR Director Maroon prevailed at every round but the one that really counted.

> *Mr. Lee Frame said that the LOWA dam was a Class I because of the probable loss of life or property damage. He noted that with the proposed emergency evacuation plan the Association believes there would be no loss of life. He said the Association is working to actively discourage further downstream development. Mr. Frame said the Association emergency plan has been provided to the Division of Dam Safety, the Orange County Emergency Coordinator and the State Emergency Management Department.*

> *Mr. Peter Taylor noted that he is President of the Lake of the Woods Civic Club with approximately 700 members … He stated that the belief of the civic club was that the possibility of the occurrence of the probable maximum flood was unlikely and unreasonable … the Civic Club supports the Association's desire to achieve the required level for the two-thirds probable maximum flood.*

> *Mr. Jim Danoy … Vice President of AARP Chapter 5239 (Lake of the Woods). Speaking on behalf of our members, we strongly support the Lake of the Woods Association Board of Directors concerning their recommendations of the Main Dam. The requirement to achieve a full 1.0 Probable Maximum Flood spillway capacity in*

our view does not meet the common sense test and would seriously impact our 350 members. The additional cost imposed on our members for meeting an unrealistic regulatory requirement would create an unnecessary financial burden on our members, many of which are on fixed and limited incomes … The heavy precipitation situation requiring the 1.0 Probable Maximum Flood spillway is extremely rare and provides more than enough warning to evacuate at risk people before any dam failure. Other dam failure situations are not mitigated (by) the expense required to achieve a 1.0 Probable Maximum Flood spillway. Therefore the AARP Chapter 5239 recommends that the Soil & Water Conservation Board accept the Lake of the Woods Association recommendation to achieve a 2/3 Probable Maximum Flood capacity …"

Mr. Doug Chidlow said that his interpretations of the regulations regarding safe operation of the impoundment is that the owner is not allowed to operate a dam that threatens life or property. He said that he disagreed with the consultants assessment that endangering life or property upstream was acceptable. He noted that if there was a strategy to lower the lake level as a protocol that would meet a portion of the PMF requirement.

Mr. Chidlow's desire to lower the lake as a protocol was pursued with a serious design effort by the Association's dam engineer, only to be dismissed by DCR after spending many months in Q&A. President Frame was successful in negotiating a builder to remove dozens of future building sites from the inundation zone, but to no avail as DCR equated one house as severe a risk as a hundred.[648] The Association set the standard for the state by their Emergency Action Plan and was the first to integrate dam safety with the county's 911 emergency system. This had no impact on DCR. In 2008, the conversation turned to the six houses that were expected to get wet from a dam break. The Association received letters from DCR that led to a response dated July 3, 2008.

Given that information, we pursued the alternative presented by DCR staff of securing the written agreement of the affected property owners that they would leave their property during an emergency evacuation event. To this end we have secured letters of commitment to evacuate from four of the owners, one is out of town and due back next week, and the sixth is a property that is not part of the Association and for which we now have a contract to purchase.

While DCR dismissed the evacuation agreements, the fact that the Association had bought a house in the inundation zone based on statements made by the DCR staff had legal and political consequences. The matter was brought to the Governor, and the negotiated result was a grant from the state for partial funding and a commitment that a loan could be obtained from a state agency for the remainder.[649,650]

LOW officials have been fighting the dam modification for eight years, but gave up in January (2009) after being assured they would get a $1 million grant from the state to help pay for it … They are hoping to see some of that money soon. They have met the state's requirements; a contract has been signed to have the work done; bank financing *has been secured; and a special assessment has been levied ... President Bruce Kay signed the $4.8 million contract with Faulconer Construction Co. of Charlottesville to build the spillway ... directors unanimously agreed to enter into a loan agreement with StellarOne Bank for $5 million ... directors also adopted a $1,200 special assessment.[651]*

On January 12, 2010, our Senator R. Edward Houck introduced SB 276 Dam safety. On January 14, 2010, Joseph Maroon resigned as Director of Natural Resources. The bill was amended and then passed the Virginia Senate unanimously. The Association of Dam Safety Officers (ASDSO) and the American Society of Civil Engineers (ASCE) campaigned to prevent its passage in the House of Delegates. On March 3, 2010, the House Agriculture, Chesapeake and Natural Resources committee reported a substitute bill written in consultation with the staff of DCR. Many of the detail requirements are the same asked for at the June 2004 SWCB meeting by Lee Frame, Peter Taylor and Jim Danoy.[652] It passed the House, with an Emergency clause added by our Delegate E. T. Scott, on March 5, 2010. The Governor signed SB 276 on April 8, 2010.[653] This action validates the many efforts made over a decade by the members of Lake of the Woods to establish cost-effective dam safety regulations.

Healthy Lakes

For over 30 years the conditions of the lakes, particularly the quality and quantity of vegetation on the lake bottom have been an issue. Healthy fishing requires a reasonable amount of healthy vegetation, called weeds by the swimmers and skiers. Stocking the lakes with carp has been the principal method of weed control.

Mr. Alan Spiher of the Maintenance & Ecology Committee reported (in 1974) his committee conducted an inspection of Wilderness Lake with members of the Board and with Mr. Frank Dugan, biologist with the Soil Conservation Service ... Steps should be taken to remove and combat siltation; the lake is in good condition although a few patches of weed growth should be eliminated ... of fertilization of the lake should be considered if the fishing pressure is high enough.[654]

We do have problems to take care of, just like everybody does ... There is a "small" weed problem in the lake, and 1,000 weed-eating carp were imported last year (1985) to take care of it. – Warren Lodge (GM), General Manager[655]

By 1998 concern for lack of lakebed vegetation led to efforts to reduce the carp population.

Ernie Meier, Lake Users Committee Chairman, reported ... The Carp Removal Project in the main lake is underway.[656]

Ernie Meier, Chairman, Lake Users Committee, announced that ... Fish habitats have been completed ... Use of the common hook and line has resulted in a catch of at least 39 carp ... Other methods of carp removal are being discussed.[657]

Mr. (Bernie) Palowitch announced the formation of a working group composed of ... M&E ... Lake Users ... and the Fishing Club ... its short term goal ... implementation of the Lake Management Plan prepared (in 1999) ... the main goal ... is to develop a long term comprehensive Lakes Management Program to monitor and preserve the quality of both ... lakes.[658]

The first Lake Manager was hired July 7, 2003. He was a qualified scientist, with a Master degree in Biology and a major in Lakes and Reservoirs Management Studies. The position has been filled twice more since by very qualified recent college graduates.

He resigned to accept a position with a Culpeper firm ... who paid him what he was really worth and not the nickel and dimes LOW paid. – Ernie Meier[659]

Seven years after the Carp Removal Project was completed, the procurement of young carp became a cause for advocacy.

(The GM) stated that 500 grass carp will be placed in the lake on Friday, October 7th, (2005) ... Later in the meeting there will be discussion whether or not more carp need to be introduced.[660]

The Water Resources Management Plan was approved by the Board of Directors their March 2006 meeting. In the end, everyone agreed, political pressure made the Lake of the Woods Association's directors decide to add more grass carp to the subdivision's largest lake. Some residents believed that the lake management plan approved by the Board of Directors the previous spring should be followed and the newly hired water-resources manager should make decisions concerning weed control.

"We have a long-term lake management plan, and that's the best thing for us to do."
- Doug Rogers, the Board Chairman [661]

By 2008 the Lake Manager position was again filled by a professional.

With April Hughes, LOWA's lake manager keeping an eye on the fish stock, the weeds, the dredging, water quality, any evidence of pollution or silting, all participants in lake activities this year should have a good experience using our primary amenity ... One sign of spring unique to LOW is the resumption of fishing tournaments, some of which begin with a lot of bass boats lined upon a starting line across the north end of the lake, and at a signal at 7 AM on a Saturday morning it looks like the Oklahoma Land Rush. Off they go to the best fishing spots! From our house midway up the lake the sound of the boats approaching is similar to a low flying prop aircraft buzzing the lake. It is nice to see the fishermen enjoying LOW's multipurpose lake – Bill Wilson, President LOWA 2009.[662]

In 2009, April Hughes proposed and the Board authorized a plan to restore Keaton's Lake.[663]

Chapter 13   It Only Takes Four Votes

Lake of the Woods is not a small business, but a big business. – General Manager Warren J. Lodge

The governing body of the Association is the Board of Directors. They are the sole authority in all matters, fiscal and legal, before the Association. Unlike some Property Owners Associations in Virginia and other communities founded by U.S. Land, Inc., in other states, members of Lake of the Woods do not vote to approve either regular assessment increases or special assessments. There was an attempt in 1989 to give members approval authority for debt financing, but that motion failed at second reading.[664,665]

"The great ... English statesman, Edmund Burke, said; 'He who hires me, hires my judgment.' I am going to paraphrase this: He/she who elected me, elected my judgment and also elected my conscience. I feel strongly that referenda are a waste of effort and time and will not support them, except when mandated by higher authority. The membership follows a democratic process by electing the Board. The Board then operates in the fashion of a republic, representing the membership. If the Board isn't doing what you want it to do, ask for a recall election. This only takes 800 signatures. Besides, I have never been around a recall election; it might be fun watching the process unfold."
–Vin McGlone, upon his election as LOWA Director 1998.[666]

Ruth Dugan and Lee Bauer

"Ruth Dugan was a state legislator in New Hampshire prior to LOW and was a very talented and smart woman. Memories of Lee Bauer were more personal as I dated her son for a span; she and my Mom worked together on LOW issues." – Ruthan O'Toole[667]

In October 1971, Ruth F. Dugan was removed as LOWA Secretary and by September 1973, she was LOWA Vice-President.[668] In the years she served on the Board of Directors, the minutes indicate that she was quite active. The minutes of the April 10, 1976, record the comments of Mrs. Dugan during open forum and President Lee Bauer's response.

Mrs. Dugan read a memorandum addressed to the President and Members of the Board of Directors with regard to violation of the Restrictive Covenants.[669]

The President responded as follows: "When I first received Mrs. Dugan's letter ... there was a thought struck me ... I found that you, Mrs. Dugan, served on the Board from January 1972 until September 1974, and I am quite sure that the (problems) ... did not accumulate in the last two years. So I do not feel you can put to this Board the ultimate task that your Board completely ignored ... ... We are working on each and every one of our problems and I can assure you that we will clear them just as fast as we can ..."

Yes, she has been on the Board, worked very hard and tried very hard to get the Restrictive Covenants supported. She was unable to do so. Mrs. Dugan ... asked ... "Do you believe the Restrictive Covenants should be enforced?" The President (Lee Bauer) said yes, that was her answer.

The above discourse raises a fundamental issue, the responsibility of the Board of Directors to enforce Association governing documents, however unpopular. This is an obstacle for many gated communities; it is not restricted to LOWA. Certainly, ignorance by a lot owner is not allowed as a defense for failure to comply with the restrictive covenants. However, failure to enforce the covenants, in lieu of the arduous task of a referendum to change them, is frequently the accepted solution.

July 17, 1976, Special Meeting

Mr. Carpenter stated he wanted to speak in favor of peace and harmony among neighbors. He listened this morning to the petition that was submitted to the Board seeking the removal of the President of the Association. He listened to the specification of charges. He heard none against her ... He wants to echo what Mr. Kesterson said, "We live here together, we can make this the finest place in the United States. All we need do is cooperate with each other." He asked for an end to the divisiveness and cynicism that is dividing us.[670]

The President stated that the purpose of the July 17, 1976, special meeting of the Board of Directors was to address the five petitions filed in the Association office for total membership consideration of the action or lack of action by the present Board of Directors.[671] This was a most unusual meeting and a watershed for this young Association. The minutes of this meeting span some thirty pages.

Mrs. Lundwall then asked "Are you saying now that you are not at this time going to make the motion to place the resolutions on the ballot?"

Mr. Nowakoski (Director) stated he is not going to make the motion.

Mrs. Lundwall stated -- very well, you have failed to do so. The petitioners will on Monday, July 19, ask their attorney to ... present our arguments before the Circuit Court to Orange ... (30 people walked out of the Board meeting).

Lavina Lundwall, a spokeswoman for the group of more than 60 property owners, said the papers have been filed in circuit court asking for the writ.[672] The case was heard in Orange County Circuit Court on August 19, 1976. Atwell W. Somerville, attorney for LOWA, argued in defense of the Board of Directors and prevailed. [673]

While the political squabbling will not be repeated herein, the meeting did produce some precedents that were very important to the Association. The Board of Directors affirmed it has a right to enter into multi-year contracts. The Board had established multi-year contracts with the Golf Pro and Dodson Security, which, by definition, imposed a financial obligation on future boards. The issues of "valid future obligations" has been debated throughout the history of the Association, but the one type of obligation that all boards have honored is multi-year contracts.

> *The Board makes the policies, so the Board can change the policies, and that is the way ... Mr. Somerville thinks it should be ... You are a non-profit corporation, it's true you are a very strange kind of a non-profit corporation ... And just like any other non-profit corporation, a Board, it is a continuing thing, you do have authority to go beyond 1 year in his (Atwell Somerville, Esq.) humble judgement.[674]*

All members must be given the ability to vote on a resolution that is submitted by petition, not just the members attending an annual or special meeting.

> *Mr. Somerville stated ... You cannot limit it to just the people who are here. You have to give your non-resident people an opportunity to vote also even if they don't come to the Annual Meeting.[675]*

Each petition required only 30 signatures, and they got almost twice that many. The procedure for petitioning the Board of Directors had been established on August 30, 1971, when the Board of Directors was controlled by the four Boise Cascade members. In addition, there was no procedure in the By-Laws for the removal of a Director or of an entire Board of Directors. In 1976, the only procedure to remove a Director or the entire Board of Directors was by court action.

The procedure for recall was established at the July 11, 1981 Board of Directors meeting, in which Lavina Lundwall (Chairperson Rules Committee) gave a report on the Committee's work on the Charters, the LOWA Bylaws and Standing Rules and Regulations. Petitions henceforth would require 800 valid signatures.

> *Article III Section C. Special Meetings ... for the purpose of initiative, referendum, or recall of a Director ... must be called by the Board of Directors upon receipt of a written petition signed by members in good standing having at least 800 of the votes entitled to be cast at such a meeting...*

Big Changes to Restrictive Covenants, Especially No. 12

The initial restrictive covenants had a restriction that no change could be made up to 1980 without approval of two-thirds of the lot owners. This effectively eliminated any effort to change any restriction until after 1980 when "only" a majority of lot owners was necessary. Given the extent of non-resident ownership, getting even a majority of lot owners to respond was difficult until several years later.

The Board of Directors on November 4, 1989, approved a list of proposed changes to the restrictive covenants. A referendum was held and the votes counted on April 2, 1990, followed by the Board of Directors approval of the changes to the Declaration of Restrictions of Lake of the Woods.[676] There were several pages of changes and deletions, many minor such as adding "unlicensed" vehicles to the prohibitions for open parking, and defining trucks as "titled/licensed as a truck." The major change was a revision of section 12. No longer would the BOD have authority to prohibit title transfer to persons who have not been approved for membership. Henceforth, "every person who acquires title … to any lot … shall become a member of the Lake of the Woods Association.[677]

The referendum must have been an arduous process as the total valid ballots were 2,631.25. Approval of each change required a majority of the approximately 4,260 numbered lots. The change, which received the least favorable votes, 2,161, was to allow the Board of Directors to set the fee for filing plans in lieu of the previous fixed fee. Two amendments were also made to the Articles of Incorporation and incorporated therein February 7, 1991. The condition for membership in the Association was changed to conform to the revised Section 12 of the covenants. This action also required a referendum, but unlike the restrictive covenants, approval by more than two-thirds of all of the votes cast constituted approval by the membership.[678] This referendum also signaled the end of an era and all that goes with a vacation community.

> *…since this has become primarily a residential rather than a vacation community, small cottages are not compatible with the de facto residential community.*[679]

Five years later, the restrictive covenants were changed by referendum to increase the minimum house size.[680]

> *Every one-story dwelling … shall contain not less than 1,600 square feet of fully enclosed floor area devoted to living purposes …*

Change was also happening all along the Germanna corridor.[681] Wilderness Shores, a 1,000-lot community originally approved by Orange County in the 1960s, was ready to begin selling lots to builders in July 1992. Many of these lots were in the LOW main dam inundation zone. Bill (Farmer) Meadows opened his 19-hole public golf course in April 1993.[682]

The mission statement, written in 1996, which appears in the current Rules and Regulations, modifies the description, "primarily a residential rather than a vacation community."[683]

> *The Lake of the Woods seeks to be a private, recreation-oriented residential community composed of single-family, owner-occupied homes. The mission of the Lake of the Woods Association is to enhance the quality of life of its members, maintain property values, and preserve the natural beauty and ambience of the lakes and their environs. The Association accomplishes its mission through the development and management of recreational amenities, security services, and the maintenance of Association-owned property.*

Assessments and Fees

The enormity of the decision to undertake the management of the largest development in Orange County by the members, without the financial and engineering resources of a major developer, cannot be overstated.

> *Counsel ... foresees a number of problems which the Board must face ... he noted that Lake of the Woods was the biggest thing in Orange County ... with its responsibility for roads, parks, and in the future the golf course, country club and lakes ...*[684]

It must have been a shock to many members to receive notice of a special assessment of $100 per lot. While the negotiated price for receiving ownership of various Boise assets was $212,500, the Board of Directors determined that they needed to immediately raise at least another $150,000 for urgent repairs to the roads and facilities.

> *The President also covered some of the problems faced by the Maintenance Department to overcome the deficiencies and deterioration ... during Boise Cascade's reign and which now required a greater expenditure of funds.*[685]

There was at that time a large percentage of delinquent accounts; the assessment was about 20% higher than would have been required otherwise.[686]

In the early annual meetings, most of the lot owners were non-residents. Most of the lots had sold by the fall of 1969. By the time the Board of Directors was exclusively lot owners in January 1972, less than three hundred homes had been built and many of them were second residences. Absentee lot owners continued to make up the majority of owners and eligible voters for the first twenty years of the Association. The social activity was centered on the summer, and weekends and holidays the rest of the year. Prior to the consolidation of the Golf and Country Club with the Association, all members were assessed $30 on May 1 for roads, other maintenance and security. Only those that elected to join the G&CC paid $7.50 per month to access the amenities. Since the sole reason to come to LOW was the amenities, most lot owners also paid the $7.50 per month. However, many owned more than one lot at $30 per year each, but had only one G&CC payment. Absentee owners, those too far to ever visit on vacation, avoided the $7.50 per month payment. All that changed upon the Boise buy-out. No longer was the true cost hidden from the members, the Board of Directors had to bring in enough income to meet the expenses. Since the covenants required all lots be assessed the same, whether you ever visited your lot or not you were expected now to pay for the amenities. In addition, those that owned multiple lots, even though they only built on one, paid multiple equal assessments. There was immediate adverse reaction from many of the members.[687]

> *I think that the Association early on set up a good procedure for setting the annual assessment ... they did a good job of studying the needs of the Lake and setting an amount. There was always a controversy between the non-residents and the residents. Early on, we had to convince the non-residents that the assessment, which helped to build the Lake, was working to their advantage because it was increasing the value of their*

lots. Jack Eckel, was strong on that, and he really helped to get that point across. Once we got that point across, the opposition seemed to disappear. – Atwell Somerville [688]

While the expected income from assessments can be determined with precision, the income from fees and sales is at best an educated guess. While the management is expected to mind the budgeted expenses, many costs are simply beyond their control. There has been since the first year, and continues to be, a basic conflict between minimizing the assessment and maximizing the services and condition of the roads and facilities. The committees provide recommended changes to the fee schedule, the General Manager prepares and submits an annual budget, and the final act is the Board of Directors setting the assessment and fees each year. The making of a budget for LOWA is a chaotic, complex adversarial process.

"My special board interest was in providing a more equitable distribution of the assessment to amenities. In my opinion, the golf course was subsidized far beyond its fair share and most of the other amenities went begging. I did find the golfer board members were reasonable, and the tennis amenity was greatly improved, as were the stables and the campgrounds." – Fran Harding, Past Director LOWA [689]

The minutes of the Annual Meeting of 1978 provide a detailed record of the process of setting the assessment.[690]

The Finance Committee was pressing for an assessment of $200, emphasizing the need for capital improvements. As a result, the Board took a tour of the maintenance facilities and equipment at LOW. It became apparent that the equipment was old and needed replacement. A lot of equipment has been cannibalized to keep one piece operating at the expense of another because we could not get parts … We announced the fact that there may be an assessment of $200. As a result, we were absolutely inundated with calls, letters and comments, primarily from non-resident property owners complaining that we were pushing the rate much too high for their expectation … We had a decision to make - we had to cut out some of the services or we had to forego the new equipment for a time or we had to find some other avenues of getting the revenues that were required. After a great deal of soul searching, the Board did not accept the Finance Committee proposal. They reduced the assessment from the recommended $200 to $182, realizing that we were going to reduce the budget about $100,000 … The important thing to remember is that in order to continue to be the community we are, we are going to have to address the fact that we have to make some changes. Higher assessment rates, different user fees or something. The only way it is going to be successful is for all of us to join together, back the Finance Committee and the Board and see this thing through.
- Ronald Duell, President LOWA 1978

Twenty years later, the Civic Club was formed by members who were reacting to years of no or low assessment increases that didn't keep up with the cost of living and did not allow LOW to keep up with their standards and expectations.

Let us stop nickel and diming. The amount of our annual assessment is laughable …

The Board of Directors should increase the annual assessment by about $360 per lot, and then adopt an annual increase at the rate of the CPI.[691]

During those years of no or low assessment increases, the expenses did increase and were paid from the revenue collected by big fee increases. By 1998, the fee increases were generating small marginal returns.

The single most important fact to know and remember is that the number of owners who pay for amenities had remained at about 1100 since 1988 even though the number of houses has doubled since that time. – Walt Velona[692]

An Attempt to Change the Assessment Covenants

In 1978, the Board proposed two radical changes to the sources of income.[693] The first was a two-tier assessment whereby unimproved lots would have a lower assessment than improved lots. The Board recognized that this required a referendum vote to change the restrictive covenants.[694] Apparently, another item was added to the referendum. Both items failed to pass.[695] The second was an attempt to make some amenities quasi-public, the so-called annual guest privilege program. The Board instituted this without referendum, apparently considering it within their right. A petition signed by 162 lot owners opposed this policy. They challenged the Board in the Circuit Court and lost the case.[696]

The annual guest privilege program never achieved its objective; as of May 1979 only three had joined and 45 expressed interest.[697] The group opposed to anything other than a "private" community eventually appealed and obtained a state Supreme Court ruling in 1982 voiding the Board action.[698]

Years later, in 1996, an ad hoc committee for restrictive covenants recommended several changes, many of which were incorporated after a referendum. The one proposal the Board of Directors unanimously decided not to include in the referendum was a proposal to delete the "uniform annual charge" requirement, required in the then current paragraph 12.1 of the Restrictive Covenants.[699]

Capital Reserves

(Board of Directors in 1978) asked the Finance Committee to research the issue and find extra means of revenues to finance capital items.

A couple of days before the 4th Annual meeting at a special meeting of the Board of Directors, the issue of needed capital items exceeding resources was addressed.

Mr. Chase (LOWA President) told Mr. Lane (Maintenace Superintendent) that the Board could not handle a big list of capital items needed in an amount as large as $143,000 and recommended that Mr. Lane and Mr. Nelson (General Manager) decide which items are most urgent and come up with a justification of not more than 2

> *or 3 items at one time. Mr. Holcomb (Board member) said he preferred to see the whole list with priorities. Considerable discussion followed …*

It would be a few years later before policies for funding and expending capital reserves would be formulated. Until then, all expenditures were either explicitly fully funded from the annual budget as a purchase or by the annual installment on bank loans. As an example, in February 1974, a local bank loaned the Association $23,000 total cost of two mowers and two pickup trucks, at the current prime rate for a period of 48 months. The financing of purchases by bank loans continued for many years until the capital reserves were built up to exceed the average capital expenditures of a few years.

By 1982, the Association had instituted the five-year planning process.[700]

> *The Planning Committee's (Lavina Lundwall, Chairwoman) recommended change was accepted by the Board. The new sentence will read as follows: "Therefore the five-year plan is tied to a capital budget. This integrated process will cause the Association property values to appreciate; and consequently, those of private owners as well."*

As has been the case with all subsequent boards, the five-year plan was considered a goal and not a binding recommendation on future boards. The plan was approved "as guidance" at a special meeting prior to the 12th annual meeting.

Later that year, at the November 1982 BOD meeting, General Manager Lodge and Finance Committee Chairman Bill Carpenter explained that questions have arisen as to what should be included in a capital budget and what should be charged as an operating expense to a cost center. The following amendment to the Standing Rules was passed unanimously.

> *For accounting purposes, capital items are defined as those single items costing $500 or more which have a life expectancy of three years, and which are not consumable, such as paper products, hand tools, feeds, gravel, etc.* [701]

By the end of the 1980s, the capital budget had developed separate reserves for the following purposes: Amenities, Expansion or Improvement of Existing Amenities and Capital Items Related Thereto, and Replacement of Existing Capital Items.

A Twenty Year Amenities Upgrade

At the November 1987 BOD Meeting, chaired by President Ron H. Pierce, the Board of Directors unanimously passed a motion to add $3,000,000 over the next 15 years to upgrade the amenities.[702] The previous month the Board of Directors had accepted the Planning Committee five-year plan.[703]

> *Funding of the Reserve for New Amenities*
>
> *Motion to approve Finance Committee's recommendation that provisions be made for financing $3,000,000 in new amenities over the next 15 years. Accordingly it recommends that the reserve for new amenities be incremented at a minimum rate of*

$200,000 per year, to be drawn first from operating surplus and, if insufficient, from assessments.[704]

This was an enormous change from the previous practice of avoiding putting financial commitments on future boards. The previous May, the Board of Directors had approved a not-to-exceed $375,000 expansion of the Pro Shop/Snack bar.[705] The following December, the Board of Directors approved $336,200 for golf course renovations.[706] Alan Polk recalls these expenditures consumed most of the reserves.

In April 1989, after extensive discussion and revision, a letter of explanation and questionnaire regarding the advisability and intended use of the proposed Recreation and Fitness Center was sent to the entire membership. The facility was designed by Greenhorne & O'Mara and was estimated to cost $1.9 million in 1988 dollars.[707] At their July 1989 meeting, the Board of Directors voted unanimously to accept the Planning Committee's report on Greenhorne & O'Mara's Master Plan and to task the Planning Committee to implement recommendations as, from time to time, the Committee determines such action to be appropriate.

Alan Polk, Chairman of the Finance Committee, proposed a policy to build reserves for replacement of existing capital items. President Gene Sorte would not put consideration of such a policy on the agenda.

"That's why I ran for the Board." – Alan Polk

Alan was elected to the Board of Directors September 1990 and was unanimously selected Vice-President by the other Directors. One of his priorities was to place the Replacement Reserve on a firm footing.

Motion by Polk, seconded by Williams, passed unanimously,

1. *Revise current Rule and treat Depreciation as a Line Budget item. This will allow for the creation of a reserve account consistent with LOWA needs at replacement time.*

2. *Utilize depreciation as an additional ingredient, similar to Maintenance, for each amenity when establishing Total Net Income or Loss during budget deliberations.*

The following month the Board of Directors approved the procedures to include treating depreciation as a funded expense item with the funds generated therefrom being deposited in this reserve account.[708] Income to Replacement Reserve was thus effectively removed from the political process, while the determination of expenditures was decided by the Board each year. The result, whether intentional or not, was less than necessary expenditures for repair, replacement and restoration of the capital components and a large increase in the restricted accounts. By the completion of the second five-year reserve study, the Association had a multi-million dollar backlog and twice the reserve funds necessary to eliminate that backlog.[709] The Association was investing their reserves in long-term bonds and deferring short-term needs. Several years before, due to income tax ramifications associated with a similar financial situation, a special meeting was called to reduce the tax liability by rebating $15 per numbered residential lot from 1983-84 income to members effective April 30, 1984.[710]

In November 1990, on a motion by Director Polk, major projects for the indoor pool and Clubhouse expansion were deferred to the "out years."[711] This effectively eliminated Warren Lodge (GM)'s "Master Amenity Plan." Three years later, when Alan Polk was President, the purpose and title of the New Amenities reserve was changed to the New Capital Reserve.

Alan recruited (Godfrey) Jeff Barber to join the Finance Committee in January 1990. Jeff retired as the Controller of NASA, and Alan wanted members with a strong financial background. They drafted a debt policy that in 1991 became the Debt By-Law.[712]

> *The Lake of the Woods Association will only enter into debt financing agreements under the following conditions:*
>
> 1. *Clearly catastrophic event that requires emergency capital relief that would be beyond the prudent use of existing LOWA funds. The Board of Directors will make this determination.*
>
> 2. *To add to existing or build new LOWA amenities that are totally revenue justified. The Board of Directors will make this determination.*
>
> 3. *To add to existing or build new LOWA operational facilities to meet the changing needs of the Association. The Board of Directors will make this determination.*

Prior to the 21st Annual Meeting, Warren Lodge (GM) had told Alan Polk that LOW needed him to be President of the Association. Alan and Phyllis took a five week trip in August and September 1991, and thus Alan was not at the meeting that selected the Association officers.

> *"When we got back from a trip, I turned on the TV and found out I'm President of the Association!"* - Alan Polk

President Polk presided at the Special Meeting of the Board of Directors convened on December 23, 1991, for the purpose of considering the award of a contract for expansion and renovation of the Administration Building and replacement of the current telephone system. It is fitting that the first Association building financed by debt, later named the Holcomb Building, was also the first building renovation and addition financed under the rules of this debt policy.

> *Passed unanimously, to fund the expansion and renovation of the Admin Bldg as follows:*
>
> *$165,000 financed at Jefferson National Bank for 5 years ... monthly payments of approximately $3248 per month or $9.17 per lot per year.*
>
> *$100,000 financed from the Reserve for Replacement of Existing Capital Items.*

1991 had been a particularly chaotic year.[713] The longstanding and outstanding General Manager, Warren Lodge (GM), was being treated for cancer and subsequently died. In the spring of 1992, the Association established the Warren J. Lodge Award for Excellence. The distinguish list of awardees includes Alan Polk in 1996.[714]

Jeff Barber was elected to the Board of Directors and served as Treasurer from September 1993 to 1995. On his recommendation, the Board of Directors transferred all 1992-93 surplus to unrestricted working capital reserves, canceled the mortgage a previous Board had approved in December l991 in the amount of $165,000 with Jefferson National Bank and funded the balance of the Holcomb Building Construction costs with an assessment charge of $22 per lot.[715]

> *There shall be established on May 1, 1993, a new account for capital items titled "Funded Reserve for New Capital Items", and there shall be transferred thereto the April 30, 1993, balance of the existing account titled "Funded Reserve for New Amenities, Expansion or Improvement of Existing Amenities, and Capital Items Related Thereto".*

President Polk tasked Director Barber with drafting a policy regarding the above, to be submitted to the Rules Committee for comments/recommendations and returned to the Board of Directors in time for the April 1993 meeting.[716] Actually, the new rule was approved at the June 5, 1993, Board of Directors meeting.[717]

The final piece of the financial reform under President Polk was the investment policy established at the August 7, 1993, BOD meeting. One of the unique features of the new policy was the placing of a committee chairperson in an executive position and one than governs financial decisions, albeit as only one of the three voting members.

> *Investment Policy*
>
> *Motion by Barber, seconded by Buchanan, passed unanimously, to approve the ad hoc Finance Committee on Investments recommendations as modified by the General Manager's recommendation. Appointed as an Investment Committee to work with Staff: President, Treasurer, and Chairman of the Finance Committee.*

The Missing Financial Reform - Road Fee or Special Assessment?

> *The President stated that currently all plans and applications for building permits must be accompanied by a check for $100 for road maintenance fee. This fee is intended to defray the cost of repairing damage to the roads caused by heavy loads of building suppliers, earth moving equipment, concrete trucks, etc. This fee is grossly inadequate.*
>
> *Motion was made by Mrs. Sumner that the road maintenance fee be raised from $100 to $200 effective July 1, 1976 ... Passed unanimously.[718]*

This fee is charged to members upon submittal of their plans to build a house. The fees collected were used to pay the operational expenses of the Association. Road fees, especially in years when the building rate was high, were used to keep the assessment low. Until the 21st century, there was no reserve for paving.

The Board of Directors at their March 1989 meeting established funding for a Road Reserve Fund to pave the main circumscribing road, Lakeview Parkway. The method was unusual; instead of a special assessment, they charged a "road fee per individual lot of $45 for four years for a Road Reserve Fund."[719] The following year, the Board of Directors at their March 1990 meeting expended some of the Road Reserve Fund for road equipment and to finance one mile of test paving. In 1991, the Board of Directors at their August meeting passed unanimously to transfer $63,619 from Road Reserve Fund to Operating Funds. Since fees are set annually by the Board of Directors, it is remarkable that the funding for the Road Reserve Fund remained intact for four years. Once the money was in the bank, it stayed there for a few years.

> *Maintenance Superintendent Bert Amidon was called upon to give his recommendations on the road upgrade project. (At the February 1995 Board of Directors meeting) a final decision on the road upgrade project was postponed until the M&E Committee restudies the upgrade project, with Mr. Amidon, and submits its recommendations to the Board of Directors.*

The following month the planned expenditure of $567,000 for the paving of Lakeview Parkway was deferred another year. The scope of the project for which the $45 for four years had been collected from each lot owner had been reduced. A planned biking/walking lane that would have required widening Lakeview a few feet had been eliminated sometime before 1996.[720] In fiscal year 1997, $434,000 was expended to pave Lakeview Parkway. Once established, a restricted reserve account takes on a life of its own. There was no intent to further expend funds for the purpose for which they were collected, but the account did provide funding for other roadwork in order to reduce the assessment for the next three years.

The previous paving of Lakeview Parkway was soon judged not able to last longer than a few years. The choices were to plan for another round of special assessments or to build up the road reserve from road fees. The 2000 Board of Directors chose the latter, and therefore imposed on future Boards that the road fees collected would be placed into the road reserve. Thus, there would be a corresponding increase in assessments. Previously, all road fees were operational income to keep the assessment low. In order to avoid too much shock, the percentage of road fees used to defray operational expenses was gradually reduced. Since there was a vibrant housing market and a brisk building rate at LOW, the road reserve rapidly grew. The Road Reserve was more than adequate to a pay for all the Lakeview Parkway paving and improvements accomplished in the first decade of the 21ˢᵗ century. However, the building rate subsequently has decreased markedly and the income from road fees has dried up. Future funding of the Road Reserve must either be from the annual assessment or some type of resale fee.

Past Presidents

Photos courtesy of Jan Eckel Griffin.

UPPER: Past Presidents Ed Law, Al Potter, Ed Harn and Jack Eckel.

LOWER: Ribbon cutting ceremony for the Holcomb expansion. From the left, Bill Carpenter, Gene Sorte, Ernie Holcomb, Alan Polk, Larry Taylor, Al Potter, and Jack Eckel.

Chapter 14   The Yellow Bus

There is no more visible sign that Lake of the Woods is not a "55 and over" community than the presence of yellow school buses inside the gate. In 1970, the Nowakoski's children were three of the seven school-aged children who lived here. Sonny Weedon's daughter was one of the first to ride the bus to Orange.[721]

> One afternoon, the bus was very late arriving here, and we waiting parents were becoming very concerned. When the bus finally arrived, the children were excited about the delay and laughing. They had had to wait for some time for a very large herd of very large cows to move from the road.[722]

Bill Howard, celebrated his 90th birthday in August 2009. When Bill and Marge became provisional members in November 1967, they would come down at every opportunity with their three-year-old daughter.[723] Few of these children would appear in a census of Orange County while the community was predominantly second homes. Nonetheless, children have always been part of the LOW membership.

> Orange County Administrator A. Terrel Baskerville said (in 1986) the County School Board is in the process of trying to purchase land in the eastern part of county for a school. That would cut down on driving time for the approximately 250 public school students who live at Lake of the Woods.

Locust Grove Elementary School opened its doors to 375 students in September 1990.[724] The bus ride was reduced to 1/3 of the time for the primary students from LOW. The Locust Grove Middle School, built on the same site, opened its doors in January 2004 to 500 students.

> Paint was still drying on the doorframes, but Locust Grove Middle opened its doors for class yesterday.[725]

In June 2009, ground was broken for a new middle school on Route 601.

> "We didn't get here easily," Orange County Board of Supervisors Chairman Lee Frame said. "The decision [to build this school] has never been unanimous. It has been a long, hard road to get here. [This shows] we care about our kids. [This] is a big step for education and progress here in Orange County. [We] know it will take continued support."[726]

The Original Children's Bus Stop Shelter

UPPER: The shelter was given by the Lions in 1987.[727] Now used as a communications kiosk.

LOWER: Photo by Dan McFarland. A few of the many yellow buses used today by LOW students.

Youth Activities

The Water Ski Club and many other youth activities have their roots in the earliest days of LOW. The Lake of the Woods Skiers placed a youth in state competition in Petersburg in September 1970; Jimmy Wilmont finished third in tricks in the boys division.[728] The swimming team was a competitive member of the Rappahannock Swim League before 1982.[729] As the number of youths grew, so did the variety of activities. A series of summer camps have been established for school-age children that had previously been considered adult activities. Golf instruction is given by the Association Golf Pro for youths seven and up. The LOW Sailing Club sponsors the Junior Sailing Program, offering spring and fall sailing clinics and summer instructional day camps for youth; beginner and intermediate classes are held for children age eight and up.

The Club Manager in September 1972 was responsible for all food service, all recreational activities, youth activities and the operation of the swimming pools. By September 1973, there were sufficient older children that the Board took action to bar them from riding their motor bikes without permit and license plates.

An erroneous article in the local paper at Christmas-time 1978, titled, "Yes, Santa was fatter – to safeguard health" reported that Santa wore a bullet-proof vest because the Sheriff's department received word from a Lake of the Woods resident who overheard some boys in the subdivision discussing their plans to shoot Santa and she had seen the weapon.

> *We have determined that (1) the lady who called was not from Lake of the Woods, (2) the boys were from a school in ... another jurisdiction. Young people in general are blamed for many things, certainly enough not to be condemned for anything incorrectly.*
> – Edwin E. Harn, President LOWA 1978

The first record of a Youth Committee appears in the minutes of the 11th Annual Meeting, September 1981. The youth activities by that year were viewed by some as an opportunity for additional income. At the following November BOD meeting, a member in open forum urged the Board not to charge fees to the various youth activities of the Lake. The youth activities are totally dependent upon the adult members for their wellbeing. In order to provide a vibrant and varied program, it is necessary that there is participation from many more than the one-third of the homeowners who are residents with children.

> *Four Silver Beavers were guests at a Court of Honor held last Sunday (June 1988) by Boy Scout troop 842, chartered to the Lake of the Woods Optimists.*
>
> *Stephen Kowalski, B. Gale Titchenell, Jack Eckel and Ed Harn all live in the Lake of the Woods area and are friends and advisers to the troop. Together they represent over 200 years of scouting experience.[730]*

The 1987 Board of Directors unanimously approved, at their July meeting, the recommendations of the Youth Activities Committee to approve the position of an Activities Director. The following month they approved funding improvements to youth facilities.

> *(1) repair Basketball Court at Clubhouse Point at cost of up to $1300 to be taken from*

> *retained earnings; (2) … improvement at Hollyfield Baseball Field in the amount up to $7500 to be taken from retained earnings; (3) Approve improvement of Soccer Field at Sweetbriar Park up to $7000 to be taken from retained earnings; (4) Fund lights and fencing for baseball field of $15,500 from Amenity Expansion Reserve Fund.*

The Board of Directors ended the year by funding an architect's drawings and cost estimates for indoor sports facility as requested by the Youth Activities Committee and the Ad Hoc Committee on Indoor Pool. This project was shelved a few years later only to reappear in a new form by 1997. No subject has polarized the LOW community more than "new amenities." The indoor pool plan was nurtured by GM Warren Lodge (GM) until his death in 1992. There followed nearly a decade of Boards that held the assessment nearly constant and spent very little on anything new. This cycle of Boards that built followed by those that froze the budget was to be repeated in the first decade of the 21st century.

As the 20th century was closing, Fran Stockdale took charge of the Youth Activities Committee and focused on a long-range plan to improve the parks in general and improve their use by youth in particular. Her plan has succeeded in improving the parks for the school age population and adding the "tot lots" for the pre-school population.

> *President McCarthy reported that … Debra Bickley, Orange County Parks and Recreation Dept., and Fran Stockdale, Youth Activities Committee, briefed the Board on Orange County recreational programs, which could be made available for residents of LOW.[731]*

> *Karen O'Donnell, Chair of Youth Activities Committee, … proposed that a portion of the new Community Center be named in honor of Fran Stockdale, in recognition of her tireless efforts in support of LOWA's youth.[732]*

Fran Stockdale received the Outstanding Service award in 1994 and the Warren J. Lodge Award for Excellence in 2002.

> *Mr. Rich Wallace commended member Fran Stockdale for her 11 years of service on the Orange County Social Service Board and read a Resolution of Appreciation for her work, time and dedication. He then presented her with the written and framed resolution on behalf of the Board of Supervisors, which Fran graciously accepted.[733]*

The Lake Youth Foundation (LYF) was formed in 2005 by Lake of the Woods residents to help support our youth. LYF is an non-profit corporation dedicated to funding programs that promote the values of citizenship, community service, leadership and creative exploration to create a lasting, positive change in the lives of our youth.

A Few of the Many Youth Activities

Photos by Dan McFarland

Co-op Pre-School

The Co-op Pre-School, originally called the Co-op Nursery, had its start in 1978.[734]

> *A request was made by the Lake Co-op Nursery, represented by Janet Wientjes, for a provision of a facility for the Nursery. A petition was presented to the Board. After a lengthy discussion the Nursery was assured space would be made available on a shared basis in the Clubhouse, and they should work with the General Manager concerning their needs.[735]*

The Board of Directors supported the Co-op Nursery fund raising and unanimously approved their request to hold a Memorial Day Carnival at Clubhouse Point on Saturday, May 26, 1984. Three years later, when the president called for a motion to provide $1,035 to the Lake Co-op Nursery school to assist in the payment of liability insurance what resulted was a unanimous directive to the General Manager to order the Nursery School closed if they did not obtain adequate liability insurance.

By the start of 1995, the Nursery School became a state certified pre-school. This certification applied standards for the faculty, the classroom space and the outside play area, the first LOWA tot-lot. The classrooms were rooms in the Clubhouse pool support building. The Pre-school certification requirements in 2006 became part of the design for the new Community Center. Concurrent with the planned move to a new facility, the Board of Directors negotiated with the Pre-school board an increased yearly fee and a contribution to the expense of post construction changes required in order to meet the certification standards.[736]

Teen Center

> *To answer Mr. Illch's suggestion that perhaps a night meeting of the Board would be more suitable, Mr. Eckel explained that the teenage program was now doing so well that he didn't want to do anything to interfere with their night gatherings in the Rappahannock Room; therefore, the next regular Board meeting would be Saturday, July 27 (1974) at 9:30 a.m.[737]*

The Teen Center is a concept and not necessarily a building. Originally, the teens met in the Rappahannock Room of the Clubhouse. In those days, the adult activity was centered on the Bottle Club in the lower level.

> *Judy Flynn needs the credit for most of the activity that we did as parents of teens in the 70's and 80's. We "created" the room in the pool building where the fitness center is now. The participation was supposed to be strictly volunteer chaperoning by the parents of the teens that used the facility. This arrangement did not last long as many of the parents did not want to do their share. We subsequently opened up our rec room to the handful of friends that were willing to participate as family units. Sad but true! - Jeff Flynn[738]*

When the Ferris property became available, the first plan was to move F&R to that area.

> *Mr. McCarthy reported that on Tuesday, April 28, 1998, the Board met with representatives of the Fire and Rescue Company to discuss plans for a new fire and rescue building on the Ferris property.*

After the purchase in August 1997 of the home of Eugene and Linda Ferris, LOWA Maintenance fixed it up, and it was dedicated as the "Teen Center."[739] The following July, President McCarthy reported a letter had been received from the Youth Activities Committee Chairman, Fran Stockdale, in appreciation of the Maintenance Department's ,particularly Bill Dwyer's, "efforts of making something out of nothing" in establishing the Teen Center at the Ferris property.[740]

A decade later, the Community Center was designed specifically to have a teen area. The Community Center allows activities that were never possible before.

> *A letter from Ms. Dunphy, co-chair of the Ski Club, thanking the Board and General Manager for supporting the "Battle of the Bands" event. Four teams, of which one was from LOW, competed in the event, which was attended by approximately 100 teens and several adults. Prior to construction of the Community Center there was no facility to put on such a show.*

Concurrent with the building of the Community Center was a heated debate over creating a skateboard park.

> *... members were vocal in their opposition to a proposed skateboard park inside the subdivision. "We olders are not anti-youngers," said Alice Drabant, as she presented a public-opinion petition signed by more than 500 residents opposed to the park. The directors are expected to discuss the skateboard park at a workshop March 15, 2006.[741]*

A compromise was reached in 2006. Funds were re-designated and the park became a "spot", an area smaller than the nearby dog park.

> *... those funds to be used to proceed with the construction of a Skate Spot in the vicinity of the Ferris House. Any additional funds needed to equip the park will be raised by voluntary donations and grants, with this activity monitored by the Youth Activities Committee.*

Chapter 15   LOW Enters the 21ˢᵗ Century

Why do things have to change? - Russell McLennan, member 1968-2008. [742]

The census of 1990 resulted in the creation of the Orange County District 5, which contains Lake of the Woods and little else.

Nolan, a first-time candidate who lives in Lake of the Woods, won a seat on the county's board (November 5, 1991) by a 3-to-1 margin in a race against Thomas C. Bledsoe.[743]

Joe Nolan did not run for re-election and on November 7, 1995, Rich Wallace beat out two opponents to grab the District 5 seat on the Board of Supervisors.[744]

LOW experienced a 57.6% growth rate over the 10-year period from 1990 to 2000. - Mr. Rich Wallace, 5ᵗʰ District Orange County Supervisor

As LOW was nearing to its 30ᵗʰ anniversary, the Association was planning to remove two of the most visible signs of the original Lake of the Woods; nothing happens fast in rural Virginia, and it would take a few years to make these changes.

Good Riddance, Green Boxes

"One of the things I wanted to change, the ugly garbage green boxes. I joined M&E and was elected chair of M&E in '96. Barbara Story asked me to run for the Board in '98; I won by a landslide of eleven votes!" – Chuck Schulle

Dumpsters had been in place at LOW since July 1974. Orange County's first manned compactor site opened in Barboursville; August 7, 1999. The compactor site in Gordonsville was opened the following October and received a number of positive comments. A compactor site was going to be located in the Locust Grove area, and the green boxes in LOW were going to be removed, the only issue was where to locate the compactor. What seemed to be a simple decision, find a place central to the population, turned out to be a rally for every xenophobe in LOW. This sanitation issue was immediately cast as a security issue - a violation of our gated community security to be specific. The compactor would be located in LOW and all Orange County residents would have access to it. President Schulle handled the matter succinctly at a BOD meeting.

"We first voted on putting it at Shoosmith, I broke the tie 3 to 3 vote, then we voted

on upper or lower level, I broke the tie again, best thing that ever happened to LOW."
– Chuck Schulle, LOWA President, 2000

The compactor, located in the Shoosmith area, has been a great success. Even the County has benefitted. The Association did not spend a penny, in stark contrast to the mailboxes. The only remnants of the green boxes are a few feral cats.

(Supervisor) Wallace noted (at the May 2005 BOD meeting) that recycling activities using the LOW compactor center produced over $32,000 in income for the county last month.

Rural Delivery

In the earlier '70's ... President Glen Barton asked his wife Doris, June Smith and me to be members of an ad hoc committee ... That is why, today, every lot has a number as originally designated by the developer and also a street address – which makes more sense. – Carolyn Nowakoski

Twenty years later, Don Nowakoski designed the 911 system for the county. It was considered the best in the state. At that time, many of the county residents outside of LOW did not have a street address.

"Don and I reviewed every phone number in the county ... Some addresses were merely, 'the third house on the left from the General Store.'" – Carolyn Nowakoski

Each LOW residence had three addresses: a section-and-lot address, which is used for legal matters including Association ballots, a street address used by F&R and visitors to locate a house, and a Highway Contract (HC) address that was used for mail service.

General Manager Michele R Brown announced (at the October 1994 BOD meeting) that Wardens are asked to bring in their Petitions for Home Mail Delivery by mid October (1994).[745]

President McCarthy (at the April 1998 BOD meeting) called upon Don Jackson of the Postal Customer Advisor Council to brief the audience on the 911 address/cluster box proposal ... LOW residents will be required to include in their return address a third line containing their house number and street location in order that the Locust Grove post office can process accurately incoming mail for delivery to a new cluster site.

If there ever was a chance to please no one, this was it. There were three choices of the form of mail delivery: no change, curbside and cluster boxes. Establishing a majority consensus was improbable. In addition, each choice was more complex than was obvious. There would be change, all addresses would be in the 911 format; it would be the end of rural delivery in the HC format.[746] The curbside service would never apply on the cul-de-sacs, the various Lanes and Courts throughout LOW. A cluster of mailboxes would have to be mounted at the entrance to all of these dead-end roads; one lot would hold up to a dozen or more mailboxes on the easement right-of–way. The modern cluster boxes were limited to LOWA property, generally the same location as the old style mailboxes on a fence. The result was that some members had a short walk to the mail and others a rather significant drive. To further complicate the issue, some members wanted door-to-door delivery, an option that was repeatedly denied by the U.S. Post Office, and they would accept nothing else. It was a classic example of the Board of Directors being accused of not listening to the people no matter what they decided. The lobbying was intense.

> *… the position of the Sheriff's department on the mail delivery curbside service is that it would be detrimental to safety and increase vandalism.* - Major Amos of the Orange County Sheriff's Dept.

> *President McCarthy reported at the August 1998 BOD meeting that the Board has approved the concept of cluster mail stations; however, this is not the final approval for the overall project. That decision rests with the review of all plans, specifications, and bids associated with this concept.*

A Board decision that is not the final approval is not uncommon, and in this case, the matter dragged on for another year. It was not until 14 months later that the matter was decided at the October 1999 BOD meeting.

> *Mail Delivery System.… task the General Manager with pricing out Option #5 ,locked cluster boxes of the larger size at current mail stations, and report back to the Board with costs and an action plan to implement. Final adoption will be voted upon receipt and agreement with the plan … to implement the 911 street address system. General Manager to investigate and deliver a plan … to fund the mail delivery project through the Association. Treasurer and President to prepare a funding plan.*

The General Manager Larry Yatchum had contracted for the manufacture of the mail lock boxes prior to his departure, but when Chuck Schulle became President in September 2000 there were no plans for building the cluster shelter to hold the key-lock mailboxes. Director Bill Mason was responsible for locating a suitable design and getting the installations completed. The entire project was not finished until 2001 at a cost of over half a million dollars.[747]

Mail Stations

LAKE OF THE WOODS VA 22508

UPPER: Old style mail station, photo courtesy of LOWA GM office.

LOWER: Mail Station today, photo by Dan McFarland.

What Has Been, That Will Be

What has been done, that will be done. Nothing is new under the sun. - Ecclesiastes 1

As we near the end of the first decade of the 21ˢᵗ century, many of the apparent changes are more a repeat of past events or a fulfillment of earlier actions, many long delayed.

Jim Foote's desire to have a memorial to the Spotswoods was finally realized forty years later.

Susannah Chandler Chapter, National Society Daughters of the American Revolution (NSDAR), has accepted the challenge of research and recognition of this rich heritage. A bronze marker will be placed in Spotswood Park along with information about the house remains and burial grounds. A special day of celebration will be planned to coincide with the 40th anniversary of Lake of the Woods in the spring of 2007. – Martha J. Sukites, Regent

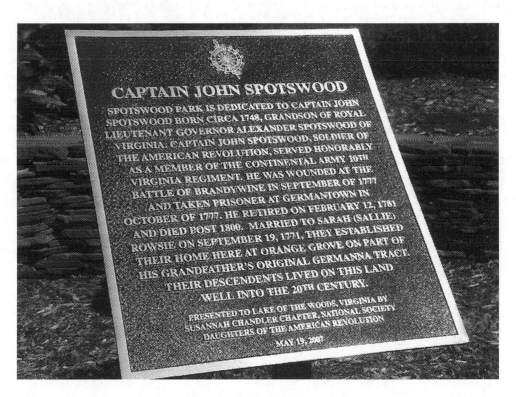

Photo by Dan McFarland.

After his term as LOWA President, Alan Polk served as an Orange County Planning Commissioner from 1993 to 1997.[748] In the spring of 1999, Vice President Gary McDaniel lost his wife, and he subsequently resigned. At the June 17, 1999, Board of Directors meeting, Alan Polk was selected LOWA Director to fill the vacancy for a 14 month period.

Phyllis had talked him into it, but on one condition, he would not be an officer. – Alan Polk

He took the job to resolve the mailbox and compactor issues. As liaison to Maintenance and Ecology, he convinced the other Directors that mailbox clusters was the right decision. After serving six months, another crisis of management occurred; Larry Yatchum resigned as GM and President Ernie Bartholomew resigned from the Board in January 2000.[749]

I'll take the job. - Alan Polk

Once again, Alan Polk was President and spent most of the working day for the next several months in the Holcomb building. He took it on himself to select a new General Manager[750] President Polk introduced Scott Devereaux as the new General Manager at the June 2000 BOD meeting. Mr. Devereaux, CMCA, was a certified manager of community associations.[751] One of the issues that once again surfaced during the FY 2001-2002 budget process was the use of facilities by non-members. Atwell Somerville wrote a letter to Mr. Devereaux, dated January 29, 2001.

"I direct your attention to Section 11 of the Restrictive Covenants relating to the use of recreational amenities. The language of this section makes it clear that the amenities are private and not public ... It has always been my position that the Association ... has the right to invite outsiders to use the amenities. It is my opinion that the invitation should be a specific one as opposed to a general one ... I fully recognize the need to increase revenues, and I support a liberal interpretation of the word 'invitee.' I cannot support a general invitation to outsiders to use the amenities at Lake of the Woods."

Within a few months, the Board of Directors chaired by President Chuck Schulle bought out the General Manager's contract, and unanimously agreed to appoint Barbara Wood the new General Manager. Barbara was an institution, a walking library and ultimate reference for any matter the Board of Directors considered.

President Schulle thanked Anne Goodwin for the assistance she had provided to Barbara Wood while Ms. Wood served as acting General Manager. He also thanked Anne for her extensive efforts in helping to recruit a new GM. Pres. Schulle then announced that Barbara Wood has accepted the position of General Manager. Vice Pres. Brown read a short poem and note written in honor of Barbara Wood.[752]

Major Project Task Force, son of Master Amenity Plan

The Major Projects Task Force was appointed by Ernie Bartholomew during October 1999, and Alan Polk was appointed Chairman. The task force published its final report September 20, 2000. The plan was much less ambitious but more inclusive than the previous Master Amenity Plan. The heart of that Master Plan had been a very large addition to the clubhouse that would house an indoor aquatic and fitness center. In contrast, the indoor pool major project was conceived as a modification to the recently replaced Sweetbriar Pool.[753] President Chuck Schulle intended to approve the "covered pool" at Sweetbriar Park. The motion had been prepared.[754]

"I had the votes until that morning (of the BOD meeting), (two Directors) told me they just cannot vote for it." – Past President Chuck Schulle

Two future presidents of the Association were on the Major Project Task Force; Al Sanborn led the study of a new Community Center, and Frank Beverina led the study of a replacement for the Pro Shop. President Frank Beverina used a novel technique to allow the membership to vote on funding a new amenity, the indoor pool. He established a cash deposit goal. It was to test if a sufficient number of fee-paying members would support the operation of such a facility. The goal was not attained due to a lack of support of the swim team families. The advocates of the indoor pool apparently did not notice the lack of support for winter swimming by the youth.

In his first month as President, Frank Beverina hired John Bailey to be the Assistant General Manager. John had been the administrator in Cumberland County and executive director of Keep Virginia Beautiful.

> *Pres. Beverina announced that on Nov. 30th the BOD regretfully accepted the resignation of Barbara Wood as GM. Mrs. Wood resigned in order to care for her husband during his illness. He stated that Mrs. Wood has 28 years of service as an employee of LOWA, and she will be greatly missed. Pres. Beverina then announced that the BOD has appointed John Bailey as LOWA's General Manager effective December 1, 2001.*

In his first year as General Manager, John Bailey proposed in December 2002 a ten-year building plan that would replace the golf Pro Shop and snack bar, build a new enclosed swimming pool and fitness center, and an indoor tennis facility. It also included a 15,000 square-foot civic center and major upgrades to the clubhouse and parking areas. These projects would have been funded by $2 million of reserves and assessment increases for the next five years.

> *"Even if assessments got to $1,000 in the next 10 years, that will not be much over the inflation rate," Frame said. He contends the improvements are necessary because Lake of the Woods is a neighborhood in change. "If we had remained a weekend or summer community, there would not be that much demand for, say, a covered pool," he said. "But we are now attracting younger families who want these things." - Lee Frame, Vice President[755]*

Clubhouse Renovation again and again

After the fire of 1980, the restored Clubhouse was partly the original, partly the 1969 addition and partly new. Over the years, the interior design was changed and minor replacements were made. In 1996, a major renovation cost $411,000 that relocated the bar. The 2002 Long Range Plan included a $350,000 requested by the Clubhouse Committee to upgrade the Sports Lounge. After years of changing the wall colors and moving furniture, a plan for another major renovation was presented to the community in 2006.[756] Unlike the last renovation, this time LOWA had professional staff in charge of Maintenance and Administration.[757] The construction contractor soon found that there were severe structural deficiencies due to among other problems the fact that some charred wood had apparently been left in place in the 1981 restoration. Parts of the building had been added to over the years without any structural analysis. Therefore, sections of the building needed to be reinforced. Contracts were authorized for $599,000 for remedial repairs and renovations.[758] While obvious improvements to the beauty of the building were accomplished by new windows and doors and an enlarged deck, the unseen improvements will guarantee a long life for the Clubhouse.

Citizens for Fiscal Responsibility

It had been 27 years since the Civic League and the petition of 1976. While the specific complaints were different this time, the basic premise was the same.

> *Doug Chidlow, Harry Ridge and Dan Elliott have formed a group called Citizens for Fiscal Responsibility (CFR) to fight the project. "We're concerned about [the board] going haywire and spending our money," Ridge said. "We want that spending constrained." The group has begun circulating a petition among the … 5,000 residents asking for a referendum to change LOW covenants.[759]*

A proposed amendment to those covenants would include language restricting future spending by the Board of Directors.

> *From one year to the next year, the Board shall not levy against any member … an increase [in] the uniform annual charge per single-family residential lot by more than three percent above the previous year's national inflation rate.*

The Board of Directors unanimously adopted the following resolution at their February 2004 meeting.

> *The Board of Directors of the Association opposes the petition and urges the membership to vote against the proposed amendment based on the following, and other considerations:*
>
> *The proposal places arbitrary limits on the ability of the BOD to discharge its responsibility to "consider the current maintenance and operational needs, the capital needs and the future needs of the Association," …*
>
> *The proposal will have a chilling effect on the efforts of the volunteer committees and staff to develop budget proposals they believe are in the best interest of our community.*
>
> *A specified upper limit on assessment increases could be viewed by future boards as an acceptable target for increases, thus encouraging higher assessment fees than necessary …*

CFR initiated petitions in 2004 and 2005 to constrain the Board's spending authority. In both cases, the referendum failed to obtain the majority of the lot owners' approval. However, both did obtain the approval of the majority of those that voted. A vigorous campaign was waged in the local press. Advocates for changing the covenants expressed their opinion.

"A referendum is the only way left for residents to voice their objection to the board's actions. The referendum didn't pass in 2004, because 2,130 votes are needed to pass a referendum. I didn't vote for the referendum in 2004, but I will vote for passage this time." - Alicia Payne, Lake of the Woods[760]

If they do not want the large increases to continue, they should vote to approve the current referendum ballot that will change the covenants to limit the amount that assessments could be increased. The most important action for all lot owners is to vote. If they do not vote, the board of directors will assume that all nonvotes are votes against the referendums ... - Elizabeth A. Tabor, Lake of the Woods[761]

Members that were against changing the Board's authority expressed their opinion.

A concern that if this referendum succeeds it could very well lead to government by referendum and render the Board powerless.[762]

The opposition to the referendum had the final word, for now.

A great feature of living at Lake of the Woods is that residents have many opportunities to participate in the development of policy, give direction to our Board of Directors, and voice our opinion. But it appears that (some do) not participate in any of these forums ["The debate isn't over at Lake of the Woods," June 12]. She wrote that the supporters of the referendum to cap assessments never advocated closing recreational facilities. (She) must have missed the April 9 open forum when the leader of the referendum effort stated that he would close the golf course or any other amenity that does not pay its own way. And perhaps she didn't read the article that stated the same thing ["LOW might hike fees 22 percent," Nov. 21]. (She) suggested that the board forced upon us a new recreational facility that will serve the youth, the seniors, and other groups at LOW, including the theater group. Did (she) miss the 15 or more public hearings on this facility? We have more than 1,500 kids under the age of 18 who need a place to hang out. Maybe her house will do. She wrote that the debate is not over. Did (she) fail to notice that the support for the cap dropped by 200 votes this election versus the election held a year ago? It is our hope that the supporters of the failed referendum will now join with us in working to keep Lake of the Woods a great place to live. - Patrick Rowland, Lake of the Woods[763]

While this debate was focused on recent large increases in the assessment used to build reserves and increase staff positions, and the building of a new facility, it was in its most basic form a contest between those that favored rule by four votes and those that favored rule by referendum. In the latter case, they wanted the majority to be defined as the majority who voted, but the restrictive covenants require the majority of lot owners.

However, it takes far less than a majority of lot owners to elect new members to the board.[764]

Incumbent President Lee Frame decided to run for re-election in 2004. Also running was Dan Elliott, a principal in CFR. Dan beat Lee by 29 votes.

> *Frame conceded that the referendum "got folks more interested in the election." He estimated that voter response in the election increased 25 percent this year. "People were ready for a change," said longtime resident Marty Caldwell. "Lee Frame embodied the free-spending, grandiose ideas the board has been following." As president of the Board of Directors, Frame had taken the lead in opposing state regulations to upgrade the spillway capacity of the dam on LOW's largest lake--a position that has won him both support and disapproval. But he says he would not have done anything differently. "I wanted to be elected on my own terms, and I wasn't going to waffle," he said.[765]*

First New Facility in 40 Years

In 2005, the Board of Directors voted to build a new $1.3 million community center. In the five years since the Major Projects Task Force report, the community center had evolved to include a stage for the Players productions, the Teen Center and the Pre-school classrooms. This was the first new building since the Holcomb building was built. Like the Holcomb addition and upgrade, this building was to be partially financed by borrowing. The Holcomb addition was financed by a bank loan soon after the Association debt policy was established without any criticism. In this case, the opposition to the use of debt to build a new building was intense, and they proceeded to court. In June 2005, a LOW property owner tried to get the judge to stop the Association from building the Community Center.[766] The following September the case was presented in Circuit Court.

> *Orange County Circuit Judge Daniel R. Bouton yesterday dismissed a lawsuit challenging the Lake of the Woods Association's decision to borrow money for a new community center ... In a nod to what he called "strong and ongoing disagreements" of Lake of the Woods residents, Bouton suggested that the residents "seek other remedies not before the court" such as elections, lobbying and attending meetings in the community.[767]*

At their March 2006 meeting, the Board of Directors accepted for first reading a proposal from the Rules Committee to revise the Bylaws. The new bylaw would allow the board to borrow money for "reasons and/or purposes determined by the Board of Directors to be in the best interests of the members of the Association." The Bylaw was finally revised in January 2008.

Community Center Ribbon Cutting

Photo by Dan McFarland.

Orange County District 5 Supervisor Wallace, Fran Stockdale and LOWA President Buttimer.

Community Center Activities

UPPER LEFT to RIGHT: Fun Bunch and Pre-school, photos by Dan McFarland.

MIDDLE: Battle of the Bands, photo from LOWA files

LOWER: Players, reproduced from LOWA.org

New Pro Shop

At their August 2006 meeting, the LOWA directors unanimously approved spending $1.6 million to remove the old and build a new pro shop and snack bar. The project was funded from the reserves in both 2006 and 2007. This was another example of the continuity of the Board and the ability for a Board to obligate future expenses beyond the budget year.

> LOWA member Doug Chidlow protested paying for the pro shop/snack bar out of association reserve funds, saying it "would bankrupt our reserves." He supported a mortgage to pay for the new building and expanded parking lot, a suggestion ignored by directors.[768]

There is no clearer sign that "things were a changing" than the demolition of the original Pro Shop. For two decades, every time a new Pro Shop was planned the task was delayed, cosmetic repairs were done and some of the planned expenditure was diverted to the golf course grounds.

> "The building is fantastic," said Lake of the Woods Association Secretary Peter Williams. "Everyone's raving about it."[769]

The project resulted in schedule slip and cost overrun that gave fuel to the fire of those opposed to replacing the old building.[770] While the focus was a golf building this time, the politics were the same as the opposition to the golf pro contract back in 1976.

The new building was named the Woods Center both to emphasize its utility to all of Lake of the Woods and to honor Barbara Wood.

> (At the 12th Annual Meeting, General Manager)Lodge presented his report ... and in closing, voiced appreciation to (President Ed) Law, (Past President Alan) Potter, (Vice President Bea) Oertel, (Legal Counsel Atwell) Somerville and Barbara Wood.

Barbara at that time was the recorder of all Board of Director's meetings. As early as 1982, she was held in esteem along with LOWA Presidents. At the 28th Annual Meeting, President Ed McCarthy introduced her as the Assistant General Manager. Barbara was exceeded only by Atwell Somerville in length of continuous service to the Association. She served as Assistant General Manager under two General Managers, and in 2001 when asked by President Schulle to be the GM, she responded, "I wouldn't mind having that job."[771]

Photos by Dan McFarland

UPPER: General Manager John Bailey with Barbara Wood at ribbon cutting, insert is close-up of Barbara.

LOWER: The Woods Center.

End of the Enclosed Pool, Birth of a Fitness Center

When President Neil Buttimer and the other Directors made the decision to fund construction of the new Pro Shop and Snack Bar, they also passed a resolution in support of the $4 million covered pool and fitness center to be built at the Locust Grove campus of Germanna Community College (GCC). The resolution mattered little as legal counsel found that the Board could not authorize the donation of money outside the Association.[772]

> *The resolution of support for the GCC facility states that LOW's efforts can "provide a model for seeking contributions from other subdivisions in the area." Buttimer reiterated this by saying that he hoped the directors' resolution would be the start of a domino effect on fundraising for the pool/fitness center.*

The funding drive did not achieve enough momentum before the Germanna administration changed and the YMCA commitment weakened. The matter died quietly.

At that time, many residents of LOW used the fitness center at Germanna Community College. There was no fee but each user had to undergo an interview with the nursing students there.

> *"While I was LOWA President, during a meeting with Germanna Community College President Frank Turnage, he said he had a community relations problem. He had to convert their fitness center to classroom space and he was concerned about the negative reaction from the LOWA members that used the equipment. In further discussion, we reasoned that if he could give us the equipment, we could put it in the soon-to-be empty Pre-school space near the Clubhouse Pool. The Pre-school was scheduled to move to the new Community Center when it was completed. (PS - I am not naive enough to believe that Dr. Turnage did not intend for LOW to get the equipment when he brought up the issue.) Because the equipment belonged to the State of Virginia, he could not "give" us the equipment. The end result, negotiated by the GM, was Germanna CC gave us a long-term loan of the equipment, which is spelled out in a contract that is on file. The only requirement is that we have to let Germanna faculty use the equipment if they wish, which rarely happens." –Neil Buttimer, LOWA President*

When the Community Center opened, the fitness equipment was moved to the Clubhouse Pool building and use started increasing. Some of the fitness center advocates, especially Dan Greene, painted and fixed-up the building. The fee was raised to $75, and the membership continued to grow. As a result, quite a bit of new equipment has been purchased. Since the income was so great, all of these pieces have been purchased using operational funds not capital reserves. This new amenity is both very popular, with one of the largest user list of any amenity, and financially self-sufficient. However, this activity has no permanent staff and is located in a part of a fully depreciated very old facility.

Referendum of 2006, Allow Use of Amenities by Outsiders

It had been 24 years since the court in Bauer vs. Harn ruled that the Association had no authority to sell to non-property owners the right of entry and access to community facilities. Once again, the desire to increase revenue led to proposals to authorize a new type of membership to people that did not own a lot at LOW. While proponents of the referendum did acknowledge that the last attempt to have an outsider membership was illegal, they failed to recognize that the earlier attempt was an economic failure. This referendum, unlike the last two, was initiated by the Association committees and the Board of Directors. It was submitted to the Board of Directors for their endorsement, but the majority decided to be non-committal.

> There are 10 proposals for Lake of the Woods' lot owners to consider on the upcoming community referendum. But there is only one really hot issue: letting outsiders in the gates to use the subdivision's amenities.[773]

President Neil Buttimer presided at the June 2006 Board of Directors meeting that authorized this referendum.

> Motion ... passed unanimously, to amend the wording ... Proposal #4: Permit Restricted Use of the Clubhouse, Golf Course and Equestrian Center by Non-members, to read: "and may, if approved by a majority vote of the lot owners, discontinue a recreational amenity."

> Motion ... to delete the first sentence of the last paragraph in the proposed cover letter to LOWA members ... that states that the LOWA Board supports these changes and believes approval will benefit member ... Motion passed.

Thus, the proposal to "let outsiders inside the gates" also included allowing an amenity to be discontinued. That proposal was the only one that received a majority of "not approved" votes (1128.54 yeas, 1547.96 nays). Other items worth noting include approval of the deletion of restrictions on radio transmitting devices, something that Don Nowakoski had sought 30 years before. The following proposals were defeated by the lack of a majority of lot owners: approving: the reduction of camping facilities, sub-dividing Life Estates and deleting the right of first refusal.[774]

F&R Upgrade

> President McCarthy reported at the May 1998 board of Directors meeting that on Tuesday, April 28, 1998, the Board met with representatives of the Fire and Rescue Company to discuss plans for a new fire and rescue building.

Seven years later at the 35th Annual Meeting, President Buttimer presented Vic Larsen of LOW Volunteer Fire & Rescue, Inc. a check for $38,000 on behalf of LOWA. Mr. Larsen gave a brief report on the progress of their Annual Fund Drive, noting that Fire & Rescue needs another $50,000 to $80,000 for the new Firehouse facility. Mr. Larsen thanked LOW members for their generous financial support over the years and asked that they continue their support now that needs are greater than ever.

At the following monthly BOD meeting, Vic Larson stated Fire & Rescue has been evaluating bids and has received tentative commitments from banks for financing. There was a tentative start date of November 2005. Flynn Construction was awarded the new firehouse contract. Financial help from the community was still needed by LOW Volunteer Fire & Rescue. Although the County helps support LOW F&R to some extent, they do not pay for new buildings. In March 2006, the building site was cleared, and in the late spring of 2007 the building was constructed.[775]

Charlie Bocook, president of the Lake of the Woods Volunteer Fire and Rescue Company, had a lot of people and institutions to thank yesterday morning. As he led the dedication ceremony for the new 7,800-square-foot fire station on State Route 3, he made sure that all the local fundraisers got a nod. And that meant thanks to everyone from the bingo workers to the mortgage holder to the people who put on the annual July Fourth celebration. But mostly it was "the generosity of the community" that made the $1.65 million building a reality, he said.

According to Public Relations Director Hank Altman, the LOW Fire and Rescue Company was first chartered in August 1971. "Our first ambulance was a station wagon," he laughed. The original building, still in use, was a double-wide trailer. A fire station was built in 1982 and is currently being spruced up for the sole use of the rescue squad.[776]

Photos by Dan McFarland

UPPER to LOWER: The F&R buildings from right to left, 1970s, 1980s and 2007. Close-up of the new fire station. New equipment responding.

From Bank to Bankrupt

As LOW entered the 21st century, the infrastructure had a multi-million dollar backlog in repair and replacement, and the Association was still staffed as if it was a summer camp facility.

The assessment in 1998 was the same as in 1992 and in between it was less.[777] During that time, the Replacement Reserve doubled as purchases of new equipment was deferred and old equipment was replaced with not-as-old equipment. Putting money in the bank for long-term bonds was preferred to spending for today's needs. In October 1998, things began to change; the Board accepted a bid from Paddock Pools, Inc., to replace Sweetbriar Pool. In 1999, President Warren Story and the other Directors increased the assessment 16%.

In 2000, the Road Reserve was increased by assigning to it a portion of the annual road fee income, a Dam reserve was created and funded from the assessment, and the New Capital appropriation from assessment was increased. There followed a series of annual assessment and fee increases, necessary to some, extravagant to others.

The Virginia Property Owners Association Act requires a Reserve Study every five years. The initial study in the 21st century determined that the Association had a backlog of major maintenance and replacement projects of over $2 million, which was slightly less than the funds in the Replacement Reserve. While not prudent to immediately eliminate the backlog and the bank balance, a five-year plan was put in place with the objective of following the Reserve Study recommended future replacement schedule and working off the backlog. While no plan is followed in detail, in general, the result was annual increases in the net worth of the Association and increases in the annual depreciation. The latter directly raised the assessment.[778]

When the Board reorganized after the election of 2004, the Directors elected Neil Buttimer as President and Doug Rogers as Vice President. Anticipating the replacement of the Pro Shop and acknowledging that the Civic Center was a new facility, the Board of Directors negotiated a loan with Wachovia Bank for about $800,000. The policies to replace old equipment and facilities with new, ensure adequate reserves, and let the assessment be what it needed to be, would remain in effect for four more years.

During this period, LOW was served by a series of very experienced and capable presidents. They, without exception, had served on LOWA committees and were officers of the Association before being elected President. Two of these gentlemen, Lee Frame and Doug Rogers, ran for Rick Wallace's seat on the County Board of Supervisors in 2007.

> *Rogers is chairman of the Orange County Republican Committee and president of the Lake of the Woods Association. Frame is a member of the County Planning Commission and a former president of the LOWA.*[779]

In September 2007, the Board of Directors consisted of Eldon Rucker, President, Tom Sheridan, Vice President, Neil Buttimer, Treasurer and a Past President, Peter Williams, Secretary, Bill Wilson, Jeff Flynn, and Bruce Kay. Differences of option among board members at the public monthly meetings became "newsworthy."

> *"We've been dipping into the cookie jar too much," said board member Bruce Kay. "The reserve funds are what we've been using to shore up our operating expenses for years."*

> *The lack of cash has been cited by Kay and others to explain why the board of directors was not able to pay off early the $860,000 loan that financed the community center.*[780]

In his August 28, 2008, President's Letter, Eldon Rucker wrote:

> *"I hope that this summary will assist in a seamless transition for the next board."*

The following month, Jeff Flynn and Margaret Darby were elected to the Board. At the Directors meeting to elect officers, the transition was a break with the past. None of the incumbent officers was elected. The new officers of LOWA were Bill Wilson, President, Jeff Flynn, Vice President, Margaret Darby, Secretary, and Olive Kelly, Treasurer. This was the first time in 30 years that a Director did not serve as Treasurer.

> *Moments before, outgoing President (Eldon Rucker) had criticized The Free Lance-Star for publishing Director Bruce Kay's comment that the Orange County homeowners association was "broke."*[781]

> *The irresponsible statement that Lake of the Woods is "broke" is untrue and not borne out by the facts. As of July 31, (2008) the Lake of the Woods Association had more than $4.9 million in cash and investment accounts. Even after completing more than $4 million in needed updates to our roads and facilities, we have more than $2.4 million in our restricted reserve accounts, which are funds set aside for future upkeep. Our recent audit confirms (there is) enough of a surplus to cover the unbudgeted costs of our new golf facility. Our current year budget ... shows that the Lake of the Woods Association is more than $43,000 to the positive side. Overall, the financial condition of the Lake of the Woods Association is solid.*[782]

Bill Wilson wrote in his President's Letter of September 28, 2008:

> *... Therefore, the Board of Directors is in a belt-tightening mode and for the time being will be putting emphasis on maintaining core amenities. The 2008 and 2009 budgets will be scoured for cost savings ... Forecasts vary about the amount of reserves remaining as of April 30, 2009, the end of the Lake's fiscal year.*

Jeff Flynn and Bruce Kay the year prior had tried to freeze, or at least cut back, the increase in employees' pay. Now that he was part of the majority, Bruce Kay proposed a freeze on the assessment. When Bill Wilson was elected in 2006, he said he would like to open up communication in the community and "in three years I would like to see this place healed and people more civil in their discourse." His year as President was one of the most difficult in thirty years. The external chaos was certainly a contributor. The real estate market showed signs of collapse a year before. When Bill Wilson was elected President, the stock market had fallen 25% over the previous year and would collapse another 25% a few days later. The impact on the community was a hiatus in building, thus no road fee income, and a drop-off in use of fee-based amenities. Foreclosures were in the news, and assessment delinquency rates rose to levels not seen in decades. A financial crisis in 2009 was predicted.

LOWA directors still have not addressed the projected shortfall in revenue for the present fiscal year. Treasurer Olive Kelly said at the Feb. 7 (2009) meeting that without cutting expenses, LOWA would be short $338,000.[783]

Treasurer Kelly reported in the August 14, 2009 *Lake Currents* that the operating revenue for the previous fiscal year had in fact actually exceeded expenses and the Association had a surplus of $80,768 as of the end of the fiscal year, April 30, 2009.

"In the aggregate, we ended the year with a capital reserve balance of $1,036,478."
– Treasurer Olive Kelly

While there were henceforth neither claims of being broke nor impending shortfalls, further changes quickly followed. Atwell Somerville's law firm, which had served the Association for 25 years, was dismissed. The legal services were retained from Whiteford, Taylor & Preston, a Falls Church, Virginia, firm specializing in homeowner-association law. The audit firm was replaced. The assessment was set at $10 above the previous year, an increase that did not cover the cost-of-living increase; the last time that happened was 1997. Dodson Security, which had provided security services to LOW since 1972, lost the competition for the security contract to U.S. Security Associates.

The board unanimously approved naming the LOW security building after George Dodson ... LOWA President Bill Wilson called Dodson a "good friend" and lauded "his years of dedicated service to Lake of the Woods."[784]

Following the path of the Holcomb debt financing in 1991, after the Board elections of 2008, the new Board of Directors reversed the old and paid off the debt by drawing down the reserves. In May 2009, the reserve balance was decreased when the collateral CD was cashed and the loan was paid off. The net result was a favorable reduction in the cost of current operations and future assessments due to eliminating future loan interest payments. However, it violated the intent of the replacement reserve by using the funds to pay for a new amenity. Once again, as in the 1990s, necessary replacement expenditures were deferred.

"This is taking replacement reserve money for new capital, the Community Center," he (Director Neil Buttimer) argued. "It's irresponsible."

"Director Buttimer, your math is not logical," said LOWA Treasurer Olive Kelly, who had earlier told him he was using "fuzzy math" to argue for keeping and extending the loan.[785]

The officers of the Association transferred all funds from Wachovia Bank to Stellar One, a state bank. They severed relations with Morgan Stanley, who had been the Association investment advisor for years.[786]

As the main dam spillway improvement project was reaching the contract award phase, John Bailey, the General Manager, announced his resignation.

He has guided the association's prolonged fight with the state over meeting safety regulations for the dam on LOW's main lake. According to (the town of Orange) Mayor Henry Lee Carter, there were 120 applications for the town manager's job, but it came down to Bailey and (one other) ..."I'm looking forward to the new challenges and new opportunities in the town," Bailey said. "Public administration is what I do, and working with the town is a good fit."[787]

John Bailey served the Association as General Manager for eight years, the longest service of a GM since the days of Col. Warren Lodge (GM). This continuity in management followed nearly a decade of frequently changing General Managers. During his years of service, he oversaw the first major facility added in thirty years, the Community Center, the long overdue replacement of the Pro Shop and a major renovation of the Clubhouse. He also replaced every cost center manager, with the exception of the golf pro, and markedly raised the education level and professional experience of the LOWA staff.

Walmart and Beyond

"All I know is, things are changing," Miss Roach said. "No, it's not what it used to be, anymore."

It is always foolish to predict the future; it is very prudent to plan for the various possibilities based on what you know today. The building in the 1990s of a grade school within a few miles, a library on our boundary and the small strip mall built in 1995 across from the entrance were pleasant additions to our lifestyle. The addition of Sheetz, McDonalds and another smaller strip mall at the corner of Routes 3 and 20 in the early part of this decade were a sign that Orange County was not protecting the panorama.

For decades, nothing has been added to LOW sections 15 and 17 until 2004 when a $4 million four-story large office building was built on Germanna Highway. It overlooks the golf course, and is across from the Locust Grove Post Office that had been built in 2001. All of the section 15 and 17 area has the potential for being a row of multi-story office buildings, albeit the one that was built 5 years ago is still only partially occupied.

The proposed big-box Super Walmart on the opposite corner of Routes 3 and 20 complies with the Orange County zoning of that area as commercial. It took over twenty years for Wilderness Shores, once zoned for residential, to start building. It may take twenty years to build out Routes 3 and 20, but it most likely will happen sooner. The build-out on Route 601 has started. There will soon be an Orange County middle school and a large quantity of county land with infrastructure in place to build more county facilities and parks.

The U.S. Census of 2010 may have a big impact on the role of LOW in the county. While gerrymandering is a possibility, it is also possible for LOW to control the election of two county supervisors.[788]

In the next eight years, we are looking forward to the 300th anniversary of Germanna, the 150th anniversary of the Battle of the Wilderness and the 50th anniversary of LOW, if we can only get through the current Great Recession!

APPENDICES

APPENDIX A - Boards of Directors Chronology

1967, VWCI members only
John S. Keating, Jr., of Hinsdale, IL
C. Daniel Clemente of Falls Church, VA
Wesley T. Butler of Springfield, VA

1967 - 1971 – Board, 5 yr term, 3 VWCI members
1969 plus Ernest J. Holcomb
1970 plus William A. Newman

1971, Four Boise Cascade members, three LOW lot owners
James H. Stewart, President
William A. Newman, Jr., Vice-President
Ernest J. Holcomb
Everett Griggs
John M. Margosian
Robert C. Goetz
James A. Moore

1971 - 1972 – Board, all LOW lot owners
James Stewart, President
William Newman, Vice President and Treasurer
Arnold Chase
Ruth Dugan
John R. Henry
Ernest Holcomb
Richard Wilbur

1972 - 1973
James Stewart, President

Arnold Chase, Vice President
William Newman, Treas.
Ernest Holcomb
Ruth Dugan
John Eckel
John R. Henry

1973 - 1974
Arnold Chase, President
John Eckel, Vice President (Arnold Chase, resigned in 1974 and as Vice President, Jack Eckel moved up as President)
John R. Henry, Vice President (when Jack Eckel became President)
Ruth Dugan
Ernest Holcomb`
F. Price Merrels
Gilbert Illch

1974 - 1975
Glen T. Barton, President
Barbara–Sue O'Toole, Vice President
Robert Frey
F. Price Merrels
Laura Sumner
John Ostby
Richard Bayless

1975 – 1976
Mrs. Lee Bauer, President
Dick Bayless, Vice President
Robert Frey

F. Price Merrels
Glen Barton
Don Nowakoski
Laura Sumner

1976 – 1977
Ronald Duell, President
John Nolan, Vice President
Donald Nowakoski
Edgar Law
Mrs. Lee Bauer
Glen Barton
Robert Frey

1977 – 1978
Ronald Duell, President
John Nolan, Vice President
Donald Nowakoski
Edgar Law
Robert Heiney
Edwin Harn
Authur Bourne

1978 – 1979
Ronald Duell, President
John Nolan, Vice President
Edgar Law
Robert Heiney
Edwin Harn
Authur Bourne
Patrica Stivers

BOD meeting January 13, 1979
Edwin Harn, President
Patrica Stivers, Vice President
Arthur Bourne resigned January 29, 1979
Don Nowakoski
Jack Eckel appointed March 11, 1979

1979 - 1980
Alan Potter, President
Donald Nowakoski, Vice- President
Patricia Stivers
Robert Heiney
Fran Harding

Bea Oertel
Edwin Harn

1980 - 1981
Alan Potter, President
Ed Law, Vice President
Don Natoli
Bea Oertel
Don Nowakoski
Patrica Stivers-Bauer
David Ivey

1981 - 1982
Ed Law, President
Bea Oertel, Vice President
Don Natoli, Treasurer
Doris Christ, Secretary (not Board member)
Ken Boheim
Bernie Walsh
David Ivey
Alan Potter

1982-1983
Ed Law, President
Bea Oertel, Vice President
Don Natoli, Treasurer
Ken Bohiem
Davis Ivey
Burnie Walsh
Brenda McCall, Secretary (not a BOD member),

1983 - 1984
Bill Carpenter, President
Ken Boheim, Vice President
David Ivey, Treasurer
Marty Stoll
Barbara Story
Bernie Walsh
Bob Frey

1984 - 1985
Bill Carpenter, President
Barbara Story, Vice President
Bob Frey, Treasurer

Marty Stoll
Bill Henterly
Gene Sorte
David Ivey

1985 - 1986
Bill Carpenter, President
Barbara Story, Vice President
Bob Frey, Treasurer
Burnett Walsh, Secretary (not Board member)
Edith Ferris
James Karr
Gene Sorte
David Ivey

1986 - 1987
Ronald H. Pierce, President
Bob Frey, Vice President
Dean Rubin, Treas.
Edith L Ferris, Secretary (resigned from BOD
June 25, 1987, remained Secretary)
Barbara Story
Gene Sorte
Jim Kaar
Larry Adams appointed July 11, 1987

1988-1989
Ronald H Pierce, President
Gene Sorte, Vice President
Dean Rubin, Treas.
Judy Williams
Neil Dickens
Andy Anderson
Mildred Droste

1989 - 1990
Gene Sorte, President
Larry Taylor, Vice President
Judy Williams, Treas.
Mildred Droste
Neil Dicken
Jesse Adams
Paula Scott

1990 -1 991

Larry Taylor, President
Alan Polk, Vice President
Betty Buchanan, Treas.
Judy Williams
Neil Dickens
Jesse Adams
Paula Scott

1991 - 1992
Alan Polk, President
Paula Scott, Vice President
Jesse Adams, Treas.
Betty Buchanan, Sec.
Les Bueng
Frank Nichols
Larry Taylor

1992 - 1993
Alan Polk, President
Mort Baratz, Vice President
Betty Buchanan, Treas.
Les Bueng
Frank Nichols
Charles Holt
Jeff Barber

1993 - 1994
Mort Baratz, President
Charles Holt, Vice President
Jeff Barber, Treasurer
Les Bueng, Secretary
Art Goodies
Dick Hollenbach
Carolyn Allen

1994 – 1995
Mort Baratz, President
Carolyn Allen, Vice President
Jeff Barber, Treasurer
Dick Hollenbach
Richard Johnson
Charles Holt
Scott Williamson

1995 – 1996

Dick Hollenbach, President
Carolyn Allen, Vice President
Richard Johnson, Secretary
Scott Williamson, Treasurer
Mike Mishkin
Gene Sorte
Ed McCarthy

1996 - 1997
Ed McCarthy, President
Dottie Cronin, Vice President
Mike Mishkin, Treasurer
Richard Johnson, Secretary
Mr. Johnson resigned October 5, 1996
Marilun Mason appointed
Scott Williamson, resigned December 7, 1996
Ernie Barthlomew appointed
Gene Sorte
Warren Story

1997 – 1998
Ed McCarthy, President
Dottie Cronin, Vice President resigned
November 2, 1997
Ernie Bartholomew – Vice President
Warren Story – Secretary
Mike Mishkin – Treasurer
Gary McDaniel
Gene Sorte resigns October 23, 1997
Marilyn Mason appointed December 13, 1997
Ione Brown appointed December 13, 1997

1998 – 1999
Warren Story, President
Gary McDaniel, Vice President
Ernie Bartholomew, Treasurer
Marilyn Mason, Secretary
Vin McGlone
Ione Brown
Chuck Schulle

June 17 1999
Gary McDaniel resigned; Ione Brown elected
Vice President,
Alan Polk appointed to fill vacancy

1999-2000
Ernie Bartholomew, President
Ione Brown, Vice President
Bill Mason, Treasurer
Chuck Schulle, Secretary
Alan Polk
Anne Goodwin
Vin McGlone

On February 18, 2000 BOD accepted
resignation of Ernie Bartholomew. Mr. Polk
was elected President. Mike Mishkin appointed
to fill the vacancy of Mr. Bartholomew.
Alan Polk, President
Ione brown, Vice President
Bill Mason, Treasurer
Chuck Schulle, Secretary
Vin McGlone
Mike Mishkin

2000-2001
Chuck Schulle, President
Ione Brown, Vice President
Bill Mason, Treasurer
Anne Goodwin, Secretary
Vin McGlone
Al Sanborn
Frank Beverina

2001 – 2002
Frank Beverina, President
Anne Goodwin, Vice President
Bill Mason, Treasurer
Al Sanborn, Secretary
Lee Frame
Mike Musatow
Peter Rainey

2002-2003
Al Sanborn, President
Lee Frame, Vice President
Mike Musatow, Treasurer
Don Weinert, Secretary
Frank Beverina
Myles Embry

Peter Rainey

2003 – 2004
Lee Frame, President
Neil Buttimer, Vice President
Mike Musatow, Treasurer, resigned December 6, 2003
Peter Rainey, Treasurer thereafter
Myles Embry, Secretary
Ken Burnett
Don Weinert
Ginny Thoms appointed January 3, 2004

2004-2005
Neil Buttimer, President
Doug Rogers, Vice President
Ginny Thoms, Treasurer
Myles Embry, Secretary
Ken Burnett
Dan Elliott, resigned June 4, 2005
Don Weinert
Ted Wessel appointed and Treasurer June 4, 2005

2005-2006
Neil Buttimer, President
Doug Rogers, Vice President
Lincoln Klabo, Treasurer
Ken Burnett, Secretary
Ginny Thoms
Eldon Rucker
Melanie Dynes

2006-2007
Doug Rogers, President
Eldon Rucker, Vice President
Melanie Dynes, Treasurer
Ginny Thoms, Secretary
Lincoln Klabo
Bill Wilson
Peter Williams

2007-2008
Eldon Rucker, President
Tom Sheridan, Vice President

Melanie Dynes, Treasurer resigns December 1, 2007
Neil Buttimer, Treasurer thereafter
Peter Williams, Secretary
Bruce Kay
Bill Wilson
Jeff Flynn appointed December 1, 2007

2008-2009
Bill Wilson, President
Jeff Flynn, Vice President
Olive Kelly, Treasurer (not a BOD member)
Margaret Darby, Secretary
Peter Williams
Bruce Kay
Neil Buttimer
Tom Sheridan

2009-2010
Bruce Kay, President
Jeff Flynn, Vice-President
Margaret Darby, Secretary
Olive Kelly, Treasurer
Tom Sheridan
Neil Buttimer
Patrick Rowland

APPENDIX B - Awards

LAKE OF THE WOODS ASSOCIATION
HONORS AWARDS RECIPIENTS

Warren J. Lodge Award for Excellence

1992   Pat Ivey
1993   Donald Nowakoski
1994   Glen Cannon
1995   John Eckel
1996   Alan Polk
1998   John Nolan
2001   John R. Henry
2002   Fran Stockdale
2003   Ione Brown
2004   Beth and Mike Ross
2005   Richard and Kathleen Bradie
2006   Lee Frame
2007   Rich Wallace
2008   William (Bill) Nowers
2009   Betty Hughes

Distinguished Service Award

1975   Ernest J. Holcomb, Ruth Dugan, and group award to John R. Henry, Arnold Chase, Ruth Dugan, Ernest Holcomb, William A. Newman, Richard Wilbur and James Stewart.
1977   Charles Wilner
1983   Roy Cassel
1985   Doris and William Christ
1989   Joyce and Robert Grim
1992   Mary Helen McFadden. Arthur Goodier
1993   Louise and James McCullough
1994   Martha Foote. Virginia Henderson
1995   Lois and Berkeley Boyd
1996   Clifford Wolfe
1997   James Bloom
1998   Carolyn Nowakoski, Patricia Woosley
1999   Marilyn Mason
2000   Henry Altman
2001   Vincent McGlone, Godfrey Barber
2002   Curtis Pendergrass
2003   Louise and James McCullough
2004   Nancy Horch, Margaret Thode

2005	Ken Haase
2006	Sid Steele
2007	Rosemary and Bill Walker
2008	Betty Beck
2009	Carolyn Nowakoski, Bob Sherba

Outstanding Service Award

1975	Wiliam H. Adrain, Richard H. Bayless, Barbara-Sue O'Toole, Clifford H. Ruffner, Edward E. Lane
1976	Janeth Page, Rolland Stoebe
1977	Dorothy Bickey, June Smith, Ray Grim
1978	Betty Law
1980	John Vogl, Norman Jack, LOW Fire & Rescue (group award)
1982	John Eckel, Homer Carpenter, William Carpenter (group award), Jim Simmons, Eldon Mills
1983	Lou Potter, Alan Potter, Edwin Harn, Glen Barton, John Eckel, Doris Christ, Marian Durden, Lee Power
1984	Edwin Harn
1985	Dorothy Finney
1986	Doris Carpenter
1992	William Dix, Stanley Clark, John Kuehn, Hugh Norton
1993	Norman Jack, Orlo Jackson
1994	Fran Stockdale, Carolyn Walker
1996	Mary and Neil Dicken
1997	Donald Nowakoski
1999	Alberta Jackson
2000	Fran Jacobeen
2001	Ione Brown
2002	Douglas Crain
2003	John (Jake) Brandt, John Hakola, Richard Martin
2004	Millie Lane, Pat Ivey, Bennie Arnold
2005	Bob Jones, Barbara Larson
2006	Ginny Thoms
2007	Pete Rainey
2008	Hank Lewis
2009	Lois Powell and Carole Roddy

Heroic Act Award (no plaque)

1994	LOW Fire Company, Dan Young, Fire Chief
1995	Mark Lane
2001	Ann Rose
2005	Greg Leita, Christine Leitz
2007	Tom Cornell

Outstanding Youth Award (no plaque)

1992   Dan Young, Jr.
1993   Norman Howard
1994   Sara Bechem
1995   Jenny Taylor
1996   Diana Weese
1998   Erin Bueng
2001   Kristin Young, Dean Johnston
2002   Sean Plant
2003   Emily Goodwin, Matt Fox
2004   Jennifer Scamacca
2006   Katherine Kulick, Kyle Townsend
2007   Carmen Moyer, Drake Williams
2008   Robert Imre Davis, Keegan George, Daniel Hawkins, Amanda Neely
2009   Allyson Dodson

Certificate of Appreciation (no plaque)

1976   Nancy Martin
1983   Janet Kildry, Ruth Dugan, Stub Stoebe, Sybil Kari Boyd
1984   Ken Boheim, Bernie Walsk, Barbara Story
1986   Bill Carpenter, Bob Frey, David Ivey, Bernie Walsh
1987   Barbara Story, Edith Ferris
1988   Jim Kaar, Larry Adams
1989   Andy Anderson, Dean Rubin, Ron Pierce
1990   Gene Sorte, Millie Droste
1991   Judy Williams, Neil Dicken, Edith Ferris, Doris Clark
1992   Paula Scott, Larry Taylor, Jesse Adams
1993   JoAnn Capewell, Walt Warner, Carolyn Allen, Al Parkinson
1994   Teresa Brown, Dan Plant, Steven Wood, Winnie and Doral Hupp
1995   Walt Velona, Ken Baer
1996   Carol Moyer, Pete Johnson, Richard Hollenbach
1999   Richard Ferguson, Richard Roso, June Stevenson
2000   Marion Henterly
2001   Charles Schulle
2002   Robert Coleman, Marion Pronk
2003   The Lakers (group award {Chuck Leslie posthumously}, Irene Robinson, Beth Goodwin, Fred Marshall
2004   Scott Jenkins, Carol and Dave Wick, The Lakettes (group award)
2005   Orange County Humane Society Members: Bob Cooke, Betty Hughes, Leo Silvan, Jancie Sweeton, Ann Walker and Dr. Anita Walton
2006   Deo Hardman, Terry Hileman, Doug Crain, Fran Stockdale
2007   LOW Garden Club, Jeff Flynn, Vera Moody

2008   Patricia Cope, Norma Ervin, Desmond Flannigan, Inez Hollm, Ken Kaltenmark, Boyce & Carolyn Wray

2009   Helga Birdsong, Dick and Kathleen Bradie, Joan Burnett, Connie Buttimer, Robert Cooke, Jim Danoy, John Martin, and Martha Sukites

1981   Citations as in D-81-65: Audrey and Lee Haskel; Joseph Maiden; Bernice Oertel

1987   Special Outstanding Leadership Award – Dorothy Bichy

1989   Plaque in Tribute – Dr. Lloyd Burke

APPENDIX C – LOWA Assessments

% CPI	Year	Assessment	% Increase	Note
6.2%	1973	100		
11.0%	1974	135	35%	
9.1%	1975	160	19%	
5.8%	1976	160	0%	
6.5%	1977	170	6%	
7.6%	1978	182	7%	
11.3%	1979	194	7%	
13.5%	1980	248	28%	
10.3%	1981	260	5%	
6.2%	1982	272	5%	
3.2%	1983	270	-1%	
4.3%	1984	253	-6%	RSA Sale
3.6%	1985	275	9%	
1.9%	1986	282	3%	
3.6%	1987	300	6%	
4.1%	1988	320	7%	
4.8%	1989	380	19%	+RR $45
5.4%	1990	405	7%	+RR $45
4.2%	1991	440	9%	+RR $45
3.0%	1992	450	2%	+RR $45
3.0%	1993	430	-4%	
2.6%	1994	425	-1%	
2.8%	1995	425	0%	
3.0%	1996	450	6%	
2.3%	1997	450	0%	
1.6%	1998	475	6%	
2.2%	1999	550	16%	
3.4%	2000	575	5%	
2.8%	2001	600	4%	
1.6%	2002	616	3%	
2.3%	2003	678	10%	
2.7%	2004	726	7%	
3.4%	2005	832	15%	
3.2%	2006	930	12%	
2.8%	2007	1068	15%	
3.8%	2008	1127	6%	
	2009	1137	1%	

RR: road reserve fee per lot

Selected Bibliography

Abercrombie, J. L. *Virginia "Publick" Claims Orange County*. Iberian Publishing Company Athens, Georgia.

Barile, Kerri Saige. Archaeology, Architecture, And Alexander Spotswood: Redefining The Georgian Worldview At The Enchanted Castle, Germanna, Orange County, Virginia, Dissertation University of Texas at Austin, December 2004

Chase, Arnold E. *The fascinating History of Lake of the Woods Area, 1976*, revised 2002 by H. Altman. Available at the Lake of the Woods Fire and Rescue Co., Locust Grove, Virginia.

English, Vera Apperson. *The Apperson Family In America*, self-published. 1977.

Fontaine, John. *The Journal of John Fontaine: an Irish Huguenot son in Spain and Virginia, 1710-1719*, edited by Edward Porter Alexander. Published by Colonial Williamsburg, 1972.

Gordon, Armistead C. *William Fitzhugh Gordon A Virginian of the Old School* 1909.

Happel, Frank, former park historian. *Fredericksburg & Spotsylvania National Military Park Administrative History*. 1955. Available at the office of the Historian and Cultural Resources Manager, Chatham, Falmouth, Virginia.

Hurst, Patricia J. "Soldiers, Stories, Sites and Fights Orange County, Virginia 1861-1865 and the Aftermath." Published by the author, 1998.

Jones, Hugh. *The Present State of Virginia Giving a Particulor and Short Account Etc.*, London: 1724.

Joyner, U. P., Jr. *Orange County Land Patents*, Orange County Historical Society, Inc., 1999.

Lacy, Elizabeth Churchill Jones. *Memories of a Long Life*, 1903.

Miller, Ann Brush. *Culpeper Road Orders 1763-1764*. Charlottesville: Virginia Transportation Research Council, 1994.

Miller, Ann Brush. *Orange County Road Orders 1750-1800*. Orange County Historical Society. Charlottesville: Virginia Highway & Transportation Research Council, 1989.

Miller, Ann Brush. *Orange Road Orders 1734-1749*. Charlottesville: Virginia Highway & Transportation Research Council, 1984.

Miller, Ann L. *Antebellum Orange, The Pre-Civil was Homes, Public Buildings, and Historic sites of Orange County, Virginia*. Orange County Historical Society. Moss Publications, 1988.

Murray, Kathleen A. *Gordon Family of Virginia, and owners of Germanna*, Report for Germanna Community College Honors History, available at The Memorial Foundation of the Germanna Colonies in Virginia, Inc.

Pecquet du Bellet, Louise. "Some Prominent Virginia Families" J. P. Bell Co. Lynchburg, Va., 1907.

Roper, John Herbert, ed. *Repairing the "March of Mars": The Civil War Diaries of John Samuel Apperson Hospital Steward in the Stonewall Brigade, 1861-1865*; Macon, Georgia: Mercer University Press 2001, 313

Scott, W. W. *A History of Orange County, Virginia*. Richmond VA: Everette Waddy, 1907.

Spotswood, Alexander. *Iron Works at Tuball: Terms and Conditions for Their Lease by Alexander Spotswood on the Twentieth Day of July 1739. Introduction by Lester J. Cappon...and map of Virginia Showing Germanna*. Charlottesville, The Tracy W. McGregor Library of the University of Virginia, 1945.

Spotswood, Alexander. *The Official Letters of Alexander Spotswood VOL. II. LIEUTENANT GOVERNOR OF THE COLONY OF VIRGINIA, 1710-1722*. Virginia Historical Society, with an introduction and notes by R. A. BROCK, published by the Society, 1885

Sweet, Palmer C. *Gold in Virginia*. Virginia Division of Mineral Resources Publication 19, 1980.

Vogt, John et.al. *Orange County Marriages 1747-1850*. Athens, GA: Iberian Publishing, 1990.

Walker, Frank S., Jr. *Remembering: A History of Orange County, Virginia*. Orange County Historical Society, Inc., 2004.

Abbreviations & Acronyms

...   Called "ellipsis," a word or words have been eliminated from the material being quoted, the author having deemed them irrelevant.

BOD   Board of Directors

DEQ   Virginia Department of Environmental Quality

DCR   Virginia Department of Conservation and Recreation

GM   General Manager

LOW   Lake of the Woods, a planned development area in Orange County, Virginia.

LOWA   Lake of the Woods Association, Inc., a non-profit corporation.

OCDB   Orange County Deed Book, available in the County Circuit Court Clerk's Office. First number is the volume and the second is the page.

OCWB   Orange County Will Book, available in the County Circuit Court Clerk's Office. First number is the volume and the second is the page.

RSA   Rapidan Service Authority.

SCDB   Spotsylvania County Deed Book. The letter is the volume and the number is the page.

VWCI   Virginia Wildlife Club, Inc., a subsidiary of U.S. Land, Inc., of Indianapolis, Indiana, and later a subsidiary of Boise Cascade Corporation.

WPA of VHI   Works Progress Administration of Virginia, Historical Inventory.

Index

Notes

1   http://image.lva.virginia.gov/cgi-bin/photo.cgi/WF/04/01/013 .

2   Walker, Frank S., Jr. *Remembering: A History of Orange County, Virginia.* Orange County Historical Society, 2004, 94. "The original Miss (Katherine) Russell had accompanied Spotswood to the New World in 1710, living wherever he lived …" Russell Run may be named for her, a Thomas Russell, or a William Russell. Alexander Spotswood conveyed land July 15, 1735, recorded in *OCDB* 1 page 87 to Thomas Russell. William Russell obtained patent recorded in Patent Book 13 page 95 of June 16, 1727, for 1,000 acres at the German Run … corner to Col. Spotswood.

3   Des Cognets, Anna Russell. *William Russell and his descendants.* Lexington, Kentucky: Samuel F. Wilson, December 1884. "It is a matter of great regret that so little can be said of the coming of William Russell from England to the Virginia Colony. The only account we have says, 'He came over with Sir Alexander Spotswood in 1710.'"

4   Des Cognets, Louis, Jr. *English Duplicates of Lost Virginia Records.* Princeton, N.J.: 1958. Recorded by a Court held on 5th day of October 1725.

5   *The Official Letters of Alexander Spotswood VOL. II. LIEUTENANT GOVERNOR OF THE COLONY OF VIRGINIA, 1710-1722.* Virginia Historical Society with an introduction and notes by R. A. BROCK, published by the Society, 1885 190 – 218. http://books.google.com/books?id=QU8SAAAAYAAJ&dq=spotswood+society&source= gbs_navlinks_s .

6   Upon his return from New York in August 1722, he learned that he had been fired as Lt. Governor. In September, the new Lt. Governor Hugh Drysdale arrived, and Spotswood became a private citizen.

7   Des Cognets, Louis, Jr. *English Duplicates of Lost Virginia Records.* Princeton, N.J.: 1958. 116.

8   The 18th century Virginia court documents, at times very difficult to read, usually refer to the value of property in terms of pounds of tobacco.

9   *Iron Works at Tuball,* The Tracy W. McGregor Library of the University of Virginia, 1945

10 Des Cognets, Louis, Jr. *English Duplicates of Lost Virginia Records.* Princeton, N.J.: 1958. 117

11 *Spotsylvania County Deeds Index 1734*

12 Many of these may be in present-day Culpeper County.

13 In 1729, Alexander Spotswood was appointed Deputy Postmaster for the American colonies. In 1732, he established New Post in Spotsylvania County as the site of postal services office in Virginia. Before then, service had not been offered south of Philadelphia.

14 Hening, William Waller. *The Statutes at Large being a collection of all the Laws of Virginia, etc.,*

Vol. VII Chapter XXVIII "An Act to enable the Executors of the Will of John Spotswood, esquire, etc." 30

15 *OCDB 14 144, 28 May 1767. Bernard Moore acting for Est of the will of John Spotswood deceased and the guardian of his son Alexander Spotswood ... to Benjamin Hawkins ... 370-acres ... Rapidan River ... corner Mr. Willis*

16 Hening, William Waller. 33. This allowed income from the ironworks to pay other debts.

17 Hening, William Waller. 31.

18 *OCDB 14 144, and 28 other deeds in 1767.*

19 *Orange County Deed Index, Grantor.* Brig. Gen. Alexander Spotswood, grandson of the Lt. Gov. conveyed 36 deeds between 1771 and 1793, two of which converted from leases. There were no sales during the war years of 1777 to 1779.

20 Joyner, U. P., Jr. *Orange County Land Patents*, Orange County Historical Society, Inc., 1999.

21 Walker, Frank S., Jr. Chapter II E "Don't Call It Dirt"

22 Joyner, U. P., Jr. *Orange County Land Patents.*

23 Barile, Kerri Saige. *Archaeology, Architecture, And Alexander Spotswood: Redefining The Georgian Worldview At The Enchanted Castle, Germanna, Orange County, Virginia*, Dissertation University of Texas at Austin, December 2004 .

24 Miller, Ann Brush. *Orange Road Orders 1734-1749.* Charlottesville: Virginia Highway & Transportation Research Council, 1984, 9.

25 Crakel, Theodore J., ed. *The Papers of George Washington Digital Edition.* Charlottesville: University of Virginia Press, Rotunda, 2007.

26 Miller, Ann Brush. *Culpeper Road Orders 1763-1764.* Charlottesville: Virginia Transportation Research Council, 1994, 464.

27 Miller, Ann Brush. *Orange Road Orders 1734-1749*, 147.

28 Miller, Ann Brush. *Orange County Road Orders 1750-1800*, 20, 30.

29 *Hill Family Papers 1787-1945* at Virginia Historical Society, #Mss1 H5565 a FA2.

30 Johnson, Elmer. *Survey Report, Reminiscences of an old lady*, March 20, 1936 Virginia W.P.A. Historical Inventory Project, Library of Virginia #000680871.

31 Paul, E.A. *The New York Times*, May 11, 1863.

32 Krick, R. K. *The Free Lance–Star*, Feb. 10, 2001.

33 *New York Times*, October 6, 1863. http://www.nytimes.com/1863/10/06/news/army-potomac-repulse-rebels-germanna-ford-foraging-party-fired-upon-artillery.html .

34 "The Campaign That History Forgot", *Civil War Times Illustrated, November*, 1969 11-37.

35 Reports of Maj. Gen. John Newton, U. S. Army, commanding First Army Corps, December 3, 1863. http://valley.vcdh.virginia.edu/OR/paynesfarmminesrun/107thpa/newton.html "Monday, November 30.--At 4 p.m. I left, pursuant to orders, for Germanna Bridge, to cover the crossing of the Fifth and Sixth Corps. Tuesday, December 1.--The recrossing of the army was effected. Wednesday, December 2.--I was ordered to leave a brigade at Germanna Ford and to send another brigade to Mitchell's Ford, and afterward proceed with the rest of my troops to Stevensburg. The brigade left at Germanna Ford was afterward relieved by a brigade of the Sixth Corps."

36 O'Sullivan, Timothy H., photographer. *Where the troops under General Grant crossed, May 4,*

1864, Library of Congress - American Memory Civil War Photos. http://hdl.loc.gov/loc.pnp/cwpb.01173

37 Scott, W.W. *A History of Orange County, Virginia: From Its Formation in 1734 to the End of Reconstruction in 1870*. Richmond, Va.: Everett Waddey Co. 90.

38 Email reply by David.Pearce@VDOT.Virginia.gov . The current bridges were completed in April of 1987. The finished grade elevation of the westbound lane bridge varies from elevation 240.15 ft. on the east end to elevation 242.58 ft. on the west end. The documented high water elevation was approximately elevation 222.7 ft. in June 1972.

39 An order of the Virginia Council passed on April 28, 1714.

40 Barile, Kerri Saige. *Archaeology, Architecture, And Alexander Spotswood: Redefining The Georgian Worldview At The Enchanted Castle, Germanna, Orange County, Virginia*, Dissertation University of Texas at Austin, December 2004 62.

41 "Fredericksburg's Origins and a History of Its Neighborhoods", *Free Lance-Star, Town and County Magazine*, March 15-June 7, 2003. http://www.nnht.com

42 Land Office Patents No. 12, 1724-1726, 484. "He held patent in 1726 to 400 acres in the fork of Rappahannock River, southwest side of the Run of a branch being corner to a patent formerly granted to Harry Beverly."

43 "Fredericksburg's Origins and a History of Its Neighborhoods" *Free Lance-Star, Town and County Magazine*, March 15-June 7, 2003. http://www.nnht.com

44 Miller, Ann Brush. *Orange Road Orders 1734-1749*, 98. "Grandjury impannelled ... We present the Overseer of the Road from upper Flat run to the Wilderness Bridge for not keeping the Road in repayr, on information of Thomas Scott."

45 Miller, Ann Brush. *Orange Road Orders 1750-1800*. 25

46 Miller, Ann Brush. *Orange Road Orders 1750-1800*. 579.
http://www.virginiadot.org/vtrc/main/online_reports/pdf/90-r6.pdf

47 OCWB 2 511, 519. Will recorded June 24, 1777 provided his grandson James Roach 600 acres "where I now live" and granddaughter Letty Roach 224 acres near Old Trap.

48 Miller, Ann Brush. 313. "James Gordon Appointed Oversr. of the Road in the Room of Richd. Collins from Germanna to the Wilderness."

49 Roper, John Herbert, ed. *Repairing the "March of Mars": The Civil War Diaries of John Samuel Apperson Hospital Steward in the Stonewall Brigade, 1861-1865*; Macon, Georgia: Mercer University Press 2001, 313

50 *A History of Roads in Virginia*. Available at
http://www.virginiadot.org/about/resources/historyofrds.pdf

51 Walker, Frank S., Jr. 224.

52 http://lcweb2.loc.gov/pp/pphome.html LC-B811-700, LC-DIG-cwpb-01173(digital file from original negative).

53 http://hdl.loc.gov/loc.pnp/cph.3a16592 (b&w film copy neg.).

54 http://www.germanna.org/

55 http://germanna.org/node/152 "Who is John Blankenbaker? For the few who might not know of John, here you go: John Blankenbaker is the unofficial historian of Germanna. John retired from being a computer engineer in 1985 (he is recognized as having produced the first commercially available personal computer) and since then he has been deeply involved in the study of the Germanna Colonies. For fifteen years he published Beyond Germanna, a newsletter/journal devoted to distributing information about the Germanna people. He

also wrote 2,500 notes, titled "Germanna History," that were distributed and archived on Rootsweb." A search engine for those notes is available at http://homepages.rootsweb.ancestry.com/~george/johnsgermnotes/germhis3.html

56 Blankenbaker, John. "Germanna History Notes page #046," note # 1141, undated, hosted by Rootsweb.

57 An order of the Virginia Council passed on April 28, 1714.

58 Fontaine, John. *The Journal of John Fontaine: an Irish Huguenot son in Spain and Virginia, 1710-1719*, edited by Edward Porter Alexander. Published by Colonial Williamsburg, 1972, 102.

59 Blankenbaker, John. "Germanna History Notes page 22," note # 537, undated, hosted by Rootsweb.

60 *Spotsylvania Co. Deed Book* A, December 19, 1722. "This indenture includes the Tract of Land and Negroes belonging to the land." Other deeds pertaining to the mines are SCDB A 54, 55 and 114

61 Blankenbaker, John. "Germanna History Notes page #046," note # 51.

62 Blankenbaker, John. "Germanna History Notes page #046," note # 58.
http://homepages.rootsweb.ancestry.com/~george/johnsgermnotes/germhis3.html
"So when the Germans (the First Germanna Colony) left, there was no iron furnace. Though Spotswood at this time could not yet say he was in the iron business, he may have had hopes but he certainly had an unclear path to the future. In fact, he seems at this time to be placing more emphasis on land development than on iron smelting. Toward this end, he, with partners, had placed seventy-odd Germans on a large tract of land. When this Second Germanna Colony arrived, there was no iron mine, yet alone an iron furnace. So there was no intention to use them in the iron operation."

63 Blankenbaker, John. "Germanna History Notes page #04."

64 Byrd, William. *A Visit To Colonel Spotswood*. Reprinted in Scott, W.W., *History of Orange County*

65 *Ibid.*

66 *Spotsylvania County Deed Book* A 201, December 20, 1725.

67 *William and Mary College Quarterly Historical Magazine* Vol XVII July 1908 No. 1. 40-41. It seems that Mr. Graeme was selected based on his connections and not based on experience. "In the clerk's office of Lancaster County, Virginia, are recorded (i) A power of attorney from Alexander Spotswood, of Spotsylvania, in Virginia, now residing in London, to John Graeme, of St. James Clerkenwell in the County of Middlesex (England), authorizing him to take possession of his iron works in Virginia, with plantations, negroes, stocks, and manage the same. Dated December 20, 1725." … (in 1732) Mr. Graeme was postmaster at Germanna with a salary of £60 a year. In 1737 he was employed by the commissioners to aid in surveying the bounds of Lord Fairfax's domain in the Northern Neck of Virginia (Ibid., 40-41). August 8, 1737, he qualified as professor of natural philosophy and mathematics in the College of William and Mary, at a salary of £80 and fees, and continued till 1749 … George Washington meets him next in Barbados … They dined together at Judge George Graeme, his brother, one of the most prominent men on the Island."

68 Byrd, William.

69 Blankenbaker, John. "Germanna History Notes page #41."

70 *Iron Works at Tuball*

71 "America and West Indies: July 1735, 16-31", *Calendar of State Papers Colonial, America and*

West Indies, Volume 42: 1735-1736 (1953). 18-28 http://www.british-history.ac.uk/report. aspx?compid=72826

72 *Probate Act Book 1742* Virginia Colonial Records Project Survey Report No. 4595, Will-Register Books 68-69 Trenley. Library of Virginia # 000699567

73 *SCDB* C 417, October 2, 1740 "... 100 slaves at Mine Tract"

74 Hening, William Waller.

75 Pecquet du Bellet, Louise "Some Prominent Virginia Families" J. P. Bell Co. Lynchburg, Va., 1907. "Brig. Gen Alexander Spotswood possessed also iron works, a foundry established by Governor Spotswood, which yielded an income of five thousand pounds per annum and which was broken up by his father's executor."

76 Northton, O. F., Jr. "The Revival Of The Iron Industry In Eastern Virginia As Exemplified By The History Of The Catherine Furnace In Spotsylvania County," *The William and Mary Quarterly*, Second Series, Vol. 16, No. 1, January 1936. 71-80.

77 Walker, Frank S., Jr. 228.

78 Orange County Historical Society, Inc., Gold Mine folder.

79 U.S. 1850 census, Orange County, Virginia 223.

80 Chenawith, Frank. Map of 1951.

81 Sullivan, Paul. "Gold and mercury found in hills," *The Free Lance-Star*, June 7, 1988.

82 *OCDB* 42 302 - 303.

83 *The New York Times*, August 25, 1929. "Henry Ford has purchased the Vaucluse gold mine, in Orange County, Virginia, said to have been worked profitably before the Civil War, but abandoned since. The deed for a 200-acre tract, purchased from Judge Alvin T. Embry of Fredericksburg, was recorded in the Orange County ..."

84 http://richmondthenandnow.com/Newspaper-Articles/Gold-Mines-1.html

85 http://supreme.justia.com/us/93/55/case.html

86 Sweet, Palmer C. *Gold in Virginia*. Virginia Division of Mineral Resources Publication 19, 1980.

87 *OCDB* 60 227 to 230.

88 Moser, James. "Virginia History is deeply Rooted in New Development", *The Free Lance-Star Town and County*, September 16, 1967

89 "Gold Mine Plan Draws Opposition," *The Free Lance-Star*, May 3, 1988, and related report published on June 11, 1988.

90 *OCDB* 49 202, 49 498, 53 130, 53 441, 53 461, 54 22.

91 *OCDB* 53 468.

92 *OCDB* 35 247.

93 *OCDB* 156 348. Lelia Spottswood Willis deed to the Goodwin brothers.

94 *OCDB* 216 450 and in Deed of subdivision recorded in *OCDB* 232 92.

95 "Trustee Sale of real Estate Located in Orange County, Virginia," *Free Lance-Star*, January 3, 1967.

96 Grinnan, Andrew G., *Two Spotswood Boys at Eton in 1760, &c* William and Mary College Quarterly Historical Papers, Vol. 2, No. 2. Oct. 1893 113-120.

97 Pecquet du Bellet, Louise

98 *Letter of Alexander Spotswood, 19 December 1775 to Dudley Digges ... and other members of the Virginia Convention in which Spotswood volunteers to raise a Virginia regiment for service in the Revolutionary War*, Library of Congress, No. mm 79001808

99 *Spotsylvania County Will Book* B 389, 6 May 1756. Their father's will assigned 9048 acres in 7 tracts for the younger brother.

100 Benjamin Grymes of Orange County, born 1751, is DAR ancestor # A055197. Others named Benjamin Grymes owned land in Orange County but did not reside therein. Another Benjamin Grymes of unknown relationship is DAR ancestor # A048526. He served in George Washington's Commander-in-chief Guard.

101 The two "t" spelling of their surname was not adopted by the family until the late 19th century.

102 Lacy, Elizabeth Churchill Jones. *Memories of a Long Life*, 1903, Virginia Historical Society No. Mss:1 L1195:1

103 *OCDB* 16 223, 321, and 360.

104 Joyner, U. P. Jr.

105 Scott, W. W. *A History Of Orange County, Virginia*.

106 Abercrombe, Janice L. et al. *Virginia 'Publick' claims Orange County*, Athens, Georgia Iberian Publishing Co.

107 Series: M805 Roll: 478 Image: 521 File: BLWT304-300

108 Heitman, Francis B.

109 *OCDB* 16 390. Alexander Spotswood, grandson of the Lt. Governor, retained the "right to enter, dig, search for stone, iron, lead, copper or other …"

110 Heitman, Francis B., 512. Maj. Gen R.C. Davis, The Adjutant General, War Department letter of January 22, 1926, to Mrs. Berkeley G. Calfee, Culpeper, Virginia, provides a service record of John Spotswood in the Revolutionary War. *Resolutions, Laws, And Ordinances, Relating To The Pay, Half Pay, Commutation Of Half Pay, Bounty Lands, And Other Promises Made By Congress To The Officers And Soldiers Of The Revolution; Settlement Of The Accounts Between The United States And The Several States; Funding The Revolutionary Debt Washington:* Printed by Thomas Allen 1838, provides additional information.

111 *George Washington to John Beatty, July 12, 1779* The George Washington Papers at the Library of Congress, 1741-1799.

112 *OCBD* 16 90. This is the earliest deed found in the Orange County Courthouse that indicates that John Spotswood possessed what later is called the Orange Grove, May 27, 1773.

113 Joyner, U. P., Jr.

114 Gordon, Armistead C. *William Fitzhugh Gordon A Virginian of the Old School*, New York: The Neale Publishing Company, 1909. One of 12 children, James was born at Urbana in 1759 and was but a child when his father moved to Richmond County, higher up the river, to live. At the age of 22, he was elected to represent that county in the House of Delegates of the General Assembly of Virginia. James Gordon, of Orange, married his first cousin, Elizabeth, daughter of Colonel James Gordon of Lancaster, and his first wife, Mary Harrison, in August 1777. Before his father's death, he removed from Richmond County to "Germanna" in Orange County, where he spent the remainder of his life as a planter and country gentleman – a career that was only briefly interrupted by his service as a delegate in the State Convention of 1788.

115 Census printed in Scott, W.W. *History of Orange County*, Appendix.

116 *OCDB* 19 144.

117 Abercrombie, J. L., *Virginia "Publick" Claims Orange County*.

118 Scott, W. W. *A History Of Orange County, Virginia*.

119 Ibid.

120 Chalkey, Lyman, *Chronicles Of The Scotch-Irish Settlement Of Va.* V. 2
   http://www.rootsweb.com/~chalkley

121 Lacy, Elizabeth Churchill Jones.

122 Abercrombie, J. L.

123 Lacy, Elizabeth Churchill Jones.

124 Johnson, Virginia. *Ellwood: A Crossroads in History,* June 1, 2006. CCRL Staff.
   http://www.historypoint.org/

125 Wilderness Bridge Society, C.A.R. http://www.dardebbie.com/WB.htm

126 http://www.germanna.org/history.html

127 Scott, W. W. *A History Of Orange County, Virginia.*

128 Gordon, Armistead C. *William Fitzhugh Gordon.*

129 Ibid.

130 *Spotswood family papers,* Library of Virginia, No. 000500720

131 The March 1761 Act to enable the Executors of the Will of John Spotswood, Esquire, deceased, to pay debts and legacies due, states that the younger son (Capt. John Spotswood) was provided nine thousand and forty-eight acres of land.

132 *Virginia Herald* obituary October 23, 1804.

133 Fredericksburg Wills Book DC 236.
   http://departments.umw.edu/hipr/www/fredericksburg/deeds/embry.tab

134 OCWB 7 516.

135 *Virginia Herald,* Fredericksburg, Va., Tuesday, August 20, 1805, 3.

136 http://leeboyhoodhome.com/fitzhugh.html

137 http://departments.umw.edu/hipr/www/fredericksburg/contracts/1820bridgeagree.htm

138 Vogt, John et.al., *Orange County Marriages 1747-1850* For example, between 1797 and 1847 there are eight marriages in the Mason family where four of their sons married Jones' daughters, two married Sanders' daughters, one a Payne, another a Roach and another a Richards, all close neighbors along current Route 601 and Route 20.

139 Payne, Brooke. *The Paynes of Virginia.* For example, Ann Roach, daughter of Robert Roach married John Thomas Payne by Parson Bennett at her parents' home just east of the intersection of Old Mountain Road and Flat Run.

140 Virginia Historical Society Mss Sp 687 b1, section 1.

141 OCDB 54 22.

142 Nowakoski, Lyn. At least twice, newly arrived residents of LOW tried to change the name of our post office from Locust Grove to The Wilderness because, they said, Locust Grove did not sound distinguished enough. Those efforts failed.

143 http://www.postalhistory.com .

144 Miller, Ann Brush. *Orange Road orders, 1734-1749 ,* 17.

145 Murray, Kathleen A. *Gordon Family of Virginia, and owners of Germanna,* Report for Germanna Community College Honors History, available at The Memorial Foundation of the Germanna Colonies in Virginia, Inc. It provides the details of transfers starting with Alexander and Elizabeth Spotswood 1,540 acre Germanna Tract in 1781 and ending with James Gordon (estate) receiving deed from Robert Jacob of Norhthampton County in 1800 for the same 1,540 acres.

146 OCDB 21 163.

147 In the late 18th century, Burgess Ball acquired a tract that adjoined the old Spotswood plantation.

He built a grist mill in 1784. He sold the tract, with additional property, to William Lovell and Charles Urquhart of Fredericksburg in 1793. Urguhart acquired and developed the mill site.

148 Historic Court Records, Collection CR-SC-H, record ID 199-6.

149 http://www.germanna.org/history.html

150 Johnson, Elmer Vivian, *Reminiscences of an old lady*. Survey Report Mar. 20, 1936, Library of Virginia #000680871. The survey describes reminiscences of Dolly Roach, daughter of Wm. Reynolds and niece of Jim Roach.

151 Eckel, Jack. "The Spottwood Family." December 2, 1997. James Somerville of Culpeper was the great-great-grandfather of Atwell Somerville, the LOWA Attorney.

152 The old James Somerville house can be seen from the tenth tee at Somerset Golf Course.

153 Miller, Ann L., *Antebellum Orange*. As pictured ca. 1988, the house appears abandoned and in decay. It is being restored by its current owners.

154 Somerville, Robert et al, *A History of James Somerville of Culpeper, Virginia*. R.S.Yates 1988.

155 Pecquet du Bellet, Louise 358 *General Spotswood …also sold forty thousand acres of leased land to James Somerville, of Fredericksburg.*

156 Tyler, L. C., ed. *Encyclopedia of Virginia History*, Volume II, 1915.

157 *OCDB* 24 514 February 26, 1810, 29 78, 29 102, 35 287, 35 323, 35 325, 37 185, 37 234, 37 237, 37 249, 37 283, 39 218, 39 505, 40 320 March 25, 1847; in the order listed above.

158 Cowherd, Charles Peyton, *Indiantown* Survey Report April 27, 1936 Library of Virginia # 000680450 In 1936 Mrs. Larkin Willis described Indiantown "This is a beautiful little village situated in the midst of four high hills and on top of each hill can be found a beautiful colonial mansion. This little village can boost of a good mill, two stores, a post office and auto shop."

159 Virginia Historical Society Mss11:2 L9437:1.

160 *OCDB* 41 35, 118 and 133.

161 Miller, Ann L., *Antebellum Orange. The Pre-Civil War Homes, Public Buildings, and Historic Sites of Orange County, Virginia*. Orange, Virginia: Moss Publications, 1988. Ann L. Miller identifies the tract as Woodland; an earlier publication by John H. Gwathney names it Woodlawn. After the death of Larkin Willis, it was simply known as the widow Willis house.

162 *OCWB* 12 193 and 235.

163 Spotsylvania County Deed Book L 535-37.

164 Wever, Hannah. "Drawing a fine line Orange – Spotsy boundary in question", *Orange County Review*, April 30, 2009. "… there have been parcels of land all along the shared border of both counties which may or may not lie in one county or the other." As explained by Frank S. Walker, Jr. in Chapter 1, the Orange – Spotsylvania county line has never been established by a known survey.

165 James P. Smith wrote to Judge Goolrick on May 11, 1922. Historic Spotswood files of Fredericksburg & Spotsylvania National Military Park

166 This is an interesting example of the errors that can appear in memoirs. The only John Spotswood born circa 1808 was the grandson of Capt. John and thus the grandnephew of General Alexander. I have not found any pension or other record of wounding of "the General" at Princeton. His brother was wounded in the leg so severely that it was a candidate for amputation.

167 Rokus, Josef W. *Caught in the Fury, the Families on the Wilderness Battlefield*, January 2009,

provides the details of how Betty Jones ended up the owner of Ellwood. See also *Free Lance-Star Town & County* April 25, 2009.

168 Miller, Ann L. *Antebellum Orange*. " … It was conveyed in that year to William (Billy) T. and Richard T. Goodwin … (part of) it was purchased by (William "Farmer" Meadows) in 1983." Meadows recently deeded it to the Civil War Preservation Trust.

169 Cowherd, Charles Peyton, *Kitty Payne Place* Survey Report Library of Virginia # 000680710. *This house is the oldest house in the Wilderness section, supposed to have been erected in 1774.*

170 Payne, Brooke Col. USA (ret.), *The Paynes of Virginia*, Richmond, Virginia.

171 *OCDB* 26 36, 4 June 1813. "John Spotswood and wife Mary of Orange County convey to Francis Jones of same county parcel of land being of the tract of land the said John Spotswood now lives on, 113 ¾ acres both sides of the Flat Run." This parcel eventually became part of Lake of the Woods.

172 Miller, Ann Brush, *Orange Road orders 1750-1800* 511.

173 Patent book 38 759.

174 *OCWB* 2 521-22.

175 Vogt, John and Kethley. T. W. *Orange County Marriages 1747-1850*. Athens, Ga.: Iberian Publishing Co. 224. http://www.livelyroots.com/gerald/2/34704.htm

176 This Absalom was grandson of the James Roach who died 1777.

177 *OCDB* 26 3.

178 *Orange County Marriage Bonds* 15 93.

179 James Roach (1760 -1823) married Elizabeth Lindsay in 1788.

180 *OCDB* 19 479.

181 Audibert, Paul. "All Four Years." *Orange County Review*, May 21, 2009 Insider section. The yellow house behind the Town Center on Rt. 20 at Locust Grove is actually the original Robinson's Tavern that has been moved back from the Orange Turnpike.

182 Hendricks, John C., *Robinson's Tavern*, Survey report Nov. 18, 1936 Library of Virginia # 00680827

183 Rokus, Josef W. *Caught in the Fury, the Families on the Wilderness Battlefield*. January 2009

184 The current church was built in 1960.

185 Johnson, Elmer Vivian *Old Mountain Road*, Survey Report, March 6, 1936 Library of Virginia #000680878.

186 *OCDB* 24 514, dated July 7, 1809.

187 *OCWB* 10 372.

188 Rokus, Josef W. *The Alexander Wilderness Cemetery: A Unique History But An Uncertain Future*. Unpublished.

189 *OCDB* 22 164.

190 *OCWB* 3 175. Will of Charles Mason lists Peter as son. In *OCDB* 21 538, the land passes to Peter Mason. In *OCDB* 22 163, Peter by indenture passes to John Mason and mentions a David Faulconer.

191 Sparacio, Ruth, ed. *Pamunkey Neighbors of Orange County, Virginia*, Baltimore: Gateway Press, Inc, 1985 1787-1788 139.

192 *OCDB* 38 246.

193 1850 U.S. Census, Orange County, Virginia.

194 *OCDB* 14 298, 17 427.

195 *OCDB* 28 449 .

196 *OCWB* 9 367.

197 *OCDB* 40 7.

198 Scott, W. W. *A History Of Orange County, Virginia.*

199 *OCDB* 16 134. This and later deeds from Alexander Spotswood are from the grandson of the governor.

200 *OCDB* 19 480.

201 *OCDB* 21 197.

202 *OCDB* 26 36, June 4, 1813.

203 *OCDB* 29 49, 30 360 and 401, and *OCDB* 32 297.

204 *OCWB* 7 304,462 and 9 212.

205 Ibid.

206 *OCDB* 34 345.

207 Hening, William Waller. "John Spotswood (esquire, deceased) agreed … to repurchase 9,048 acres of land and 50 slaves, in order to make provision for his younger son (Capt. John Spotswood)."

208 Hening, William Waller. Court order of 1761 established his rights to 9,700 acres of his grandfather's land.

209 *OCDB* 16 90. Lewis Craig lease of May 27, 1773 "John Spotswood line."

210 *SCDB* J 381, January 10, 1779. "Jno of Orange … slaves …" This is the earliest record of Capt. John Spotswood residing in Orange County.

211 Miller, Ann Brush, *Orange Road orders 1750-1800* 50.

212 Grinnan, Andrew G. "Two Spotswood Boys at Eton in 1760, &c." *William and Mary College Quarterly Historical Papers*, Vol. 2, No. 2. (Oct., 1893). 113-120.

213 *OCDB* 25 253.

214 *The Virginia Herald*, February 10, 1816 3:5.

215 *OCDB* 26 16. On page 140 of said deed book, the tract is identified as Chesterfield and the reason for the sale is to pay off the debt to Robert Patton of Fredericksburg.

216 *OCDB* 18 412. In 1814, 26 140 and in 1818, 27 285.

217 *OCDB* 34 452.

218 *Spotswood Family Papers, 1741-1934 Section 38.* Consists of one item, a bond, March 2 , 1846, of Mary (Goode) Spotswood (1776-1847) to Lelia Maria (Allison) Spotswood (ca. 1809-1868) for the sum of $100.00 received from a bond of John Rowzie Spotswood (1799-ca. 1888) concerning Orange Grove, Orange County, Virginia. Virginia Historical Society: Mss1Sp687b.

219 U.S. Census 1850 223.

220 *OCDB* 32 205.

221 *OCDB* 39 508.

222 *OCDB* 41 333.

223 Joyner, U. P., Jr.

224 Mary Bland Spotswood, only daughter of John Jr., to John E. Lemione July 2, 1825.

225 Willis, Anna Townsend. "Cousin Lelia Our Own Lady Spotswood," *Willis-Gordon-Garnett and Allied Families Journal* Vol. 1 No. 8 (August 13, 1978). 3-7.

226 Moser, James. "Virginia History is deeply Rooted in New Development," *The Free Lance-Star* September 16, 1967, Town and County.

227 Ruffner, Clifford H., Jr. *The Spotswood Willis House at Orange Grove*, 1976. Interview of Mr. and Mrs. Willis of Culpeper, Virginia, on March 30, 1976.

228 Lelia Spottswood Willis died at the age of 95 in January 1967 at her home in Culpeper.

229 Willis, Anna Townsend. "Cousin Lelia"

230 Moser, James. *The Free Lance-Star* September 16, 1967. Jim Foote of Virginia Wildlife Club, Inc. may have had such good intentions as reported, but none of them were implemented by Boise Cascade.

231 All Orange County deeds spell the surname with an "A", but several Civil War era maps spell it with an "E".

232 *OCDB* 40 136. He had also purchased 50 acres March 25, 1847, from James Somerville for $125 adjoining Robert Roach duly recorded in *OCDB* 40 320.

233 Herndon, Dudley L., et.al. *The Herndons of the American Revolution*. Gateway Press 1992.

234 Apperson, Terry interview by Josef W. Rokus, Orange County, Virginia. The historic site of Alfred Apperson's house is located in Section 5 lots 47-48 across Lakeview Parkway from the cemetery.

235 Vogt, John et. al. *Orange County Marriages 1747-1850*. "Melinda Jones married Alfred September 3, 1836; she was a daughter of James Jones and Caty Robeson, granddaughter of John Robeson (probably Robinson)."

236 Tyler, Lyon G. *Men of Mark in Virginia Ideals of American Life Collection of Biographies of the Leading Men in the State* Vol. III. "Apperson, John Samuel, M. D., was born August 21, 1837, in Orange County, Virginia, and his parents were Alfred Apperson and Malinda Jones, his wife. The Apperson family came to Virginia at a very early period and dwelt for many years in New Kent County, from which it scattered its branches over Virginia and the South. Dr. Apperson's grandfather was Peter Apperson, who married Miss Lobb, of Caroline County, Virginia. His father, Alfred Apperson, was in the early part of his life an overseer on a plantation, and afterwards a small farmer on his own account. He was a man of industry and economy and very loyal to his convictions."

237 Fredericksburg Court Record: Green vs. Fitzhugh, collection CR-CI-V, record 284-160 dated 1854. http://www.historiccourtrecords.org/default.asp

238 Roper, John Herbert.

239 Apperson, Terry. Interview with author on March 11, 2010

240 *OCWB* 8 96.

241 Library of Virginia Digital Collection, http://image.lva.virginia.gov/cgi-bin/GetRev.pl?dir=0613/A0001&card=14 Document Images

242 Henry D. Roach was a son of Robert Roach, brother of James W. Roach.

243 *Orange county Marriage bonds* 15 93.

244 *OCDB* 40 291, 24 Sept 1846. Wild Cat Road is part of the current Flat Run Road. U. P. Joyner, Jr., lists Robert Roach as a Justice in 1852 for (current) District 5.

245 *OCDB* 26 36, 4 June 1813.

246 Hendricks, John C. *Old Roach Place*, Survey Report Jan. 5, 1937. Library of Virginia #000680726

247 Johnson, Elmer Vivian, *Reminiscences of an Old Lady*, Survey Report Mar 20, 1936. Library of Virginia #000680871.

248 Roper, J. H. 152.

249 Courtesy of Library of Congress, LC-USZC4-5968. Inscribed below image; Spotswood

house, on the plank road from Germanna Ford, Sedgwick. Green sheet and tan sheet joined. Tan sheet is overleaf to second scene, inscribed: Plank road, Wilderness, Sedgwick, Friday.

250 *Chataigne's 1888 Directory for Orange County, Virginia*. Lists the 1880 Orange County census as white 6,210 and colored 6,842 for a total of 13,052.

251 Scott, W. W. *A History Of Orange County, Virginia*. Chapter XX.

252 Scott, W. W. *A History Of Orange County, Virginia*. Appendix H.

253 Roper, John Herbert, 314. Eli is his brother and his father was Alfred Apperson, the farm was on the east side of Flat Run Road.

254 Roper, John Herbert 314.

255 Lacy, J. Horace, Major. *The Century Illustrated Monthly Magazine* (Vol. 32; New ser. Vol. 10, 605-8), August 1886.

256 Paul, E. A. *The New York Times*, May 8, 1863.

257 http://www.nps.gov/nr/twhp/wwwlps/lessons/45chatham/45facts1.htm .

258 Johnson, E. V. *Tanyard* Survey Report January 27, 1936. Library of Virginia #000680874.

259 Hendricks, John C. Library of Virginia #000680726.

260 Find a Grave. http://www.findagrave.com/index.html.

261 Hendricks, John C. *Robinson's Tavern*, Survey Report OR 166. Library of Virginia #000680827.

262 *Pension Application for a Widow of a Confederate Soldier*, May 20, 1927. Library of Virginia # 000598824. She reported an annual income of $200, the value of land of $3,000 and personal property of $150.

263 Roper, John Herbert. 436.

264 *Daily Express*, Petersburg, VA, Wednesday, ?, 1863. Obituary. "Died in this city, Saturday, June 6th, of disease contracted from the cruel treatment of the enemy while a prisoner, John Rowzie Spotswood, Jr., of Orange County Va., second son of John R. and Lelia A. Spotswood, aged about 28 years, a private in Co. E 9th Va. Cavalry. He answered the first call of his country promptly, and under Gen. J.E.B. Stuart, has participated in every important battle, skirmish and raid which has distinguished the command of that notable chieftain. While at home recovering from a severe cold, he was captured on his father's farm, near the Wilderness, having stood the fire of some ten to fifteen shot from the invaders before surrendering was marched to Falmouth, there paroled and might have been saved if sent across to Fredericksburg, but no, he too was wanted to swell the pageant, and was to be driven to ?? procession a prisoner through Washington and Philadelphia and then ?? led to Fort Delaware, where the putrid water and loathsome food ?? ?? to our poor soldiers developed the disease, which has deprived our country of a brave, modest, steadfast, and efficient defender. One of ?? unnoticed, unhonored private soldiers of whom there are thousands in the service doing their daily duty manfully and heroically without hope of honor or reward. He bore his trying illness with the fortitude of one inured of suffering but though blessed with the ?? care of kind physicians and friends, all was unavailing to stay his ?? of Death. He peacefully breathed out his ?? about 9 o'clock on Saturday morning, ?? ?? to his afflicted parents and relations the consolation of an expressed truss in his redeemer the hope of meeting in Heaven, and the pre?? legacy to his country of another gallant life sacrificed, no not sacrificed, by freely offered up for her freedom."

265 Rhea, Gordon C. *The Battle of the Wilderness May 5-6, 1864*, LSU Press, 2004 178.

266 Adams, John R. *Memorial and Letters of Rev. John R. Adams D.D., Chaplain of the Fifth Maine*

and the One Hundred and Twenty-first New York Regiments during the War of the Rebellion, 1890; Library of Congress Control No. 12016466.

267 Chase, Arnold E. *The fascinating History of Lake of the Woods Area, 1976,* revised 2002 by H. Altman.

268 Nowakoski, Lyn. *Living in LOW in the Early Days,* unpublished.

269 Hurst, Patricia J. "Soldiers, Stories, Sites and Fights Orange County, Virginia 1861-1865 and the Aftermath." Published by the author, 1998.

270 "THIS WILDERNESS BATTLE-FIELD.; Gathering up the Wounded The Place Where Wadsworth Died." *The New York Times,* from the Rochester Evening Union, published: July 20, 1864

271 Ewell, Richard S. Lt. Gen. "May 4 – June 12,1864 – Campaign from the Rapidan to the James River, Va. March 20, 1865." Richmond, Va.

272 Rhea, Gordon C. *The Battle of the Wilderness.* 80.

273 Cutcheon, Byron M. Formerly Colonel of The Regiment. *The Story Of The Twentieth Michigan Infantry July 15th, 1862, To May,1865 Embracing Official Documents On File In The Records Of The State Of Michigan And Of The United States Referring Or Relative To The Regiment.* Lansing, Michigan: Robert Smith Printing Co. 1905.

274 A different version is found in Ann. L. Miller's *Antebellum Orange.* "... nine sons and three grandsons of Larkin Willis served in the Civil War." The Orange County Death Records Index lists the deaths in Orange County during 1864 of two of his sons, Benjamin and Joseph. Many of the Willis-Gordon-Garnett records list the other sons as surviving many years after the war and three grandsons died during the war, two of which were infants born after 1860. The quote is similar to one that appears in the W. W. Scott History of Orange, "Ah, Mr. W-, I wish I had a million sons, even though they all had to go the same way!"

275 Hurst, Patricia J., *Soldiers, Stories, Sites and Fights Orange County, Virginia 1861 – 1865.*

276 Bones dug up in the construction of the main dam at Lake of the Woods were quickly covered up; else construction of the entire project would be delayed.

277 Cowherd, Charles Peyton, *The Willis boys,* Survey Report, Library of Virginia # 000680400.

278 Moser, James. *The Free Lance-Star* September 16, 1967.

279 "Ancient Spotswood Fireback is Stolen," *The Free Lance-Star,* August 21, 1931. An interesting coincidence is the fact that a fireback similar to the one owned by Mrs. Lelia Spotswood Willis is currently on display at the Virginia Historical Society. It was part of the Dr. and Mrs. Henry P. Deyerle Collection, Harrisonburg, VA. The figure of the crowned Indian princess was derived from one of Virginia's colonial seals. Fireback was excavated in 1984 at Germanna Mansion at the site of Gov. Alexander Spotswood's home.

280 Willis, Anna Townsend. "Cousin Lelia Our Own Lady Spotswood," *Willis Gordon Garnett & allied Families Journal, Vol. I, No.8 , August 13, 1978,* 3.

281 Lacy, Betty Churchill. *Memories Of A Long Life,* Fredericksburg, VA. April, 1903 http://homepages.rootsweb.com/~elacey/chatham.htm

282 *OCDB* 46 51.

283 Fisher, Therese. *Marriages in Virginia Orange County 1851-1867,* Heritage Books, 1992.

284 Gordon, Armistead C. *William Fitzhugh Gordon.* The memory of James Gordon is preserved in the designation of one of the four magisterial districts.

285 Joyner, U. P. *Supervisors of Orange County Virginia 1734 – 2006,* A fifth district, Spotswood, was created, in 1965. Names of election districts were changed to numbers in 1992.

286 Scott, W. W. *A History Of Orange County, Virginia*. 11.

287 *Chataigne's 1888 Directory*. J. Lesson, E. S. Woodville, H. C. Woodville, Wm. Willis, Isaac Willis, E. W. Willis, R. T. Jones, Wm. M. Watson. http://www.newrivernotes.com/va/oran1888.htm .

288 http://www.nps.gov/nr/twhp/wwwlps/lessons/45chatham/45facts1.htm

289 Lacy, Elizabeth Churchill Jones, *Memories of a Long Life (1903)*, Virginia Historical Society # Mss:1 L1195:1.

290 William Lacey is buried at Alexander Chapel Wilderness Cemetery.

291 *OCWB* 13 387, 420.

292 *OCDB* 49 637.

293 *OCDB* 65 446.

294 English, Vera Apperson, *The Apperson Family In America*, self-published. 1977.

295 *OCDB* 125 39 and 134 71. Alphonzo conveyed 80 acres more or less to his son William Ray Apperson and his wife Pauline L. Alonzo's widow conveyed 75 acres to their son Clarence G. Apperson and his wife Alice P.

296 *Application of widow of a Soldier... of the Confederacy* Nov. 25, 1927, She reported in 1927 an annual income of $200, the value of land at $3,000 and personal property at $150.

297 Born on June 18, 1836 in Virginia, Lucy Harrison Gordon Spottswood died on Feb. 8, 1922 and was buried in Spotswood Family Cemetery, Lake of the Woods, Orange County, Virginia.

298 Gordon, Armistead, C. *Gordons of Virginia*, 1918. http://freepages.genealogy.rootsweb.com/~duffy/reports/gordon/rr01_037.htm#P322 .

299 Gordon, Lindy H. "Gordon Genealogy Home Page." http://freepages.genealogy.rootsweb.ancestry.com/~duffy/gordon.htm

300 *OCDB* 52 480.

301 Murray, Kathleen A. *Gordon Family of Virginia, and owners of Germanna*, Report for Germanna Community College Honors History available in the files of the The Memorial Foundation of Germanna Colonies in Virginia, Inc.

302 *OCDB* 134 507.

303 *OCDB* 53 319.

304 *Fredericksburg Daily Star*, February 9. 1923, 1x7.

305 *OCWB* 17 310. He signed with his mark "X" between the A. and D. This appears strange, as he was literate.; it may indicate his poor state of health. As magistrate he had signed documents recorded in the court in 1901, *OCDB* 60 227.

306 Willis, Anna Townsend, "'Cousin Lelia' Our Own Lady Spotswood," *Willis-Gordon-Garnett and Allied Families Journal*, Vol. 1 No. 8 August 13, 1978: 3-7. Many of the documents are at the Virginia Historical Society, Richmond, Virginia. Lelia Spottswood Willis lies buried at Flat Run Baptist Church along with her husband.

307 Rokus, Josef W. *Caught in the Fury, The Families of the Wilderness Battlefield*, January 19, 2009.

308 Willis, Anna Townsend. "Alice in Lake of the Woods", *Culpeper Star – Exponent*, April 7, 1967.

309 *OCDB* 49 202, 49 498, 53 130, 53 441, 53 461, 54 22.

310 *OCDB* 53 468.

311 *OCDB* 35 247.

312 School House No. (?) W (White) does appear on the circa 1870 Gordon District map. It was located along Flat Run on the north side of Germanna Road. A school in the same location appears on the Frank Chenawith map.

313 Joyner, Ulysses P., Jr. *Glimpses of Orange County History, a collection of essays and articles on Orange County, Virginia.* 2005.

314 *OCDB* 97 368.

315 *OCDB* 209 9, 187 383. Russell Udell Allen & wife Nan Aitken Allen sold to the Ayers. They had bought from R. S. Knighton estate in 1960.

316 *OCDB* 87 91.

317 *OCDB* 67 125.

318 Happel, Frank, former park historian, *Fredericksburg & Spotsylvania National Military Park Administrative History.* 1955. Available at the office of the Historian and Cultural Resources Manager, Chatham, Falmouth, Virginia.

319 Mayor A. P. Rowe, Chairman, letter to Wm. Taliaferro of April 7, 1896.

320 *Ellwood Family History from 1862 to 1977,* unpublished Ellwood Training Manual. His grandson, Gordon Willis Jones, sold 97 acres to the NPS in 1971 and provided 86 acres as a life estate to live at Ellwood until his death in 1977.

321 "CCC Projects in Virginia" http://www.arscse.org/qCCCVA.htm .

322 http://lvaimage.lib.va.us/cgi-in/photo.cgi/VCC/N/images/003167-009 .

323 *CCC Projects in Virginia.* http://www.arscse.org/qCCCVA.htm

324 Johnson, Elmer Vivian. *Old Mountain Road* Survey Report March 6 1936. Library of Virginia No.000680878.

325 University of Mary Washington, Department of Historic Preservation, http://umwhisp.net/germanna/node/23 .

326 Davidson, D. N., General, Chairman of the Orange County Bicentennial Committee in 1934. *Orange County [Virginia] 1734-1934.*

327 Pezzullo, Elizabeth. "Sharing the Past Deal protects Mine Run campaign site, *The Free Lance-Star,* May 10, 2003.

328 "Final Contract Let to Complete Work on Last Section of Rt. 20 East", *Orange County Review,* July 1967. "The final link (from Mine Run) to Rt. 3 will be welcomed." The road was slated to complete the summer of 1968.

329 Biographical Directory of the United States Congress, 1771-Present. http://bioguide.congress.gov/biosearch/biosearch.asp .

330 http://waldo.jaquith.org/blog/2007/12/byrd-massive-resistance/ "Orange County native Lindsay Almond was elected governor of Virginia against Harry Byrd's wishes in 1957. Almond had managed to get the Democratic nomination and elected without kissing Byrd's ring. What the two did share — or appeared to share — was the zealous support of segregation. Almond went on TV in January of 1959 and told the state's citizens that, despite the Virginia Supreme Court's demand that schools be opened up again, he was determined to "destroy every semblance of education for thousands of the children of Virginia" before he'd give in "to those who would overthrow the customs, morals and traditions of a way of life which has endured in honor and decency for centuries and embrace a new moral code prepared by nine men in Washington whose moral concepts they know nothing about." Just a week later, Almond spoke before the General Assembly and, to the shock of the assembled legislators, had come 180° on the matter. The courts had ruled, and it was time to integrate the schools."

331 Trask, Roger *Oral History of Atwell Somerville*, unpublished 2008.

332 Brown, Dr. Katherine L. *The First Fifty Years*, The Germanna Record Number Seventeen July 19, 2006, ed. Faircloth, Thomas W., The Memorial Foundation of the Germanna Colonies in Virginia, Inc.

333 McKelway, John. *The Evening Star*, Washington D. C. February 21, 1967.

334 Library of Congress. Complete map DIGITAL ID g3883o cwh00052 available at http://hdl. loc.gov/loc.gmd/g3883o.cwh00052

335 "Development Underway in Orange," *Richmond Times Dispatch*, April 9, 1967.

336 Raymond, Linda. "Wilderness Area Land on Rise," *The Free Lance-Star*, January 24, 1969. "Lake of the Woods started things off ... land prices are rising."

337 Zitz, Michael. "Lake of the Woods," *The Free Lance-Star*, November 1, 1986.

338 *OCDB* 156 348 The same land to which the boundary line adjoining the Orange Grove mining tract was settled by a deed between the party of the first part and Claire. D. Schlemmer et ux, said deed having been dated October 28, 1952. Her title to the same having been adjudicated perfect by decree the Circuit Court of Orange County, Virginia, entered in the chancery cause styled Lelia Spottswood Willis vs. Edwin Spottswood et al on the 20th day of April 1953

339 *Orange County Supervisors Minutes* Vol. 8. 188.

340 *OCDB* 215 603 and 217 69.

341 Goodwin, William T. interview by author and Roger Trask, 2007. Orange, Virginia.

342 *OCDB* 211 666.

343 *OCDB* 211 624.

344 *OCDB* 62 191.

345 *The Washington Daily News*, March 17, 1967.

346 Nowakoski, Carolyn. *Living in LOW in the Early Days*, unpublished 2007. Lyn later stated that the house was unoccupied at the time of the fire. Mrs. Nowakoski is the sole surviving founder of the LOW church and spouse of Don Nowakoski, deceased, former LOWA Director 1975-1981. She received the Distinguished Service Award in 1998 and 2009.

347 *The Evening Star* April 21, 1967

348 *LOWA BOD Meeting minutes*, October 20, 1973. Anne M. Roach lies buried at Zoar Cemetery Burr Hill Orange County, Virginia. She apparently had moved out of the Life Estates between 1969 and 1972.

349 *LOWA 6th Annual Meeting minutes*, September 6, 1976. ... the problems of how you are going to use a piece of property that was willed to us as a life estate which is called the Roche (Roach) property which became ours because Mrs. Roche (Roach) passed away ...What is the date set for getting rid of the Old Roche (Roach) house and barn? Mr. Warren (General Manager) stated that life estate property was discussed at a previous Board meeting and a decision was made to have it burned down and Fire and Rescue had been contacted and they plan to do this. A date has not been set. It depends on the weather, etc. Probably some time in September. It is doubtful there will be a lot of publicity. All safety precautions will be taken.

350 Clemente, C. Daniel, Attorney for VWCI and Director of LOWA. Email to the author, July 8, 2008.

351 PRNewswire, April 30, 2008, Vienna, Virginia. C. Daniel Clemente, Chairman and Chief Executive Officer of Clemente Development Co., Inc. and Manager of Clemente, LLC, announced today the formation of the CDC Real Estate Opportunity Fund I, a private equity fund established to take advantage of extraordinary investment opportunities in income

producing commercial real estate created by the current disarray in the global financial markets. Clemente reports that with $200,000,000 in committed funds he is in serious negotiations to leverage the new fund to $2 billion.

352 *OCDB* 215 605- 683.

353 Additional land was acquired later.

354 *OCDB* 195 233. Howard R. Masters, deceased, to Ada Masters Gibson, July 22, 1961.

355 *OCDB* 103 444.

356 *OCDB* 96 135 and 89 110.

357 *OCDB* 80 181 and 182.

358 Apperson, Terry. Interview by Josef Rokus, 2009. The cemetery is located in Lake of the Woods Section 5 between lots 214 and 215. Peter Apperson was a Revolutionary War veteran.

359 *OCDB* 134 507.

360 *OCDB* 60 227 to 230.

361 *OCDB* 51 461.

362 Henry, John R. *The Fascinating Development of the Lake of the Woods*. Locust Grove, Va.: John Henry Publishing Company, 2007.

363 *OCDB* 63 161.

364 Scott, W. W. *A History Of Orange County, Virginia*. Company C, 7th Va. Inf., was called the Culpeper Rifles. Many of the families surrounding the future Lake of the Woods also had their sons join Company C, commanded by J. W. Almond of Orange, including Bledsoe, Dempsey, Hawkins, Morris, Richards, Webb and Willis families.

365 *OCDB* 40 136, 1846. The land and house may have been in the possession of his wife's family. The property seems to be the same area as conveyed to Francis Jones by Spotswood in 1813. A strange coincidence is the fact of an Apperson house in Culpeper was recorded by the WPA VHI as being from 1800.

366 Spohn, Ralph and Joanne, present owners. Email to author, December 20, 2008.

367 Apperson, William Ray. Interview with author March 11, 2010.

368 "Fire destroys old home at Lake of the Woods," *The Free Lance-Star*, January 17, 1972.

369 "Fire official is charged with arson," *The Free Lance-Star*, May 31, 1972.

370 Nowakoski, Carolyn. Unpublished memoirs, December 8, 2008.

371 *OCDB* 225 717, November 16, 1967.

372 Their son, John, has contributed pictures and memories.

373 *OCDB* 248 592. 400 ft Highway 20 in Gordon District Orange County Virginia, 12.37 acres previously acquired from C. Apperson October 30, 1946, recorded *OCDB* 128 438.

374 *OCDB* 149 414.

375 *OCDB* 124 254.

376 *OCDB* 98 14 and 99 88.

377 *OCDB* 228 10, February 13, 1968.

378 *OCDB* 228 14 to 18.

379 Moser, James. "Bulldozers Changing the Face of Orange Countryside," *The Free Lance-Star*, November 1966.

380 *OCDB* 237 246, survey dated June 20, 1969 Map Book 2 66.

381 *OCDB* 237 323, survey dated March 13, 1969 Map Book 2 61.

382 Permits for home construction issued by the Environmental Control Committee: 1967 – 11, 1968 – 62, 1969 – 47.

383 *OCDB 240 371 to 522.*

384 Moser, James. *The Free Lance-Star*, November 1966.

385 *Declaration of Restrictions Lake of the Woods*, November 18, 1969.

386 *LOWA BOD Meeting minutes*, March 4, 1989, (D-89-14).

387 Jim Foote had an aerial photograph marked-up to show the planned addition of Mr. Middlebrook's property.

388 *OCDB 594 359.* The property is associated with the land of W. Johnson and Martha, his wife, sold to VWCI recorded in *OCDB 215 611* and the survey of February 17, 1950, recorded in *OCDB 146 237.*

389 Aitken-Cade, Phil. Interview May 3, 2010. Although the county map, http://www.onlinegis. net/VaOrange/ , shows that 9.9 has a pipe-stem to Flat Run road, Mr. Aitken-Cade stated his property abuts Ms. Winn's parcel.

390 *LOWA BOD Meeting minutes*, December 2, 1995.

391 *LOWA BOD Meeting minutes*, April 2, 2005.

392 *Time Magazine*, Sep. 23, 1966. http://www.time.com/time/magazine/article/0,9171,842824-2,00.html

393 Other U.S. Land, Inc. lake projects included Holiday Lakes, just outside of Cleveland; Lake of the 4 Seasons near Gary, and Lake Holiday near Chicago.

394 Clemente, C. Daniel, attorney for VWCI and member of the first Board of Directors of LOWA. Email to author. "I did not meet Tom Perine. I do not recall him ever visiting the project. His man on the ground in Virginia was Jim Foote. The home office visitor was always a vice president named Robert Washburn."

395 Willmann, John B. "Developer Likes Lakes and Nature" *The Washington Post*, February 11, 1967, Real Estate Section E.

396 "Lake of the Woods Developers Report Million and a Half dollars in Sales," *The Orange Review*, April 6, 1967.

397 "Lake Developer Starts Project," *The Free Lance-Star*, September 19, 1969.

398 *OCDB 250 430.*

399 *OCDB 261 341.*

400 *Time Magazine*, July 21, 1967. http://www.time.com/time/magazine/article/0,9171,941574-2,00.html

401 *The Orange Review*, April 6, 1967.

402 Passin, Glen. *Lake of the Woods How Boise Cascade Raised Money.* "The program worked well initially … Buyers liked the idea … However, Boise Cascade found itself in a new business, the financing business. … they had to wait years to collect all the payments. There was a gap between the time the money was spent and when it was collected." As a result, Boise Cascade contacted General Electric Credit Corporation (GECC, now called GE Capital), about GECC buying its "paper" …GECC determined that there were two risks associated with "buying" Boise Cascade's portfolio of lot paper. The first risk was whether the individuals … made the payments on a regular basis … The second risk was … If the buyers felt that the value of the lots and the communities were not being maintained and instead was deteriorating, then the likelihood individuals would not continue to make payments on the lot would increase. This made it important to know what Boise Cascade planned to do in the future and what steps they were taking to maintain the properties."

403 Foote, James C. Interview by author at Lake of the Woods, 2008.

404 Virginia Wildlife Clubs, Inc (VWCI), assembled 2475.1958 acres surveyed by Calvin Burns, CLS, recorded November 18, 1966, in Orange County plat book 1.

405 Clemente, C. Daniel. Email to author.

406 *Orange County Supervisors Minutes*, Vol. 8 465.

407 *OCDB* 216 402 to 454.

408 *OCDB* 215 686.

409 For example, on June 22, 1967, twelve lots of Section 1 were released and recorded in *OCDB* 219 762.

410 Jim Foote said he put together the Articles of Incorporation and Bylaws along with Jack Keating, President of U.S. Land. They decided on the wording based on their experience. He stated they neither used a standard format nor a previously approved community model.

411 *OCDB* 216 618 to 702 and June 8, 1967 *OCDB* 218 750 to 758.

412 Keating, John S., Jr. President of Virginia Wildlife Clubs, Inc. letter August 10, 1967, available in LOWA historic files.

413 Foote, James C. Letter to author December 2008.

414 The Articles of Incorporation section 12 was amended February 7, 1991.

415 "Lake of the Woods Developers Report Million and a Half dollars in Sales," *The Orange Review*, April 6, 1967.

416 *The Free Lance-Star*, September 28, 1966.

417 "$4.8 Million Recreational Facility Approved For Co." *The Orange Review*, September 29, 1966.

418 Bilanow, Alex. "We took to the Air for a Visit to Lake of the Woods," *The Washington Daily News*, October 13, 1967, Home Section.

419 Bilanow, Alex. *The Washington Daily News*, October 13, 1967.

420 Moser, James. "Virginia History is deeply Rooted in New Development," *The Free Lance-Star*, September 16, 1967, Town and County.

421 Moser, James. *The Free Lance-Star*, November 1966

422 Chase, Arnold. *The fascinating History of Lake of the Woods Area*. *The Free Lance-Star*, November 1966.

423 *The Evening Star*, April 21, 1967, Week-End Real Estate, Washington, D. C.

424 "Lake of The Woods to Hold Official Opening This Sat.," *The Orange Review*, June 15, 1967.

425 "Land Sale Response Reported," *Richmond News Leader*, September 27, 1967.

426 Bilanow, Alex. *The Washington Daily News*, October 13, 1967.

427 Foote, Jim C. Phone conversation with author June 23, 2008.

428 Willis, Anna Townsend. "Alice in Lake of the Woods," *Culpeper Star – Exponent*, April 7, 1967.

429 For many years, it has been the ECC Building.

430 Pullen, Rick. "High Pressure? No such thing says developer," *The Free Lance-Star*, March 5, 1986. Descibes the different recreational land developments and sales practices of James C. Foote for twenty years after LOW.

431 Nowakoski, Carolyn. *Living in LOW in the Early Days*, unpublished 2007.

432 Willmann, John B. "Developer Likes Lakes and Nature," *The Washington Post* February 11, 1967, Real Estate Section E.

433 Ibid.

434 *The Evening Star*, February 21, 1967, Washington, D. C.

435 *The Washington Daily News*, March 17, 1967.

436 Chase, Arnold. *The fascinating History of the Lake Of The Woods Area.*

437 Bilanow, Alex. *The Washington Daily News*, October 13, 1967.

438 Henry, John R. *The Fascinating Development of the Lake of the Woods.*

439 *The Washington Daily News*, March 17, 1967.

440 *The Evening Star,* April 21, 1967.

441 Bilanow, Alex. *The Washington Daily News*, October 13, 1967.

442 Willis, Anna Townsend. "Society and Women; Party By Lake Enjoyable Affair," *Culpeper Star Exponent*, February, 1968.

443 Ruffner, Clifford H. Interview of Mrs. E. O. Willis on March 30, 1976. She was quite concerned over the fate of the portrait of Lt. Gov. Spotswood, which originally hung in the LOW club.

444 Willis, Anna Townsend. *Culpeper Star Exponent*, February, 1968.

445 Middlebrook, Warren. Interview April 15, 2010. "Jim Foote bought the relics from a collector on Route 3."

446 Davis, L. J. "Unlikely, But Boise Means Big Business," *New York Times*, June 11, 1989.

447 Holcomb, Ernest J. *Lake of the Woods Association Its Early Years*, 1977. Available in LOWA historic files.

448 *LOWA BOD Special Meeting minutes*, January 29, 1972.

449 Holcomb, Ernest J. Written in 1977, it provides the most details.

450 Chase, Arnold. *The fascinating History of the Lake of the Woods Area*, 1976.

451 Eckel, Jack. *Talk Before Lake of the Woods Lioness Club*, September 13, 1990.

452 The Board of Directors held several meetings during the negotiations from October 1971 to August 1972. The August 25, 1972, minutes provide the details of the two parties splitting the difference between their positions of $250,000 offered and $175,000 bid. At the 4th Annual Meeting it was reported that members had paid a total of $257,364 for the equipment, furnishings and land, including attorney's fees and other transfer fees from Boise.

453 Henry, John R. Interview by the author and Chris Burr, May 15, 2009.

454 http://www.fundinguniverse.com/company-histories/
Boise- Cascade-Corporation-Company-History.html

455 In 1969, Mr. Stewart was president of the Wilderness Club, vice president of the Lake Residents Association, and an officer of the Lake of the Woods Association. In February 1971, Mr. Holcomb resigned as president of LOWA, and Mr. Stewart became president and a director. Boise voted to increase the Board to seven with four Boise members and three lot owners, Mr. Holcomb, Mr. Stewart and Mr. Newman.

456 Eckel, Jack. *Talk before Lake of the Woods Lioness Club*, September 13, 1990. "In Sept. 1973, LOW property owners for the first time elected its own Board of Directors, and Arnold Chase was chosen by the Board to be its president. He was the first president selected by an elected property owners' Board. Arnold, for personal reasons, resigned in 1974 and as Vice President, I moved up as President."

457 Joyner, Ulysses P., Jr. Mr. Somerville also served as Orange County Attorney for the years 1982 to 1996.

458 Interview with Roger Trask and author.

459 *LOWA 3rd Annual Meeting*, September 4, 1972. Mr. John Henry briefly outlined the activities of the Top Management Personnel Committee in soliciting and reviewing applications for

the "key" positions and in making recommendations to the Board for employment of such personnel. He noted that a number of applications had been received - 27 for General Manager, 19 for Club Manager, 10 for Golf Pro, 10 or more for Superintendent of Maintenance. To date only the Controller had been appointed to one of the "key" positions.

460 *LOWA BOD Special Meeting minutes*, July 30, 1972.

461 Eckel, Jack. September 13, 1990. "Shortly after the inception of the Lake of the Woods, Boise had employed Glen Marburger as the General Manager, and he still is a resident here."

462 *LOWA BOD Meeting minutes*, April 27, 1974.

463 Even to this day, the remoteness of Lake of the Woods from population centers results in the fact that many, if not most, of the staff of the Association are also members.

464 "Lake of the Woods manager moving on to new position," *The Free Lance-Star*, August 24, 1979.

465 "New Lake of the Woods manager is Texan, retired colonel," *The Free Lane-Star*, Januaray 31, 1980. "Directors of LOWA picked Warren J. Lodge form a list of some 200 applicants."

466 *The Orange Review*, April 6, 1967.

467 The first zoning ordinance for the county was adopted in May 1968 providing, among other classifications, Planned Residential Communities (R-3) specifically designed to cover Lake of the Woods or any similar development in the County.

468 Weedon, Larkin (Sonny). Interview by author, 2009. Sonny served as a building inspector for 3 years.

469 Epstein, Daniel. "Lake airs building woes," *The Free Lance-Star*, May 11, 1977.

470 *LOWA BOD Meeting minutes*, May 14, 1977.

471 *LOWA BOD Meeting minutes*, June 29, 1974.

472 http://digital.library.cornell.edu/r/ruffner/

473 "Deaths in the city and area, Clifford Ruffner, Jr.," *Free Lance-Star*, March 17, 1979, Fredericksburg, Virginia.

474 Ruffner, Clifford H., Jr. *The Spotswood Willis House at Orange Grove*, 1976. Interview of Mr. and Mrs. Willis of Culpeper, Virginia, on March 30, 1976.

475 Flynn, Jeff. Email to author, June 10, 2009. Jeff currently is Vice-President of LOWA.

476 *LOWA 6th Annual Meeting minutes*, September 6, 1976.

477 *LOWA BOD Meeting minutes*, December 2, 1989.

478 Holcomb, Ernest J. 1977.

479 Reaffirmed after the purchase from Boise Cascade at July 30, 1972, Board meeting.

480 Eckel, Jack. "LOW also secured bids for security from the National and Pinkerton agencies."

481 *LOWA BOD Special Meeting minutess*, July 17, 1976.

482 *LOWA BOD Meeting minutes*, member comments, February 14, 1976.

483 *LOWA BOD Meeting minutes*, August 14, 1976.

484 *LOWA BOD meeting minutes*, February 11, 1978.

485 In response, Mr. Warren stated that the contract was submitted to the Finance Committee by the Board of Directors for their review. They revised it where appropriate and have now recommended it to the Board of Directors. Mr. Warren believes it is an excellent contract and would endorse it. The contract is available at the office for review

486 The security contract with Dodson Security expired in 2009 and was not renewed.

487 Knepper, Robin. "New LOW squad house a far cry from double-wide trailer days," *The Free Lance- Star*, April 22, 2007.

488 Zitz, Michael. "Lake of the Woods," *The Free Lance-Star*, November 1, 1986.

489 *LOWA BOD meeting minutes*, October 7, 1971.

490 *LOWA BOD meeting minutes*, June 18, 1972.

491 The donations have been set by the Board of Directors each year, for example: Bob Kitchen, President of the LOW Fire and Rescue Company, presented his annual report following which Potter presented the Association's check in the amount of $8,000 to the F&R Company -- 11th Annual Meeting September 7, 1981 A check in the amount of $32,000 was given to Jack LeMay, President, LOW Fire and Rescue Company, as the Association's annual donation.—19ᵗʰ Annual Meeting September, 4 1989. Tom Reeder, on behalf of the Fire & Rescue Company, spoke briefly and accepted a $25,000 check from the Association—24ᵗʰ Annual Meeting September 5, 1994.

492 *LOWA BOD Meeting minutes*, June 29, 1974.

493 *LOWA BOD Meeting minutes*, April 14, 1979.

494 "Ten lake of the Woods residents are honored," *The Free Lance-Star*, September 4, 1975. The awards have continued to be awarded at the annual meeting. They are listed in the Appendix.

495 Henry, John R. *The Fascinating Development of the Lake of the Woods.*

496 *LOWA 25ᵗʰ Annual Meeting minutes*, September 4, 1995. Mr. Wade was introduced as the new general manager. At that meeting, it was announced that Larry Yatchum has replaced Bert Amidon as Maintenance Supervisor.

497 Holcomb, Ernest J. 1977.

498 Harding, Fran. Email to author, January 5, 2009.

499 Nowakoski, Carolyn. *Living in LOW in the Early Days.*

500 Henry, John R.

501 Email to author, February 2, 2009

502 Holcomb, Ernest J. "Action of Board with respect to the Wilderness Club," December 15, 1972. "We have continued a privileged class of fewer than 10 percent of the property owners … we have established an unacceptable precedent …and will be terminated immediately when the Association obtains its A. B. C. club license …"

503 *The Wilderness Club Newsletter*, June 1973.

504 O'Toole, Ruthan. Email to author, November 19, 2009.

505 6th annual Meeting September 1976.

506 Ms. Bauer was the first woman President of LOWA.

507 "Lake of Woods Civic Leaque carnival slated," *The Free Lance-Star*, September 7, 1973.

508 *LOWA BOD Meeting minutes*, May 25, 1974.

509 *LOWA BOD Meeting minutes*, June 29, 1974.

510 Bob Kitchen, President of the LOW Fire and Rescue Co. presented at the 11ᵗʰ Annual LOWA Meeting 1981.

511 *LOWA BOD Meeting minutes*, January 26, 1974.

512 *LOWA BOD Meeting minutes*, May 25, 1974. Action accomplished at the BOD meeting of August 21, 1976.

513 *LOWA BOD Meeting minutes*, July 27, 1974.

514 Schulle, Chuck. Interview with author, July 20, 2009.

515 http://www.lowa.org/clubs.htm . Although every effort has been made by LOWA to offer a complete listing, new clubs form and inactive clubs disband from time to time. Some clubs are

closed to new members or have unique membership requirements and have chosen not to be included on the LOWA website.

516 Wednesday Bridge is still going strong – Carolyn Nowakoski.

517 Krietsch, Elizabeth. "Square-dance club celebrates," *The Free Lance-Star*, May 22, 2007.

518 Cook, Ralph E. *History of the Lake of the Woods Lions Club, 1982-2000*. An eighty-one page detailed history of the club. The follow-on, *History of the Lake of the Woods Lions Club, 2000-2008* was written by Don Rogers.

519 Rogers, Lion Don. "History of the Lake of the Woods Lions Club 2000-2008."

520 *LOWA BOD Special Meeting minutess*, August 20, 1972.

521 *LOWA BOD Special Meeting minutess*, September 1, 1972.

522 Mr. Robert Corber, Legal & Compliance Committee; Mr. Robert Frey, Finance Committee; Mr. Price Merrels, Planning Committee; Mr. William Heimbach, Maintenance and Ecology Committee; Mr. Robert Clark speaking for Mrs. M. Lee Bauer, Public Relations Committee; Mr. Rolland Stoebe, Environmental Control Committee.

523 Mr. Jack Eckel, Sanitation Committee; Mr. John Hendrix, Nominating Committee; Mr. Charles Willner, Elections Committee; Mr. Ernest Storrs, Awards Committee; Mr. Ernest Storrs, Golf Committee; Mrs. Frances Harding, Tennis Committee.

524 Mr. Ed Harn, Legal & Compliance Committee; Mr. Arthur Bourne, Finance Committee; Mr. Don Nowakoski, Planning Committee; Mr. John Loughlin, Maintenance & Ecology Committee; Mr. Roy Cassell, Public Relations Committee; Mr. Stub Stoebe, Environmental Control Committee. Mr. John Nolan, Rules Committee; Mr. Russell McLennan, Campground Committee; Mrs. Janet Kennedy, Nominating Committee; Mr. John Thaxter, Elections Committee; Mr. Lyle Warren, Golf Committee; .Mr. Bob Kitchen, Tennis Committee; Mr. Gerry Beal, Stables Committee. Mrs. Barbara Pittman, General Recreation Committee.

525 Campgrounds was chaired by a departed neighbor who taught the author the game of golf, Russell McLennan.

526 Willmann, John B. "Developer Likes Lakes and Nature," *The Washington Post*, February 11, 1967, Real Estate Section E.

527 Most employees lived at LOW and were members in good standing. It was not until October 2, 1993, that it was passed unanimously by the BOD, to delete from LOWA Regulations VIII.F that portion that restricts LOWA employees from sitting down to eat at the Pro Shop Snack Bar or Clubhouse during normal work hours; and adjust the Personnel Manual accordingly.

528 McFarland, Dan. "Highs of L.O.W.," *Orange County Review*, April 12, 2007. Dan reports his interviews of John Henry, John and Barbara-sue and daughter Ruthann O'Toole, and Jeff Flynn.

529 McFarland , Dan. "LOW History," *Orange County Review*, July 6, 2006, Country Living.

530 *LOWA BOD Meeting minutes*, Feb 23, 1974.

531 *LOWA BOD Meeting minutes*, Apr 27, 1974.

532 Smiders, Duke and Carla. Interview by the author, 2008.

533 Unfortunately, the book later was lost in the 1980 fire.

534 *LOWA BOD Meeting minutes*, June 12, 1976.

535 *LOWA BOD Meeting minutes*, December 27, 1993.

536 *LOWA 11th Annual Meeting minutes*, September 7, 1981.

537 Joyner, Ulysses P., Jr.

538 *LOWA BOD Meeting minutes*, July 7, 1990.

539 Warren Lodge (GM), the General Manager, replaced Norm Howard by Rich Wallace the following December. Since it is impossible to get Warren's side of the story, only Norm's version can be told. Norman Howard is still a resident and member of LOW.

540 *LOWA BOD Meeting minutes*, March 9, 1974.

541 Willner, Charles. Letter to BOD LOWA, December 10, 1976.

542 Don Nowakoski served six years as a LOWA director. He was mainly responsible for bringing cable TV to LOW and served as the Orange county technical representative for cable services for five years. He designed the Orange county 911 system in the 1990s.

543 *LOWA BOD Meeting minutes*, June 12, 1976.

544 Knepper, Robin. "Battling weeds at LOW," *The Free Lance-Star*, November 5, 2006. "In other action, (at their November 2006 meeting) the (LOWA) directors voted unanimously to rescind a regulation that requires user fees for all amenities. Finance Committee Chairman Pete Rainey called it 'a regulation that can't be implemented.'"

545 *LOWA BOD Meeting minutes*, February 4, 1984.

546 Howard, Norman. Interview by author, August 4, 2009. Not only groups but also individual member sponsored parties were charged much less than the amount quoted by the Clubhouse Manager. After "making a profit" in October 1984, Norm was told by the General Manager that LOWA is a non-profit association.

547 "Lake of the Woods golfers second," *The Free Lance-Star*, December 6, 1971.

548 Buttram, Bill. "Bill's briefs," *The Free Lance-Star*, April 27, 1971.

549 "Plug to play at Lake of the Woods," *The Free Lance-Star*, June 28, 1972.

550 Henry, John R. email to author September 29, 2009.

551 *OCDB* 288 272. He sold the lot in September 1982, *OCDB* 341 856.

552 http://en.wikipedia.org/wiki/Lee_Elder. Leading up to the (Masters) tournament, he received substantial amounts of hate mail. Fearing for his safety, during the week of the tournament he rented two houses in town and kept moving between them, and always had people around him when he went to eat. At the Monsanto Open in 1968 in Pensacola, Florida, the same tournament at which he claimed his first victory, Elder and other black players on tour were forced to change their clothes in the parking lot because members of the club would not allow non-whites in their clubhouse.

553 Only seven years earlier, Prospect was used as a black school until the Orange County Schools were finally integrated in 1968. Prior to integration of the county schools, after finishing seventh grade at Prospect Heights, African-American students continued their studies, not at the local high school in Orange, but at a regional school for blacks, the George Washington Carver High School in Culpeper County. – http://www.ocaahs.org

554 "Elder good scores possible," *The Free Lance-Star*, May 7, 1975.
http://news.google.com/newspapers?id=wFIQAAAAIBAJ&sjid=_YoDAAAAIBAJ&dq=lake%20of%20the%20woods&pg=6533%2C880967

555 Weedon, Larkin (Sonny). Interview by author, 2009.

556 Eckel, Jack. September 13, 1990.

557 Woolf, Lee. "Lee Elder suit 'still pending' etc." *The Free Lance-Star*, June 17, 1976.

558 Howard, Bill. Interview May, 2009, by author and Dan McFarland.

559 "Lake of the Woods awarded Open," *The Free Lance-Star*, January 14, 1975.

560 One of the accusations in the petition discussed at the Board of Directors special meeting July 17, 1976, was that the Board of Directors had no authority to award a multi-year contract to

the PGA Golf-Pro. There also were accusations that he, as a member of the Association, had violated the regulations.

561 Nicoll, Kurt. "Post, LOW to go separate ways," *The Free Lance-Star*, April 7, 1981.

562 Rhodes, Gary. "Lehnhard still shoots for golf improvement," *The Free Lance-Star*, October 25, 1988.

563 "A Wee History of Lake of the Woods Golf Course," compiled by Sandy Kenyon with help from Tommy and Janet Thompson, Don Show and Ted Ludvigsen, undated. Available in the LOW Pro Shop.

564 Hargraves, Rea. Email to author September 19, 2009.

565 "Lake of the Woods Skiers Place in State," *The Free Lance-Star*, September 30, 1970.

566 "Mead sets water ski," *The Free Lance-Star*, September 12, 1972.

567 "Wilmopt, Gay among winners in water skiing tournament," *The Free Lance-Star*, June 20, 1977.

568 "Jennings Pond, LOW to host skiing events," *The Free Lance-Star*, June 10, 1981.

569 "Tykes slide into water-skiing Members of Lake of the Woods," *The Free Lance-Star*, September 5, 1992.

570 http://www.potomacbassmasters.com/. Potomac Bassmasters of Virginia (PBV) is one of the oldest bass angling clubs in the greater Washington, D.C., area. The club is a not-for-profit organization dedicated to the advancement of bass fishing, conservation and youth involvement in angling. Its members generally come from Virginia, Maryland and Washington, D.C., and share a common passion for bass fishing.

571 *LOWA BOD Meeting minutes*, February 11, 1978.

572 "Competition for open space on waterways fierce," *The Free Lance-Star*, July 20, 1989.

573 Summer of 1989 there were 1871 houses and 1528 registered boats.

574 This compares with, on average, an additional two cars registered for each new home built.

575 Smith, Peggy. "Lake of the Woods enjoyed," *The Free Lance-Star*, May 8, 1980.

576 *LOWA BOD Meeting minutes*, attachment D-87-108, November 13, 1982.

577 Daniels, Rickey. "The Horse Scene," *The Free Lance-Star*, March 15, 1984.

578 Carter, Betsy. "Excellence rewarded at Lake of the Woods," *The Free Lance-Star*, January 15, 1987.

579 Carter, Betsy. "Lake of the Woods greets new season," *The Free Lance-Star*, March 26, 1992.

580 Carter, Betsy. "Lake of the Woods a fine place to start," *The Free Lance-Star*, April 13, 2007.

581 McFarland, Dan. "Filling the lake first with water, then with people", *Orange County Review*, July 11, 2006, Country Living.

582 Henry, John R.

583 Goolrick, John. "Clubhouse burns at Lake of Woods", *Free Lance-Star*, April 7, 1980.

584 Ibid.

585 Harding, Fran. Email to author March 6, 2009. Ms. Harding was elected Director in the very late seventies, to fill out the term of Mr. Bourne, who had resigned from the Board of Directors. She served during the 1980 deliberations on the clubhouse reconstruction.

586 "Lake of the woods gets $557,000 for clubhouse fire," *The Free Lance-Star*, August 22, 1980.

587 Nowakoski, Carolyn.

588 *LOWA BOD Meeting minutes*, December 11, 1982. The fire sprinkler installation was still an issue a year after reopening. President Law reported that the Board had discussed in

Executive Session … the clubhouse sprinkler system, which must meet the Fire Marshall's specifications.

589 Harding, Fran. Email to author, January 5, 2009.

590 *LOWA BOD Meeting minutes*, November 14, 1981.

591 *LOWA BOD Meeting minutes*, November 13, 1982.

592 *LOWA BOD Meeting minutes*, December 11, 1982.

593 During reconstruction of the Clubhouse, the Morton building that is currently the Maintenance building served as the community center.

594 *LOWA BOD Meeting minutes*, July 11, 1987; July 8, 1989; June 5, 1993; October 1, 1994; May 6, 1995, and July 8 , 1995.

595 *LOWA BOD Meeting minutes*, February 10, 1996. "Approval of Clubhouse Renovation Contract and an Adjustment to the Maximum Amount to Include Contingencies … enter into a letter of intent contract with a revised authorized planned expenditure of $328,000."

596 Mead, Eileen. "Church honors a variety of traditions," *The Free Lance-Star*, September 20, 1986.

597 *The Wilderness Club Newsletter*, December 1971. "So now who has an excuse for not going to church. Come as you are – God doesn't care as long as you come."

598 Howard, Norman. Interview, 2009.

599 *LOWA BOD Meeting minutes*, April 8, 1978.

600 "St.Patrick's starts fund drive," *The Free Lance-Star*, July 23,1983.

601 Howard, Norman. Interview 2009.

602 http://www.lowchurch.org/history.htm "The facilities encouraged many different activities and a growth in membership. Due to the need for more space to hold various meetings and Sunday School classes, a fund drive for a building addition was started in April 1993. This new construction, dedicated in June 1996, included the Friendship Hall, kitchen, added classrooms, restrooms and office space. Renovations in 1999 multiplied this space opening additional room for new offices and small group ministries. Based upon a strategic plan developed by the Board of Elders and Trustees and the Pastors, the facilities were expanded once more with the construction of a 22,000-square-foot Worship Center and Education Center, which was dedicated in December 2004."

603 Zitz, Michael. "Lake of the Woods," *The Free Lance-Star*, November 1, 1986.

604 Ibid.

605 Ibid.

606 Resales of lots were typically below cost during the 1970s. A significant downward adjustment of the Association was made by the County tax appraisers in the spring of 1978. All land in Orange County eventually had a large increase due to the prices paid by the LOW developer.

607 Zitz, Michael.

608 Holcomb, Ernest J., 1977.

609 McFarland, Dan. "Highs of L.O.W.," *Orange County Review*, April 12, 2007, East Orange Laker. James Stewart was joined by Holcomb, Dugan and Newman, all future LOWA Directors, in filing a lawsuit against Boise to repair and improve the conditions of the private roads. Boise accomplished some work, and the lawsuit was dropped.

610 *LOWA BOD Meeting minutes*, October 20, 1973.

611 *LOWA BOD Special Meeting minutes*, July 17, 1976.

612 *LOWA BOD Meeting minutes*, February 7, 1987.

613 *LOWA BOD Meeting minutes*, May 4, 1996.

614 "Letter to the Editor," *The Free Lance-Star*, August 5, 2008.

615 "BOD Storm Water Management Guidance report," September 22, 2009. A summary of the report appears in *Lake Currents*, November 6, 2009.

616 Foote, Jim C. Phone conversation with author June 23, 2008.

617 *OCDB 218 756*.

618 The changes to the restrictive covenants in 1990 changed the set fee to "at rates established by said utility."

619 *LOWA BOD Meeting* minutes, February 10, 1979. "Mr. Harn (President, LOWA) stated that, in connection with the sale of the utility system at Lake of the Woods, there have been several discussions with General Counsel, and General Counsel has had several discussions with Boise Cascade and other people. Mr. Harn announced that the stock of Boise Cascade in the LOW Utility Co. has been sold and transferred to a firm called Atlantic Pacific Land Co. This was accomplished in January of this year. Mr. Ron Bodecker, who worked in utilities operations, including LOW, will be with the new company as the President of the Operations Managing segment. The new owner, referred to as ATPAC, intends to operate Lake of the Woods, Ocean Pines and a new development in Hawaii. Representatives of ATPAC have been requested to visit Lake of the Woods to discuss with us the system and their intentions. They have agreed to do so, although no firm date has been set."

620 "REPORT:Health Department chronicles spills," *The Free Lance-Star*, April 2, 2003. This article provides a detailed history from 1970 to 2003 of the sewer problem.

621 United States Court of Appeals, Fourth Circuit, docket no. 76-1890, July 8, 1977.

622 Polk, Alan. Interview with author April 21, 2009. The bond liability applied to all of RSA, not just the LOW portion.

623 *LOWA BOD Special Meeting minutes*, August 31, 1987.

624 "State Water Control Board Enforcement Action Special Order by Consent Issued to Rapidan Service Authority for Lake of the Woods Sewerage Collection System" (VPDES Permit No. Va0083411), 2003.

625 Patttie, Dudley. "RSA Unveils Plan for Upgrades," *Lake Currents*, Vol. 6 No. 7, August 29, 2008. In 2003, questions arose about the vacuum system at the Lake. The main reason for the notoriety came as a result of a LOW sewer user wrongfully and illegally manipulating his own vacuum sewer valve and then calling the newspaper and claiming a sewer overflow. With that, RSA came under intense scrutiny from both the federal Environmental Protection Agency (EPA) and the Virginia Department of Environmental Quality (DEQ). As a result of their inquiries, RSA voluntarily entered into a Court Order with Virginia DEQ.

626 *LOWA BOD Special Meeting minutes*, March 11, 1972

627 Chase, Arnold. 1976

628 *LOWA BOD Meeting minutes*, November 13, 1982.

629 *Orange Review*, June 2009

630 *The Free Lance-Star*, September 28, 1966.

631 "$4.8 Million Recreational Facility Approved For Co.," *The Orange Review*, September 29, 1966.

632 Holcomb, Ernest J. 1977.

633 Current national building guidelines place the lowest level of a house at least two feet above the top of the dam.

634 Moore, Nancy. "Nearly 5-inch rain tops Camille output," *The Free Lance-Star*, August 28, 1971.

635 *LOWA Special BOD Meeting* minutes, June 18, 1972.

636 *LOWA BOD Meeting minutes*, July 27, 1974.

637 Jones, Edward. "No State Inspections for Embry Dam," *The Free Lance-Star*, August 16, 1997.

638 *LOWA BOD Meeting minutes*, August 12, 1978. The recommendations, D-78-219, are missing.

639 *LOWA BOD Meeting minutes*, October 14, 1978 and February 10, 1979.

640 *LOWA BOD Meeting* minutes, March 7, 1987.

641 Virginia Soil and Water Conservation Board minutes, July 15, 2004. "Mr. Maroon (Director, Department of Conservation and Recreation) noted that the original dam was built before the regulations were in place. When the state regulations were adopted, originally the dam was classified as a Class 1. <u>For reasons that were not clear, the dam was later reclassified as a Class 2</u>."

642 *LOWA BOD Meeting* minutes, July 11, 1987.

643 Interview with author, 2009.

644 Bailey, John. Interview with author October 3, 2009. The agreement was successfully negotiated to re-plat of several lots in Wilderness Shores so that no building would occur in the inundation zone, fix the low level drain and upgrade the spillway to 2/3 PMF.

645 Presentation, "Virginia Impounding Structure Regulations and the Dam Safety Program" by Ms. Dianna Sheesley.

646 Knepper, Robin. "State to review dam standards Lake of Woods hails decision," *The Free Lance-Star*, July 22, 2005.

647 McFarland, Dan. "Dam could cost LOW big money," *Orange Review*, August 28, 2008.

648 Wilderness Shores, a 1,000-lot subdivision on the east side of Germanna Highway was revived in 1991 when developers revised a 1960s plan and funded RSA development of new water and sewer treatment plants to serve both them and LOW. Their plat included dozens of lots in the LOW main dam inundation zone. LOWA successfully negotiated with Wilderness Shores and the county to remove all lots in the flood zone and designate them as open space.

649 Knepper, Robin. "Did state mislead LOW leaders? WHAT'S NEXT," *The Free Lance-Star*, August 31, 2008.

650 Knepper, Robin. "LOW may pay for special tax for dam upgrade," *The Free Lance-Star*, April 30, 2009.

651 Knepper, Robin. "LOW officials set to fix dam," *The Free Lance-Star*, October 4, 2009.

652 1. That § **10.1-605** of the Code of Virginia is amended and reenacted as follows:

    § **10.1-605**. Promulgation of regulations by the Board.

    A. The Board shall promulgate regulations to ensure that impounding structures in the Commonwealth are properly and safely constructed, maintained and operated. Dam safety regulations promulgated by the State Water Control Board shall remain in full force until amended in accordance with applicable procedures.

    B. *The Board's Impounding Structure Regulations shall not require any impounding structure in existence or under a construction permit prior to July 1, 2010, that is currently classified as high hazard, or is subsequently found to be high hazard through reclassification, to upgrade its spillway to pass a rainfall event greater than the maximum recorded within the Commonwealth, which shall be deemed to be 90 percent of the probable maximum precipitation.*

Additionally, such an impounding structure shall be determined to be in compliance with the spillway requirements of the regulations provided that (i) the impounding structure will pass two-thirds of the reduced probable maximum precipitation requirement described in this subsection and (ii) the dam owner certifies annually that such impounding structure meets each of the following conditions:

1. *The owner has a current emergency action plan that is approved by the Board and that is developed and updated in accordance with the regulations;*
2. *The owner has exercised the emergency action plan in accordance with the regulations and conducts a table-top exercise at least once every two years;*
3. *The Department has verification that both the local organization for emergency management and the Virginia Department of Emergency Management have on file current emergency action plans and updates for the impounding structure;*
4. *That conditions at the impounding structure are monitored on a daily basis and as dictated by the emergency action plan;*
5. *The impounding structure is inspected at least annually by a professional engineer and all observed deficiencies are addressed within 120 days of such inspection;*
6. *The owner has a dam break inundation zone map developed in accordance with the regulations that is acceptable to the Department;*
7. *The owner is insured in an amount that will substantially cover the costs of downstream property losses to others that may result from a dam failure; and*
8. *The owner shall post the dam's emergency action plan on his website, or upon the request of the owner, the Department or another state agency responsible for providing emergency management services to citizens agrees to post the plan on its website. If the Department or another state agency agrees to post the plan on its website, the owner shall provide the plan in a format suitable for posting.*

   A dam owner who meets the conditions of subdivisions 1 through 8, but has not provided record drawings to the Department for his impounding structure, shall submit a complete record report developed in accordance with the construction permit requirements of the Impounding Structure Regulations, excluding the required submittal of the record drawings.

2. That the Virginia Soil and Water Conservation Board may amend its Impounding Structure Regulations to conform with the provisions of this act through a regulatory process that is exempt from the requirements of the Administrative Process Act (§ **2.2-4000** et seq.) of the Code of Virginia.

653 The BOD had authorized that all dam alteration contracts be terminated and unexpended funds returned to the members upon the notification of this action.
654 *LOWA BOD Meeting minutes,* June 29, 1974.
655 Zitz, Michael. "Lake of the Woods," *The Free Lance-Star,* November 1, 1986.
656 *LOWA BOD Meeting minutes,* June 6, 1998.
657 *LOWA BOD Meeting minutes,* July 11, 1998.
658 *LOWA BOD Meeting minutes,* March 6, 1999.
659 Meier, Ernie. Email to author October 19, 2009.
660 *LOWA BOD meeting minutes,* October 1, 2005.
661 Knepper, Robin. "Battling weeds at LOW," *The Free Lance-Star,* November 5 , 2006.

662 Wilson, Bill. "President's Letter," *Lake Currents*, March 27,2009.

663 Hughes, April. "Keaton's Lake Restoration Plan," *Lake Currents*, July 31, 2009.

664 *LOWA BOD Meeting minutes*, June 3, 1989.

665 *LOWA BOD Meeting minutes*, July 8, 1989.

666 McGlone, Vin. Letter to "Interested Members of LOWA," October 3,1998. The letter also stated, "The only written comment, I received was from a group of 8 former LOWA Presidents, who were worried about my ability to understand the difference between majority and minority. My example: Majority, 2600-2700 members who didn't vote; Minority, -8." Vin McGlone was awarded the Distinguished Service Award in 2001.

667 O'Toole, Ruthan. Email to author October 15, 2009.

668 *LOWA BOD Special Meeting minutes*, October 7, 1971, and September 1, 1973.

669 *LOWA BOD Meeting minutes*, April 10, 1976.

670 *LOWA BOD Meeting minutes*, June 12, 1976

671 These petitions were submitted by Mrs. Levis Lundwall on June 8, 1976.

672 Goolrick, John. "Some owners at Lake of the Woods unhappy with association's moves," *The Free Lance-Star*, July 28, 1976.

673 "Lake of the Woods directors are big winners in court decision," *The Free Lance-Star*," August 20, 1976.

674 *LOWA BOD Special Meeting minutes*, July 17, 1976.

675 Ibid.

676 *OCDB 443 page 693* dated April 12, 1990.

677 Zitz, Michael. "Lake of the Woods," *The Free Lance-Star*, November 1, 1986. "There are restrictions governing the sale of lots. Owners must first be accepted for membership in the Lake of the Woods Association. To sell a lot, an owner must offer it first to the owner on the right, then to the owner on the left and then to the Association. If all three decline to buy, then the owner may offer his property to other buyers – at the same price."

678 *LOWA Annual Meeting minutes*, reconvened September 6, 1990.

679 *OCDB 443 page 703* is the rational for change to restrictive covenants.

680 *LOWA BOD Meeting minutes*, May 4, 1996. In addition, changes were made to ECC rules, parking rules, limit number of rentals, and prohibit radio transmission stations.

681 Grace, Susan. "Germanna corridor changes, Major projects in the works for Orange County area," *The Free Lance-Star*, July 3, 1992.

682 That summer there were 5,000 fewer rounds of golf at LOW; within two years the number of annual golf members had fallen 20%.

683 *LOWA BOD Meeting minutes*, May 4, 1996. LOWA Mission Statement (D-96-43).

684 *LOWA BOD Special Meeting minutes*, March 5, 1972.

685 *LOWA 4th Annual Meeting minutes*, September 3, 1973.

686 This problem persisted for years. The 1976 Annual Meeting minutes reported that in 1975, "$562,058 was collected, or 82% of total billing. Total billing is the total amount of billing of all the lots. It is not what we use for budget purposes. In 1976, $607,546 was collected or 89% of our total billing - an increase of 7%." In 1985, LOWA sought judgment against builders that held many lots with unpaid assessments, the largest due was $15,830, others were $6,740 and $2,669, duly recorded OCDB 364 page 849.

687 Nowakoski, Carolyn. The few primary homeowners at LOW considered it "quite a bargain."

688   Somerville, Atwell. Interview by author and Roger Trask, October, 12, 2007. Orange, Virginia.

689   Harding, Fran. Email to author January 5, 2009.

690   *LOWA 8th Annual Meeting minutes*, September 4, 1978.

691   McClullough, Jim. "An Open Letter from this directory publisher," *LOWA Directory*, 1998.

692   Velona, Walt. Letter to Jim McCullough, July 8, 1998. Cook, Ralph. "Lion Walt Velona drew up plans for a storage shed and following conversations with the general manager of the Association, the Lions Club received permission to construct a building at the Shoosmith site."

693   The Finance Committee had examined 11 potential income sources. The Board of Directors had further refined the list down to five and subsequently presented two.

694   *LOWA Public Hearing minutes*, October 21, 1978.

    #1   Proposal that a referendum should be conducted, designed to amend the Restrictive Covenants (number 12D), to permit the Association to levy a rate of assessment at a different level for unimproved lot owners than for owners with single family dwellings. ---and---

    #2   Proposal that a trial program be initiated to offer use of LOW amenities to non-owner paying guests on a one-year basis at the rate of $300 per guest (family). Rates are subject to Board review on an annual basis. Further, it was proposed there be a special off-season introductory offer at $150, to cover the remainder of the current fiscal year - September through April 30, 1979. Guests would be subject to payment of users' fees, depending upon recreation facility selected, not to include boat privileges.

695   *LOWA BOD Meeting minutes*, March 10, 1979. "Mr. Harn reported on the results of the referendum. On Proposition 1 (split assessment) - 1,597 for, 544 against; on Proposition 2 (interest on delinquent accounts) - 1,766 for, 328 against. Neither item had sufficient votes to meet the Restrictive Covenant requirements."

696   *LOWA BOD Meeting minutes*, April 14, 1979. "Another legal matter discussed was the suit related to the annual guest privilege program. Mr. Somerville read a letter received from Judge Purcell which states that the Board of Directors does have the authority to establish the annual guest program. The Court has not yet entered the official order. Mr. Somerville expects it will be done shortly. Mr. Harn stated that under the circumstances, the Association will go ahead with the annual guest program."

697   *LOWA BOD Meeting mintues*, May 12, 1979.

698   Bauer v. Harn 223 Va. 31, 286 S.E.2d 192 (1982) (From the Circuit County of Orange County). M. Lee Bauer President of LOWA 1975-76, Edwin Harn President of LOWA 1978-79. "Owners contended that association had no authority to sell to non-property owners the right of entry and access to community facilities.

Restrictive covenants are not favored and should be strictly construed against the party seeking to enforce them - substantial doubt or ambiguity is to be resolved against the restrictions and in favor of the free use of property. However, if it is apparent from a reading of the whole instrument that the restrictions carry a certain meaning by definite and necessary implication, then the thing denied may be said to be clearly forbidden, as if the language had been in positive terms of express inhibition (citing, Friedberg v. Building Committee).

For example, permitting the sale of use rights to 250 owners could have been expanded to an unlimited number of guests--which would permit the destruction of the entire concept of this planned residential community. If economic pressures were so great, the community would need to amend its own covenants to permit sale."

699 *LOWA BOD Meeting minutes*, May 4, 1996.

700 Some of the files are unreadable, some minutes are very brief and cryptic. Further research is required to identify which year the Association started the five-year planning process.

701 Over the years, the minimum has risen to $3,500.

702 At the same meeting, Alan Polk was appointed a member of the Finance Committee.

703 *LOWA BOD Meeting minutes*, October 3, 1987 (D-87-102).

704 *LOWA BOD Meeting minutes*, November 7, 1987.

705 *LOWA BOD Meeting minutes*, May 2, 1987.

706 *LOWA BOD Meeting minutes*, December 5, 1987.

707 *LOWA BOD Meeting minutes*, April 1, 1989 (D-89-31).

708 *LOWA BOD Meeting minutes, December 1, 1990*. Motion by Dicken, seconded by Polk, passed unanimously, to approve the following modification to the Standing Rules on Funded Reserve

A. FUNDED RESERVE FOR REPLACEMENT OF EXISTING CAPITAL ITEMS

WHEREAS the Board of Directors of the LOWA is charged with the financial management of the Association by its Charter (Article 5) and its Bylaws (Article 5, Section A) and,

WHEREAS the Board of Directors has established a Reserve Fund for the replacement of existing capital assets,

THEREFORE, it is resolved that the Association's annual budget shall include an amount for a funded reserve to be determined by the Board of Directors. This funded Reserve shall be maintained solely for the replacement of existing capital assets of the Association.

RESOLVED further that these funded reserves shall be identified in a separate reserve account in the Association's accounting records and shall represent uncommitted funds and that no disbursements shall be made from these funded reserves for any purpose other than the replacement of existing capital items.

IN ADDITION, it is resolved that any funds generated by the investment of such reserve funds shall accrue to and increase this reserve fund.

1. This schedule will be revised annually to reflect additions and deletions for the current year by the General Manager and will be provided to the Finance Committee no later than 1 January of each year with a list of recommended replacement items to be funded from this reserve fund in the next fiscal year.

2. Effective May 1, 1991, the total amount of the depreciation of existing capital items will be carried as a line item in the budget and will be treated as a funded expense item with the funds generated therefrom being deposited in this reserve account.

3. The depreciation expensed to each cost center will appear monthly on the financial statement for that cost center, and will be shown as a line entry after the initial income or expense has been determined, but prior to the below the line maintenance costs. This breakdown of depreciation expense for each cost center will be effective May 1, 1991.

4. Any funds derived from the net proceeds of a sale of capital assets will accrue to this fund.

709 Required by POA 55-514.1 Reserves for capital components. Conduct at least once every five

years a study to determine the necessity and amount of reserves required to repair, replace and restore the capital components.

710 *LOWA BOD Special Meeting minutes*, March 17, 1984.

711 *LOWA BOD Meeting minutes*, November 3, 1990.

712 "Revision to Bylaws Article VI Debt Financing," *LOWA BOD Meeting minutes*, item D-91-21.

713 Due to a series of circumstances, including the change of the computer system some Association records were lost. For example, there is no record of boat registrations for 1991-92. In particular, sometime after October 1991 the Standing Rules are replaced by Regulations. The Standing Rules included Board of Directors policies that applied to operation of the Association and regulations that applied to members. The last mention of Standing Rules appears in the BOD minutes of 1991. A few of these rules have been made Bylaws.

714 The entire list of awards is presented in the Appendix. Jeff Barber was honored in 2001 with the Distinguish Service Award.

715 *LOWA BOD Meeting minutes*, March 2, 1993.

716 Ibid.

717 These accounts will be expended only for the purposes stated in the fund title. Should a situation arise in which expenditures for a capital asset or group of assets promise materially to exceed the amount available in the appropriate reserve account, funds from other reserve accounts may be drawn upon to cover the deficiency, PROVIDED:
   a.   The Board of Directors of LOWA, by vote of at least three-fourths of its membership, declares a condition of emergency and thereby authorizes an exception to the policy governing usage of its reserves.
   b.   Use of the funds in this situation shall be restricted to existing Association assets and limited to restoring them to their original condition, and
   c.   Any insurance proceeds received associated with the declared emergency should be used exclusively for replenishing the reserve funds used to address the emergency situation.
   Paragraph B.2 to read: Funding for this reserve will be provided from budget depreciation built into the assessment.

718 *LOWA BOD Meeting minutes*, July 12, 1976.

719 *LOWA BOD Meeting minutes*, March 4, 1989.

720 Schulle, Chuck. Interview with the author July 20, 2009. Mr. Schulle was Chairman of the M&E Committee in 1996 and elected to the Board of Directors in 1998.

721 Walker, Frank. *Remembering*, 204. "The Orange public school system was not fully integrated until 1968." The integration of the school buses required parent supervision, which Sonny provided.

722 Nowakoski, Carolyn, *Living in LOW in the Early Days*.

723 Bill has retained his membership card and wishes that such artifacts could be put on display by the Association.

724 http://www.ocss-va.org/schools/lges/

725 Hannon, Kelly. "Orange county opens school," *The Free Lance-Star*, January 6, 2004.

726 Hart, Gracie. "County breaks ground for new school," *Orange Review*, June 11, 2009.

727 Cook, Ralph E., Lion, *History of the Lake of the Woods Lions Club 1982 – 2000*, 22. The shelter was given by the Lions Club to the community in 1987.

728 "Lake of the Woods Skiers Place in State," *The Free Lance-Star*, September 30, 1970. The

Water Ski Club included adults for many years; Mr. and Mrs. Gordon Gay placed second in their respective competitions. The club is currently open to children 7 to 18.

729 "Rappahannock Swim League preview," *The Free Lance-Star*, June 17, 1982.

730 "Scout Log" *The Free Lance-Star*, June 18, 1988.

731 *LOWA BOD Meeting minutes*, May 2, 1998.

732 *LOWA BOD Meeting minutes*, October 1, 2005.

733 *LOWA BOD Meeting minutes*, July 8, 2006.

734 http://www.freewebs.com/lakeco-oppreschool/

735 *LOWA BOD Meeting minutes*, July 11, 1981.

736 *LOWA BOD Meeting minutes*, February 4, 2006, and August 17, 2006.

737 *LOWA BOD Meeting minutes*, June 29, 1974.

738 Email to author, July 22, 2009.

739 The county tax records indicate the house was built in 1964.

740 *LOWA BOD Meeting minutes*, July 11, 1998.

741 Knepper, Robin. "LOW seeks input on state dam regs, Some Lake of the Woods residents are opposed to a proposed skateboard park." *The Free Lance-Star*, March 5, 2006.

742 "Russell E. McLennan," *The Free Lance-Star*, January 18, 2008. Mac was the author's neighbor for several years. He had been one of the first campers, Chairman of the Campgrounds Committee in the 1970s, and LOW men's golf champion. He played against John Daly for the LOW course title.

743 Lease, Daryl. "Orange ousts Faulconer; Nolan joins supervisors." *The Free Lance-Star*, November 6,1991.

744 Brown, Tanya. "Eastern Orange gets new supervisor." *The Free Lance-Star*, November 7, 1995.

745 Michele R. Brown was the Assistant GM under Warren Lodge (GM); upon his death, she was appointed General Manager. At the January 1995 BOD meeting, President Baratz announced the resignation of General Manager Michele R. Brown to be effective August 1, 1995, or earlier. Rick Wade was appointed GM by the July 1995 BOD meeting. In less than two years, Rick Wade was replaced by acting GM Larry Yatchum. President McCarthy appointed a search committee on April 5, 1997. On Friday June 13, 1997, the Board of Directors unanimously appointed Larry Yatchum as the Association's GM.

746 *U.S. Post Office's Publication 28*, "Postal Addressing Standards." Highway Contract Route Addresses. "Print highway contract route addresses on a mailpiece as: HC N BOX NN. "

747 Schulle, Chuck. Interview by author, July 20, 2009.

748 *LOWA BOD Meeting minutes*, March 17, 1998. "It is the recommendation of both Lois Boyd and Alan Polk, present and prior Planning Commissioners, that the Board of Directors of Lake of the Woods take the following action with the Orange County Planning Commission and Board of Supervisors. Defer any action on commercial development at the Route 3 and 20 intersection until a comprehensive revision of the Germanna Highway Corridor Land Development Plan has been accomplished."

749 *LOWA BOD Meeting minutes*, January 8, 2000. Dear Larry, It is with deep regret that Lake of the Woods Association Board of Directors accepts your resignation effective on or about February 3, 2000. Your contribution to our community has been numerous and substantial … On a personal note, I have felt a … kinship since our first meeting involving the Maintenance budget some five years ago. – Ernie Bartholomew, President

750 Ibid. The official record is that a special committee was appointed, past Presidents Polk and Hollenbachm, Vice President Brown and President Bartholomew to locate a successor for the General Manager; Barbara Wood was appointed Acting General Manager.

751 The National Board of Certification for Community Association Managers (NBC-CAM) administers the Certified Manager of Community Associations˙ (CMCA˙) certification program. NBC-CAM is affiliated with Community Associations Institute (CAI), which provides education and resources to community association homeowners, managers, and other industry professionals.

752 *LOWA BOD Meeting minutes*, June 2, 2001.

753 Rock ballasting was required to put in the Olympic size pool in 1999, a change not in the construction budget. The budget had included funds to have high tolerances for flatness of the pool deck and proper footings to allow a future "sliding enclosure." The as-constructed pool deck was not suitable for such an enclosure. In addition, it was later learned that the enclosure manufacturer had never built such a large span, thus the feasibility of the entire project was called into question. The GM had been authorized in March 1997 to develop a replacement plan for the Sweetbriar Pool to be implemented in the fall of 1997. Two years passed before the work was started.

754 Schulle, Chuck. Interview by author, July 20, 2009.

755 Johnston, Donnie. "Vision causes LOW tiff," *The Free Lance-Star*, March 17, 2003.

756 Knepper, Robin. "Lake of the Woods budget raises residents'eyebrows," *The Free-Lane Star*, March 16, 2006.

757 Salaries are the largest part of the cost of LOWA. A part of the increase in assessments from 2001 to 2008 was the hiring of experienced professionals to fill staff vacancies and the addition of staff positions.

758 *LOWA Master Plan FY 2006-2010*, March 6, 2006.

759 Johnston, Donnie.

760 "Letters to the Editor," *The Free Lance-Star*, April 10, 2005.

761 "Letters to the Editor," *The Free Lance-Star*, April 7, 2005.

762 *LOWA BOD Meeting minutes*, April 2, 2005.

763 "Letter to the Editor," *The Free Lance-Star*, July 1, 2005.

764 Knepper, Robin. "Lake of the Woods elects two to board," *The Free Lance-Star*, September 9, 2004. Three of the seven seats on the board were up for election this year. Voting began in midsummer and ran until Monday. Rogers received 1,369 votes, Thomas 1,061 and Elliott 1,049. Incumbent President Lee Frame finished fourth with 1,020 votes in his bid for a second term.

765 Lee Frame ran against Doug Rogers for Orange County Supervisor of District 5 in 2007 and won.

766 Knepper, Robin. "Court rejects LOW resident's effort to block loan for facility," *The Free Lance-Star*, June 28, 2005.

767 Knepper, Robin. "Judge tosses lawsuit over LOW borrowing," *The Free Lance-Star*, September 23, 2005.

768 Knepper, Robin. "Lake of the Woods to build Pro Shop," *The Free Lance-Star*, August 6, 2006.

769 Knepper, Robin. "Golf center prompts audit," *The Free Lance-Star*, January 17, 2008.

770 *LOWA BOD Meeting minutes*, August 6, 2006. The Board action was specifically to set a cap

on the construction contract of $1.6 million. The Board never did establish a project cost limit nor establish an increase in the Maintenance budgets for 2006 and 2007 for all the work done in the parking lot, which later became part of the overrun.

771 Schulle, Chuck. Interview by author, 2009.

772 Knepper, Robin. "Lake of the Woods to build pro shop," *The Free Lance-Star*, August 6, 2006. Although LOWA could not donate, the Orange County Board of Supervisors did donate $150,000 of taxpayers' funds.

773 Knepper, Robin. "Community may open its gates," *The Free Lance-Star*, May 8, 2006.

774 The final count was tabulated on November 13, 2006.

775 Henry, John R.

776 Knepper, Robin. "New LOW squad house a far cry from double-wide days," *The Free Lance-Star*, April 22, 2007.

777 *LOWA Long Range Plan*, March 2002. During those six years, the marina fee increased 38%, the annual family golf fee 27%, the annual family pool fee 30% and the boat registration fee 11%.

778 Appendix includes a table of the annual assessments.

779 Knepper, Robin. "Orange election contests shape up," *The Free Lance-Star*, May 21, 2007.

780 Knepper, Robin. "LOW takes up dips into reserves," *The Free Lance-Star*, June 29, 2008.

781 Knepper, Robin. "New LOW board president vows to improve subdivision finances," *The Free Lance-Star*, September 4,, 2008.

782 Buttimer, Neil. "Lake of the Woods' finances are just fine," *The Free Lance-Star*, September 14, 2008. The statement printed on September 2, 2008, attributed to Bruce Kay was, "I was going to expose the fact that LOW is broke, so we were excluded."

783 Knepper, Robin. "LOWA board OKs $10 per lot increase," *The Free Lance-Star*, March 1, 2009.

784 Knepper, Robin. "Five hopefuls file for two LOWA seats," *The Free Lance-Star*, May 3, 2009.

785 Knepper, Robin. "No deal on fee, budget in LOW," *The Free Lance-Star*, February 8, 2009.

786 Wachovia was rescued from bankruptcy by the government action to have it absorbed by Wells Fargo. Morgan Stanley was one of the surviving major investment houses and never was in peril.

787 Knepper, Robin. "Lake of the Woods manager hired to be town manager of Orange," *The Free Lance-Star*, August 5, 2009.

788 *LOWA BOD Meeting minutes*, May 5, 2001. Final layout has been reached in connection with redistricting of Orange County. District 5 consists of LOW and approximately 32 residents in the area near the Wilderness Branch Library. The area <u>surrounding</u> LOW is part of District 4.